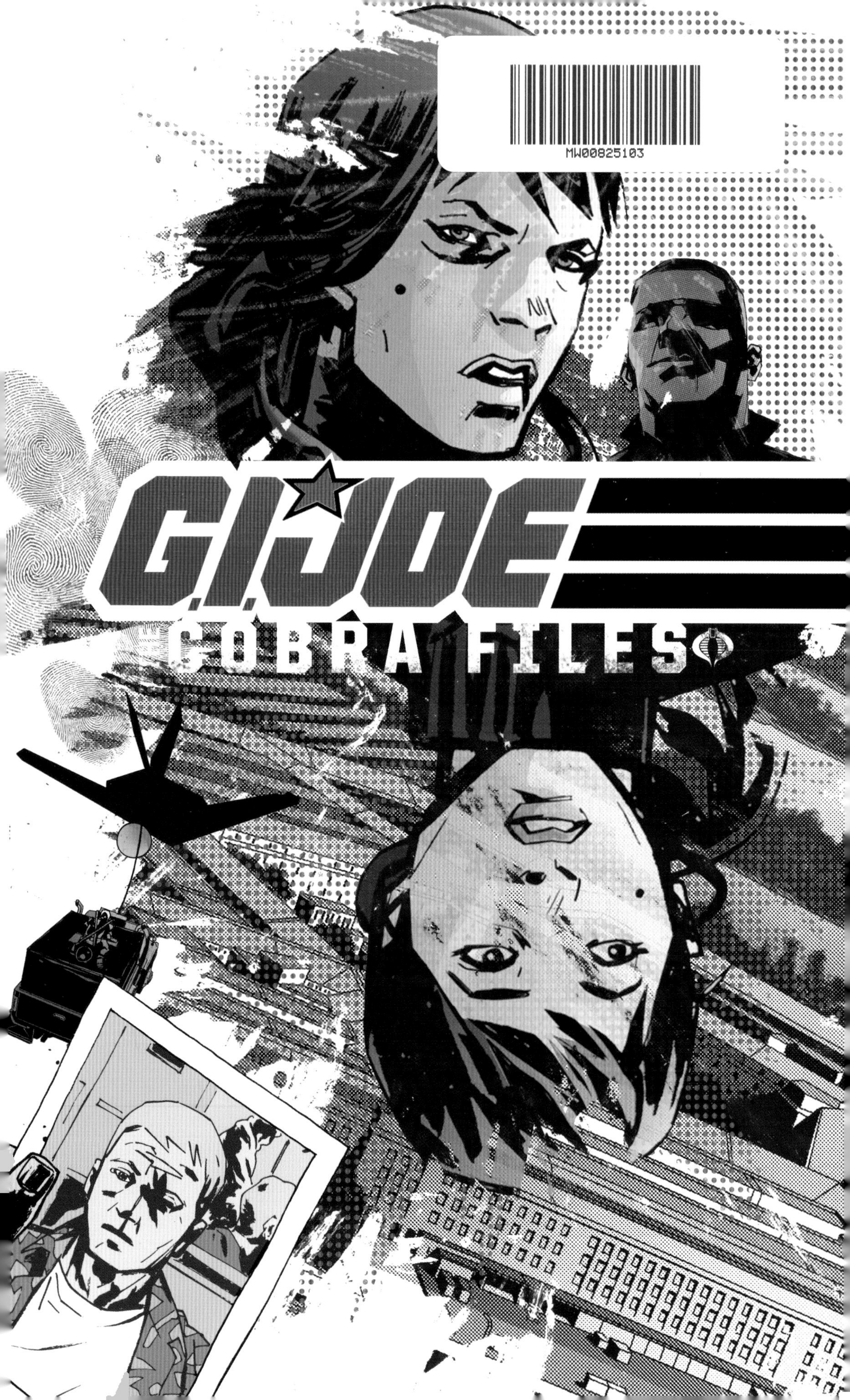
G.I. JOE
COBRA FILES

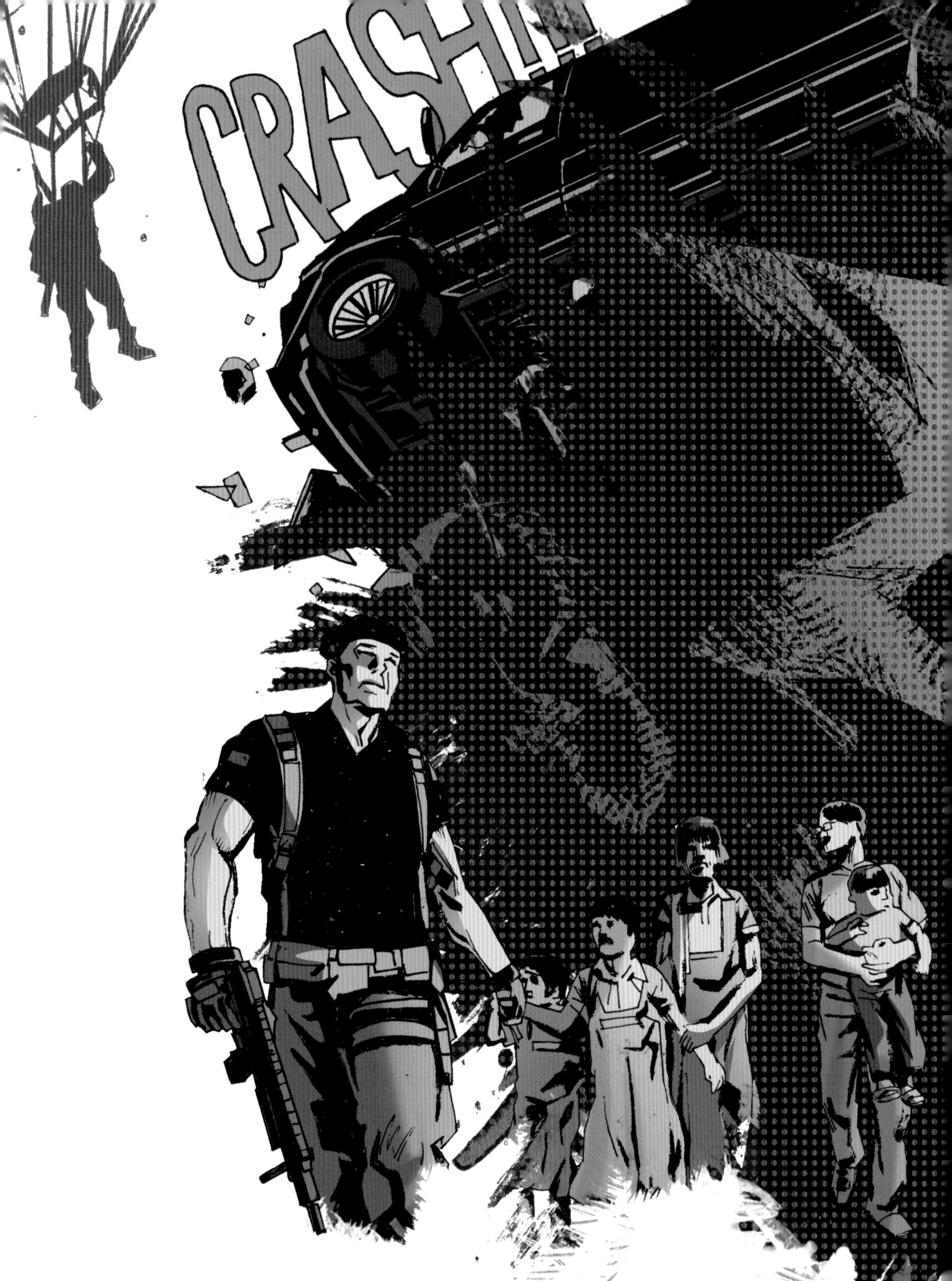
CRASH!!

Special thanks to Hasbro's Aaron Archer, Derryl DePriest, Joe Del Regno, Ed Lane, Joe Furfaro, Jos Huxley, Heather Hopkins, and Michael Kelly for their invaluable assistance.

IDW founded by Ted Adams, Alex Garner, Kris Oprisko, and Robbie Robbins

ISBN: 978-1-61377-731-2

16 15 14 13 1 2 3 4

IDW

Hasbro

Ted Adams, CEO & Publisher
Greg Goldstein, President & COO
Robbie Robbins, EVP/Sr. Graphic Artist
Chris Ryall, Chief Creative Officer/Editor-in-Chief
Matthew Ruzicka, CPA, Chief Financial Officer
Alan Payne, VP of Sales
Dirk Wood, VP of Marketing
Lorelei Bunjes, VP of Digital Services

Become our fan on Facebook **facebook.com/idwpublishing**
Follow us on Twitter **@idwpublishing**
Check us out on YouTube **youtube.com/idwpublishing**
**www.IDWPUBLISHING.com**



Originally published as G.I. JOE: THE COBRA FILES issues #1–4.

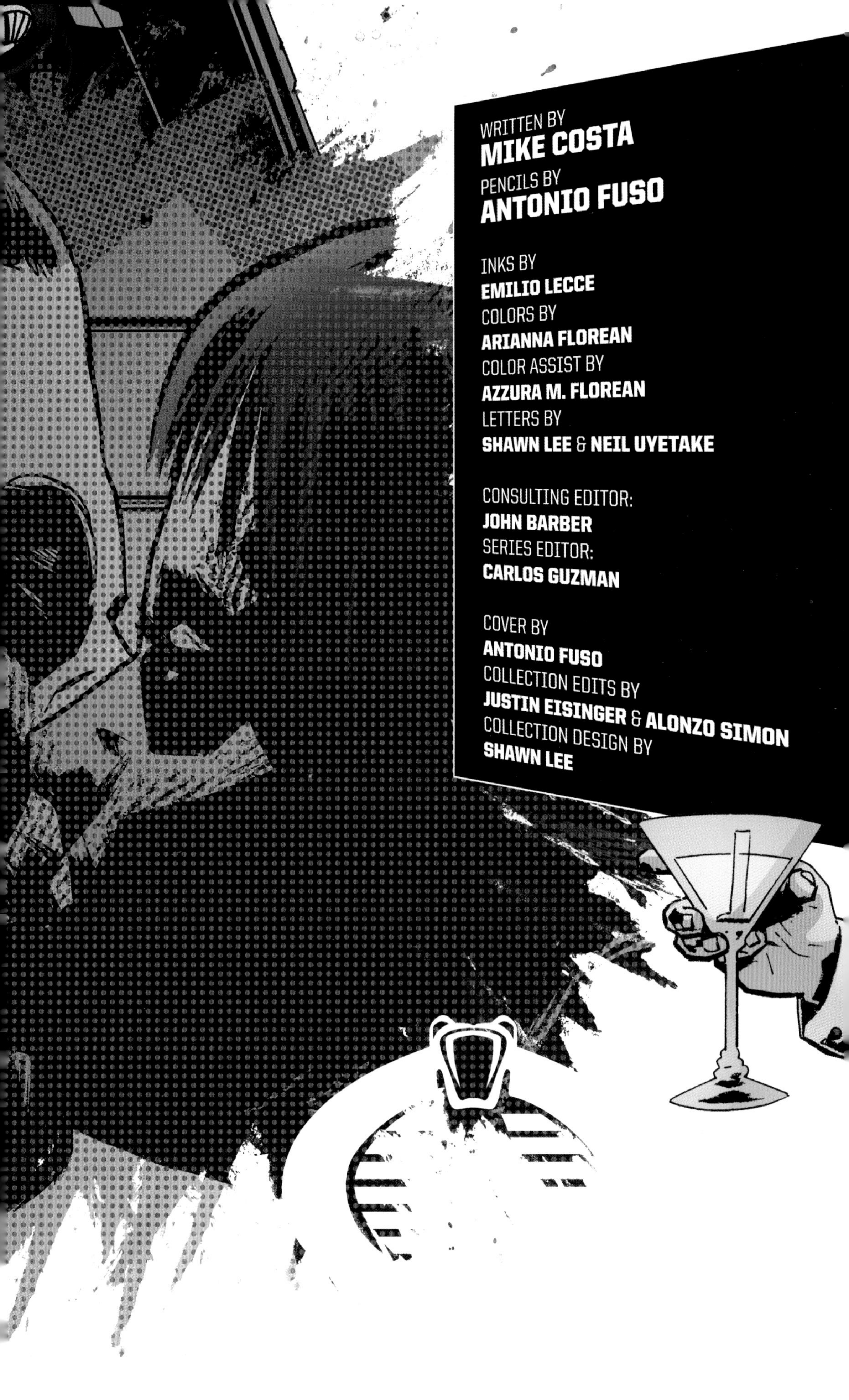

WRITTEN BY
**MIKE COSTA**
PENCILS BY
**ANTONIO FUSO**

INKS BY
**EMILIO LECCE**
COLORS BY
**ARIANNA FLOREAN**
COLOR ASSIST BY
**AZZURA M. FLOREAN**
LETTERS BY
**SHAWN LEE** & **NEIL UYETAKE**

CONSULTING EDITOR:
**JOHN BARBER**
SERIES EDITOR:
**CARLOS GUZMAN**

COVER BY
**ANTONIO FUSO**
COLLECTION EDITS BY
**JUSTIN EISINGER** & **ALONZO SIMON**
COLLECTION DESIGN BY
**SHAWN LEE**

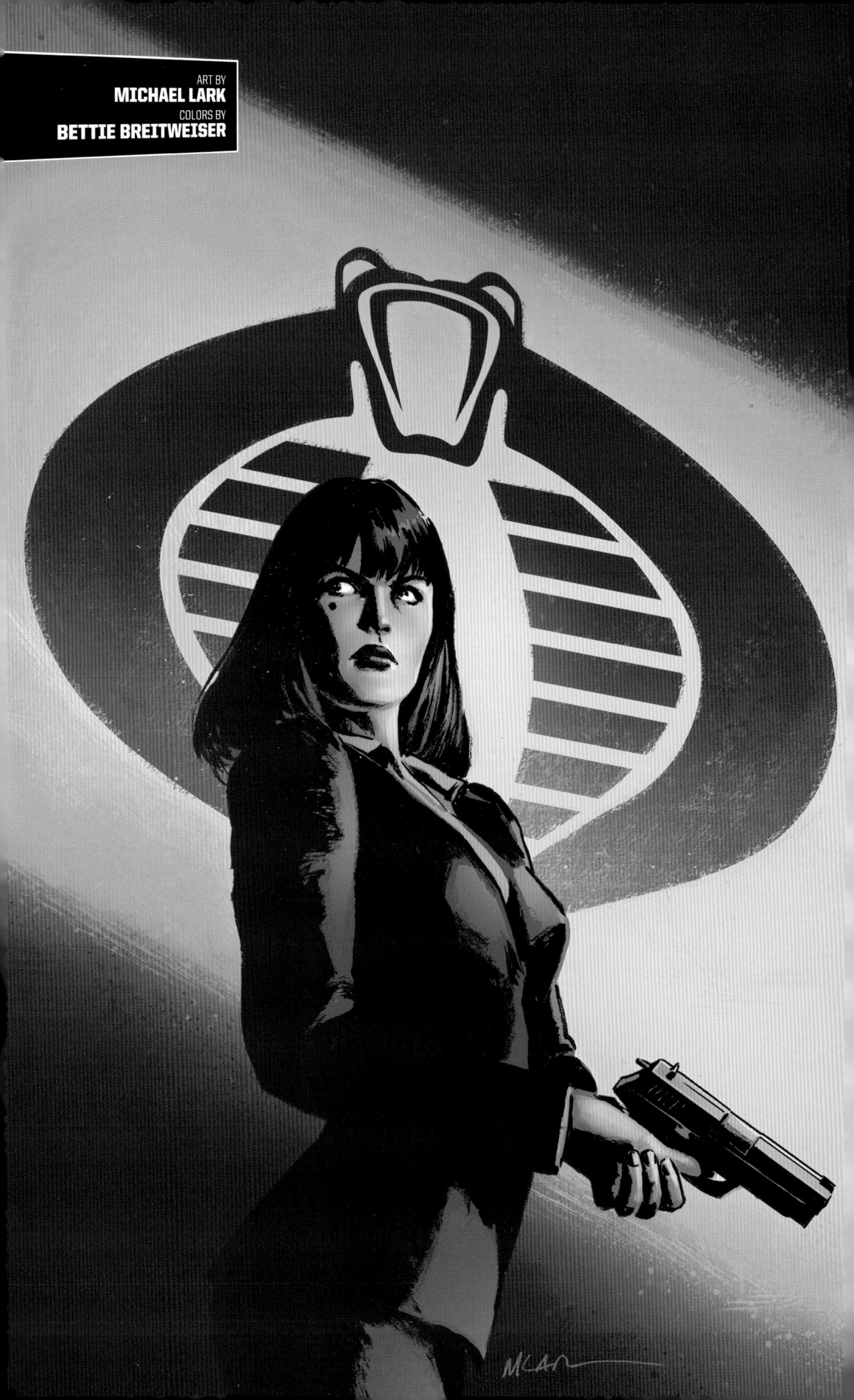

ART BY
**MICHAEL LARK**
COLORS BY
**BETTIE BREITWEISER**

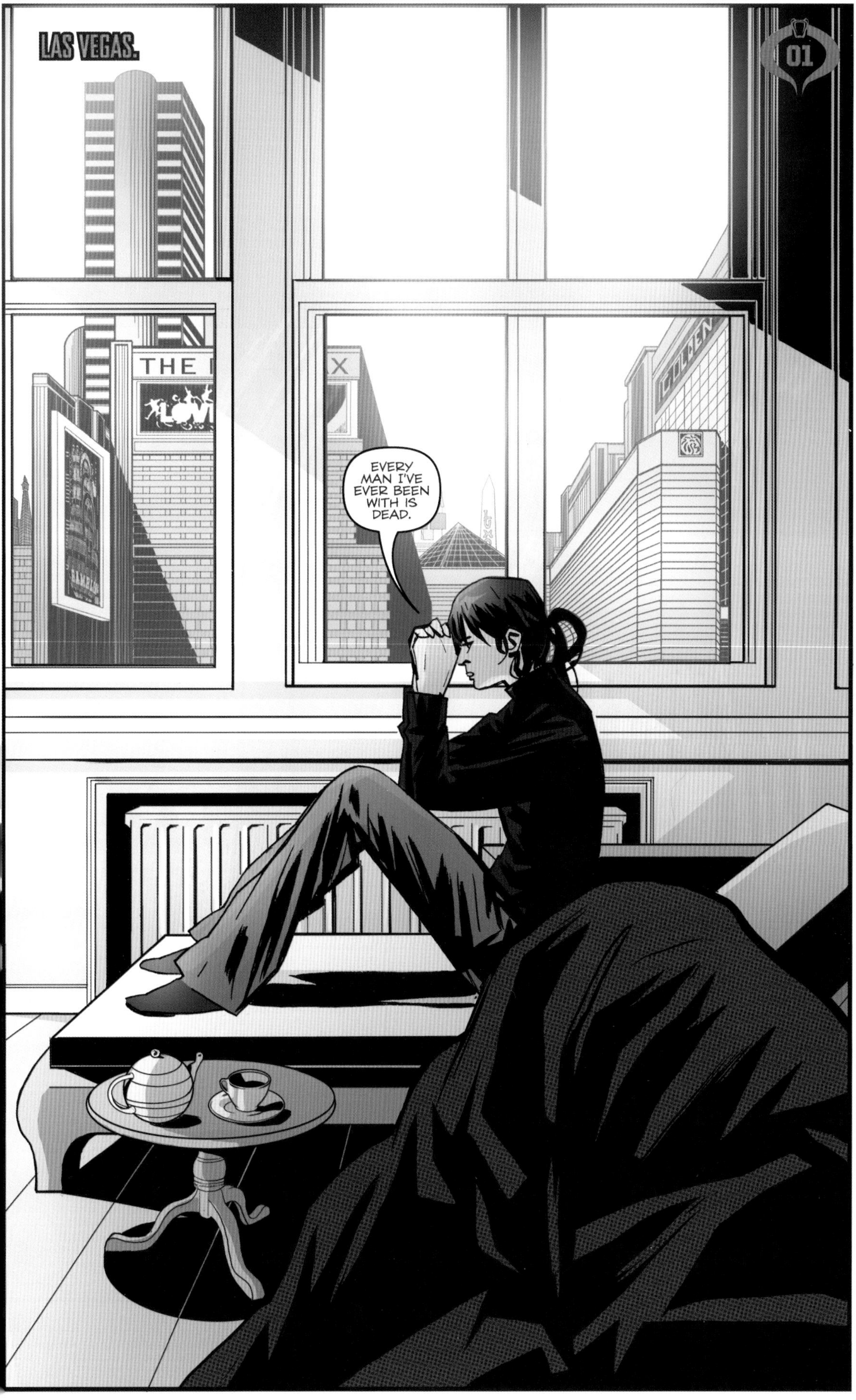
LAS VEGAS.
01
THE
X
EVERY MAN I'VE EVER BEEN WITH IS DEAD.

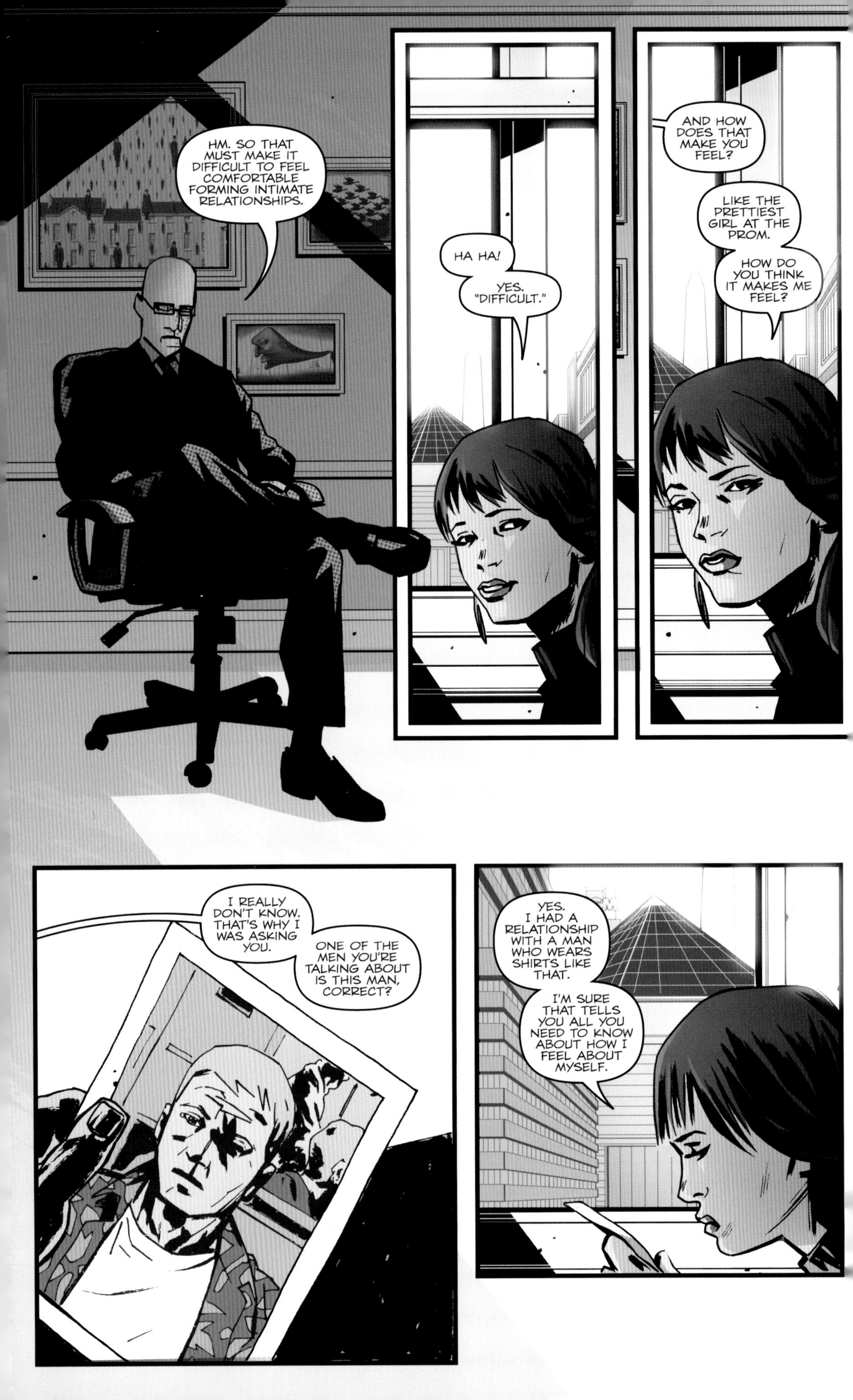

HM. SO THAT MUST MAKE IT DIFFICULT TO FEEL COMFORTABLE FORMING INTIMATE RELATIONSHIPS.
HA HA!
YES. "DIFFICULT."
AND HOW DOES THAT MAKE YOU FEEL?
LIKE THE PRETTIEST GIRL AT THE PROM.
HOW DO YOU THINK IT MAKES ME FEEL?
I REALLY DON'T KNOW. THAT'S WHY I WAS ASKING YOU.
ONE OF THE MEN YOU'RE TALKING ABOUT IS THIS MAN, CORRECT?
YES. I HAD A RELATIONSHIP WITH A MAN WHO WEARS SHIRTS LIKE THAT.
I'M SURE THAT TELLS YOU ALL YOU NEED TO KNOW ABOUT HOW I FEEL ABOUT MYSELF.

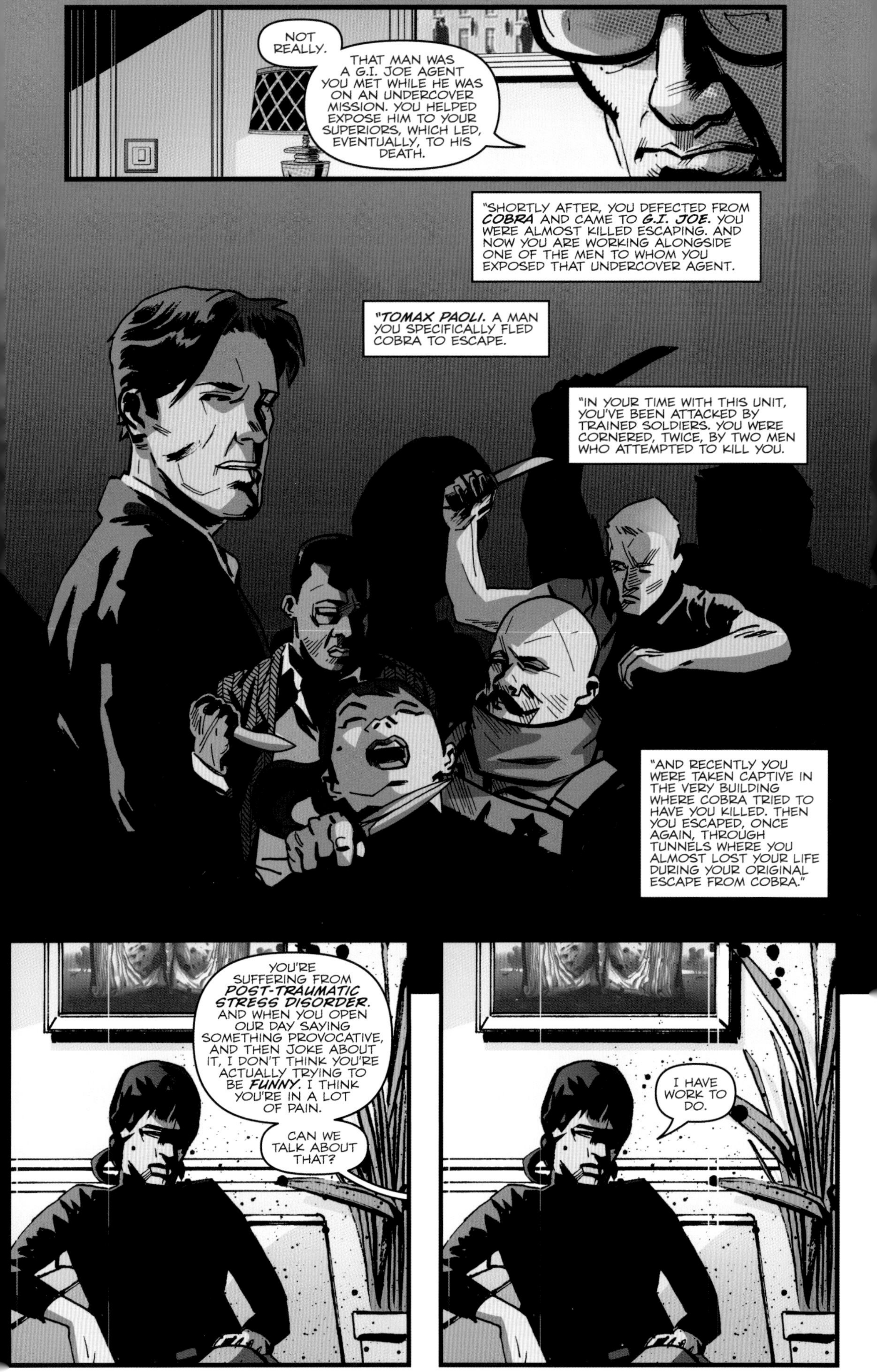
NOT REALLY.
THAT MAN WAS A G.I. JOE AGENT YOU MET WHILE HE WAS ON AN UNDERCOVER MISSION. YOU HELPED EXPOSE HIM TO YOUR SUPERIORS, WHICH LED, EVENTUALLY, TO HIS DEATH.
"SHORTLY AFTER, YOU DEFECTED FROM COBRA AND CAME TO G.I. JOE. YOU WERE ALMOST KILLED ESCAPING. AND NOW YOU ARE WORKING ALONGSIDE ONE OF THE MEN TO WHOM YOU EXPOSED THAT UNDERCOVER AGENT.
"TOMAX PAOLI. A MAN YOU SPECIFICALLY FLED COBRA TO ESCAPE.
"IN YOUR TIME WITH THIS UNIT, YOU'VE BEEN ATTACKED BY TRAINED SOLDIERS. YOU WERE CORNERED, TWICE, BY TWO MEN WHO ATTEMPTED TO KILL YOU.
"AND RECENTLY YOU WERE TAKEN CAPTIVE IN THE VERY BUILDING WHERE COBRA TRIED TO HAVE YOU KILLED. THEN YOU ESCAPED, ONCE AGAIN, THROUGH TUNNELS WHERE YOU ALMOST LOST YOUR LIFE DURING YOUR ORIGINAL ESCAPE FROM COBRA."
YOU'RE SUFFERING FROM POST-TRAUMATIC STRESS DISORDER. AND WHEN YOU OPEN OUR DAY SAYING SOMETHING PROVOCATIVE, AND THEN JOKE ABOUT IT, I DON'T THINK YOU'RE ACTUALLY TRYING TO BE FUNNY. I THINK YOU'RE IN A LOT OF PAIN.
CAN WE TALK ABOUT THAT?
I HAVE WORK TO DO.

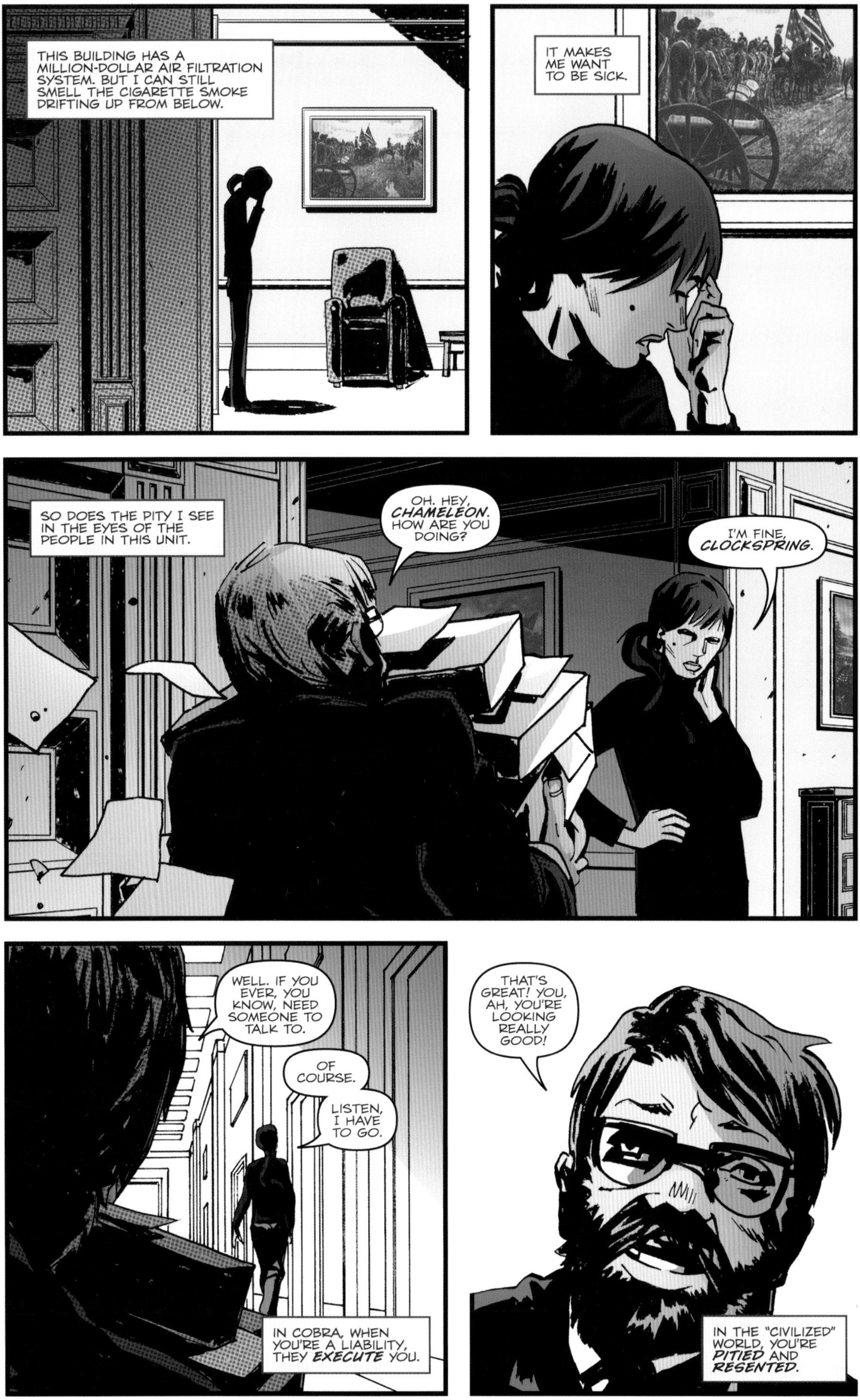
THIS BUILDING HAS A MILLION-DOLLAR AIR FILTRATION SYSTEM. BUT I CAN STILL SMELL THE CIGARETTE SMOKE DRIFTING UP FROM BELOW.
IT MAKES ME WANT TO BE SICK.
SO DOES THE PITY I SEE IN THE EYES OF THE PEOPLE IN THIS UNIT.
OH. HEY, CHAMELEON. HOW ARE YOU DOING?
I'M FINE, CLOCKSPRING.
WELL. IF YOU EVER, YOU KNOW, NEED SOMEONE TO TALK TO.
OF COURSE.
LISTEN, I HAVE TO GO.
IN COBRA, WHEN YOU'RE A LIABILITY, THEY EXECUTE YOU.
THAT'S GREAT! YOU, AH, YOU'RE LOOKING REALLY GOOD!
IN THE "CIVILIZED" WORLD, YOU'RE PITIED AND RESENTED.

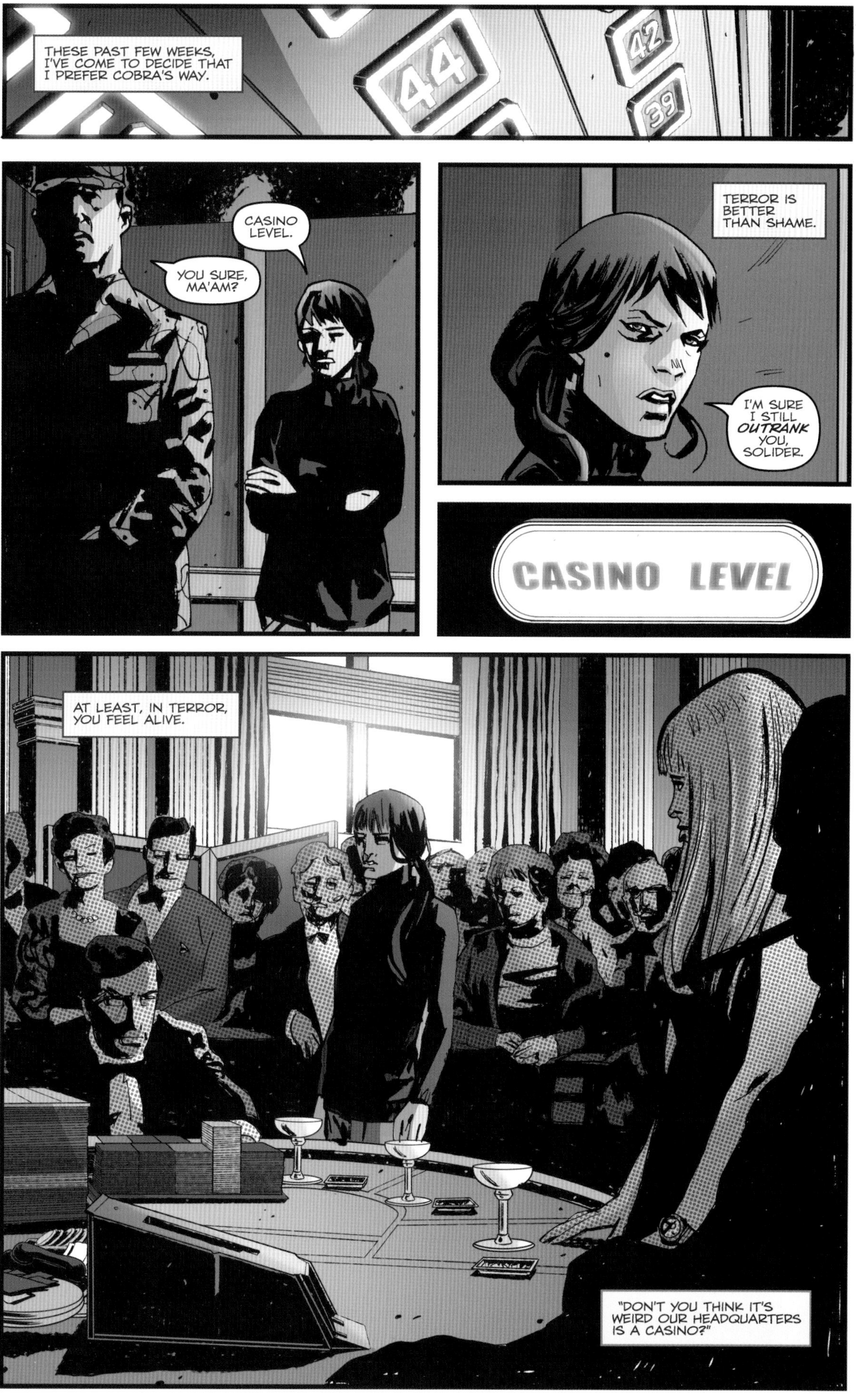
THESE PAST FEW WEEKS, I'VE COME TO DECIDE THAT I PREFER COBRA'S WAY.
44
42
39
CASINO LEVEL.
YOU SURE, MA'AM?
TERROR IS BETTER THAN SHAME.
I'M SURE I STILL OUTRANK YOU, SOLIDER.
CASINO LEVEL
AT LEAST, IN TERROR, YOU FEEL ALIVE.
"DON'T YOU THINK IT'S WEIRD OUR HEADQUARTERS IS A CASINO?"

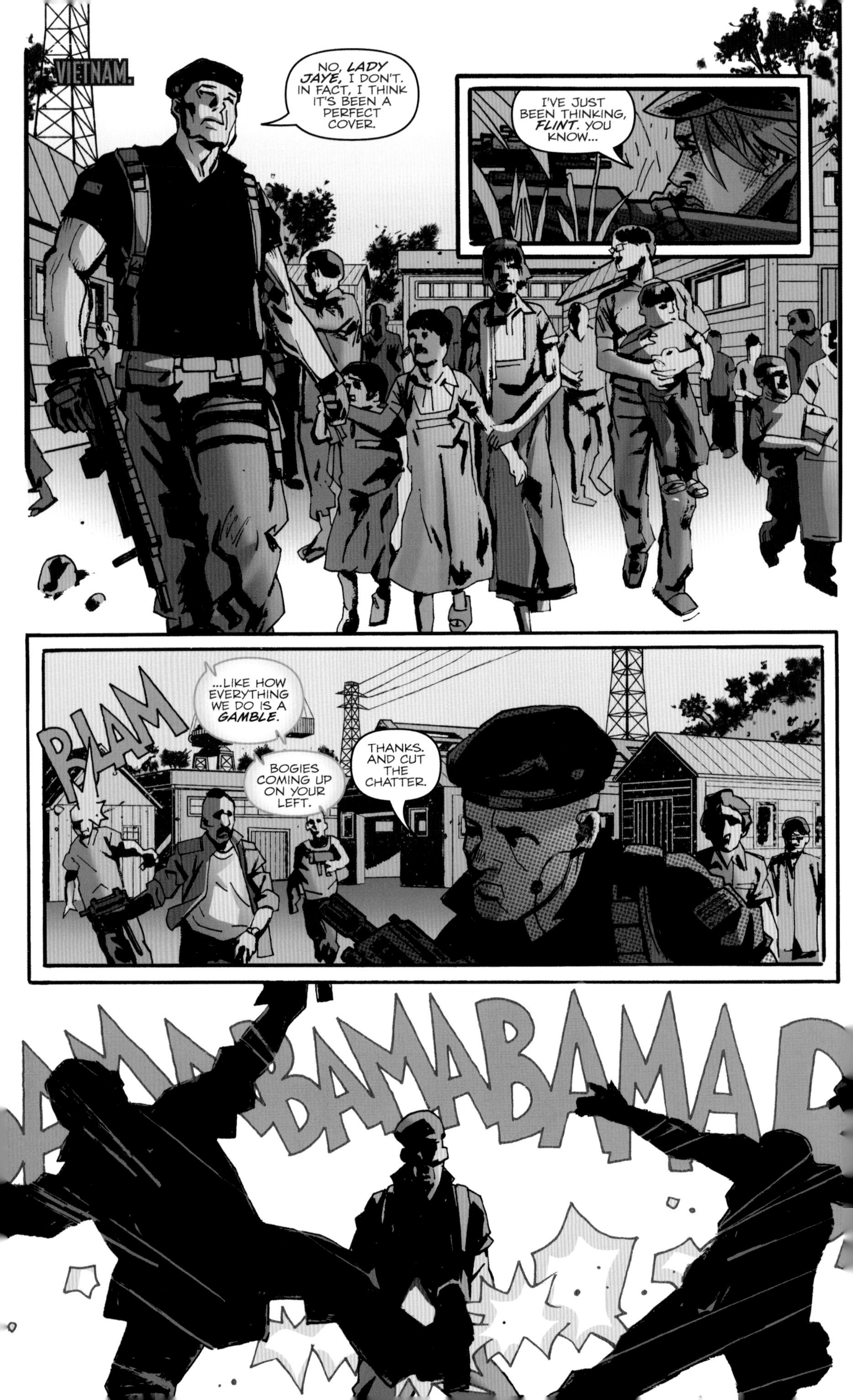
VIETNAM.
NO, LADY JAYE, I DON'T. IN FACT, I THINK IT'S BEEN A PERFECT COVER.
I'VE JUST BEEN THINKING, FLINT. YOU KNOW...
BLAM
...LIKE HOW EVERYTHING WE DO IS A GAMBLE.
BOGIES COMING UP ON YOUR LEFT.
THANKS. AND CUT THE CHATTER.
BAMABAMABAMA

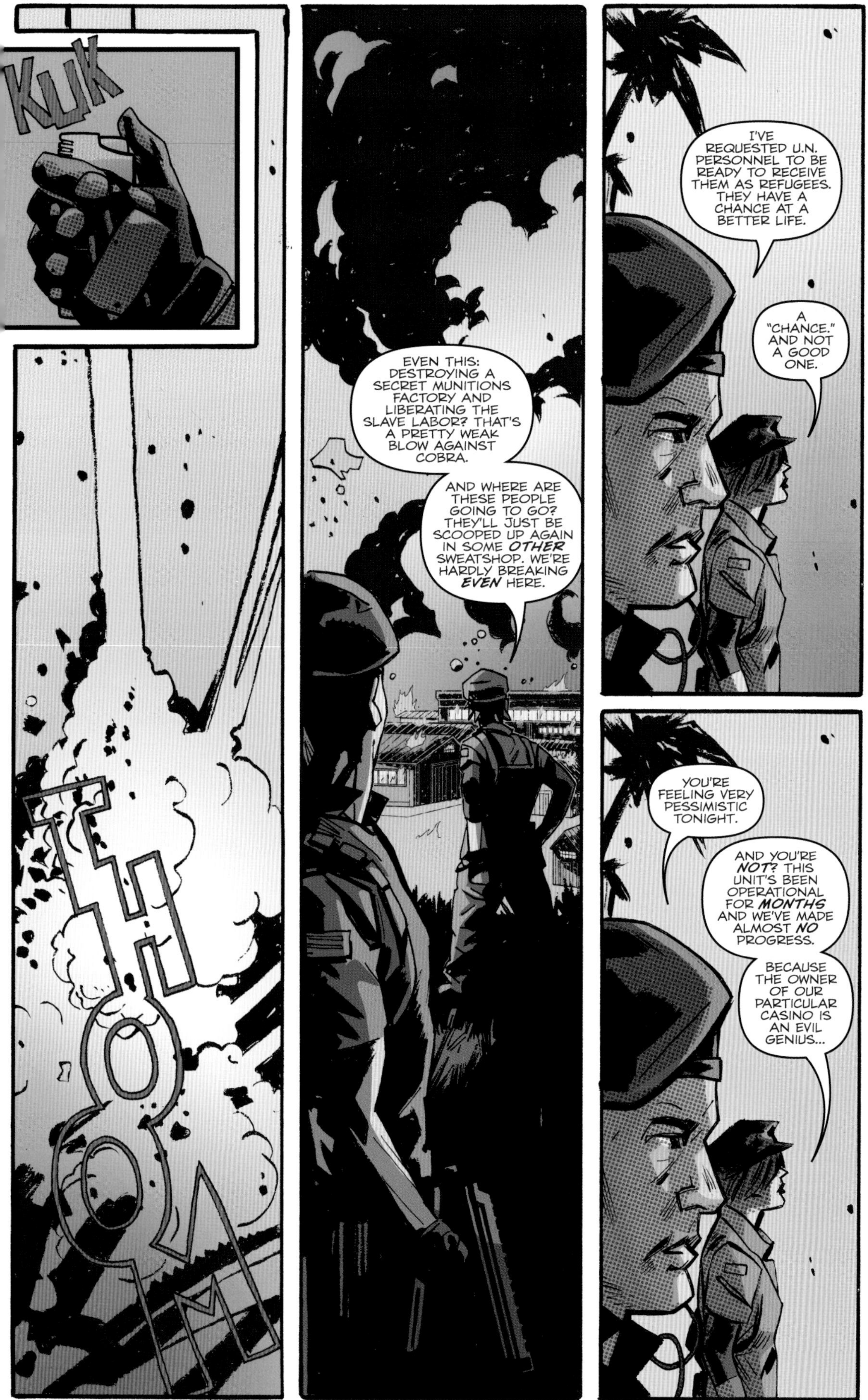

KLIK
THOOOM
EVEN THIS: DESTROYING A SECRET MUNITIONS FACTORY AND LIBERATING THE SLAVE LABOR? THAT'S A PRETTY WEAK BLOW AGAINST COBRA.
AND WHERE ARE THESE PEOPLE GOING TO GO? THEY'LL JUST BE SCOOPED UP AGAIN IN SOME *OTHER* SWEATSHOP. WE'RE HARDLY BREAKING *EVEN* HERE.
I'VE REQUESTED U.N. PERSONNEL TO BE READY TO RECEIVE THEM AS REFUGEES. THEY HAVE A CHANCE AT A BETTER LIFE.
A "CHANCE." AND NOT A GOOD ONE.
YOU'RE FEELING VERY PESSIMISTIC TONIGHT.
AND YOU'RE *NOT?* THIS UNIT'S BEEN OPERATIONAL FOR *MONTHS* AND WE'VE MADE ALMOST *NO* PROGRESS.
BECAUSE THE OWNER OF OUR PARTICULAR CASINO IS AN EVIL GENIUS...

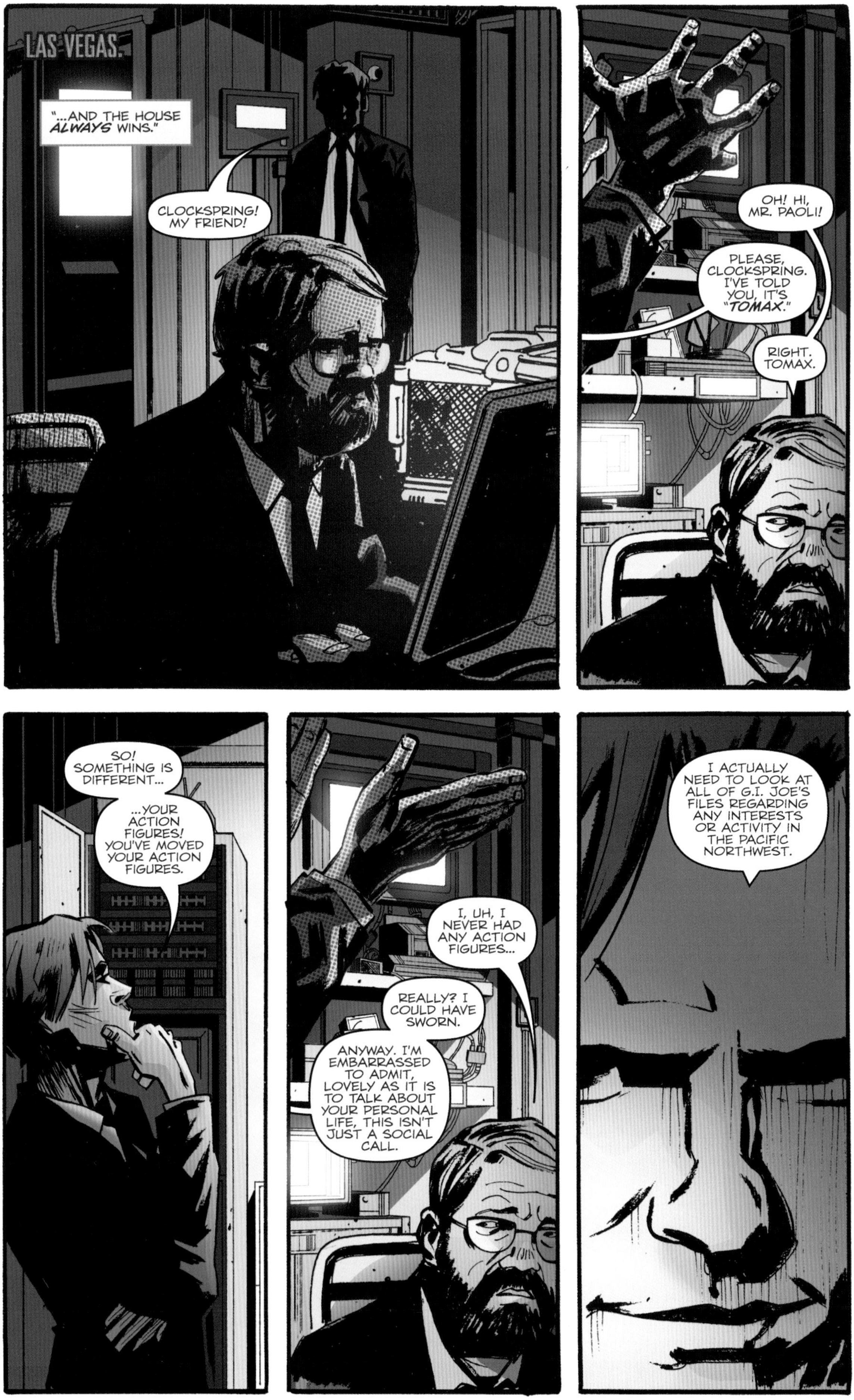
LAS VEGAS.
"...AND THE HOUSE ALWAYS WINS."
CLOCKSPRING! MY FRIEND!
OH! HI, MR. PAOLI!
PLEASE, CLOCKSPRING. I'VE TOLD YOU, IT'S "TOMAX."
RIGHT. TOMAX.
SO! SOMETHING IS DIFFERENT...
...YOUR ACTION FIGURES! YOU'VE MOVED YOUR ACTION FIGURES.
I, UH, I NEVER HAD ANY ACTION FIGURES...
REALLY? I COULD HAVE SWORN.
ANYWAY. I'M EMBARRASSED TO ADMIT, LOVELY AS IT IS TO TALK ABOUT YOUR PERSONAL LIFE, THIS ISN'T JUST A SOCIAL CALL.
I ACTUALLY NEED TO LOOK AT ALL OF G.I. JOE'S FILES REGARDING ANY INTERESTS OR ACTIVITY IN THE PACIFIC NORTHWEST.

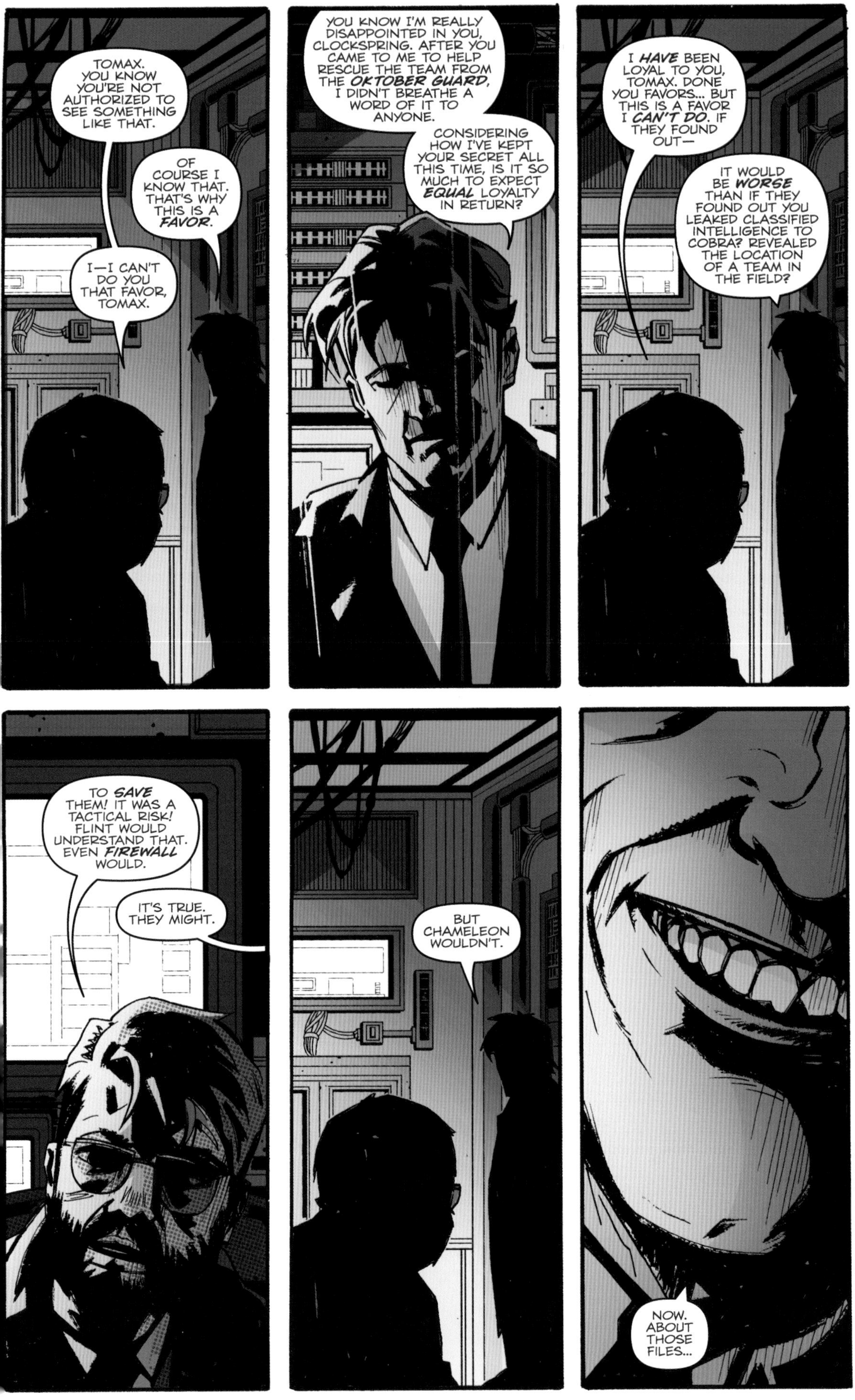
TOMAX. YOU KNOW YOU'RE NOT AUTHORIZED TO SEE SOMETHING LIKE THAT.
OF COURSE I KNOW THAT. THAT'S WHY THIS IS A FAVOR.
I—I CAN'T DO YOU THAT FAVOR, TOMAX.
YOU KNOW I'M REALLY DISAPPOINTED IN YOU, CLOCKSPRING. AFTER YOU CAME TO ME TO HELP RESCUE THE TEAM FROM THE OKTOBER GUARD, I DIDN'T BREATHE A WORD OF IT TO ANYONE.
CONSIDERING HOW I'VE KEPT YOUR SECRET ALL THIS TIME, IS IT SO MUCH TO EXPECT EQUAL LOYALTY IN RETURN?
I HAVE BEEN LOYAL TO YOU, TOMAX. DONE YOU FAVORS... BUT THIS IS A FAVOR I CAN'T DO. IF THEY FOUND OUT—
IT WOULD BE WORSE THAN IF THEY FOUND OUT YOU LEAKED CLASSIFIED INTELLIGENCE TO COBRA? REVEALED THE LOCATION OF A TEAM IN THE FIELD?
TO SAVE THEM! IT WAS A TACTICAL RISK! FLINT WOULD UNDERSTAND THAT. EVEN FIREWALL WOULD.
IT'S TRUE. THEY MIGHT.
BUT CHAMELEON WOULDN'T.
NOW. ABOUT THOSE FILES...

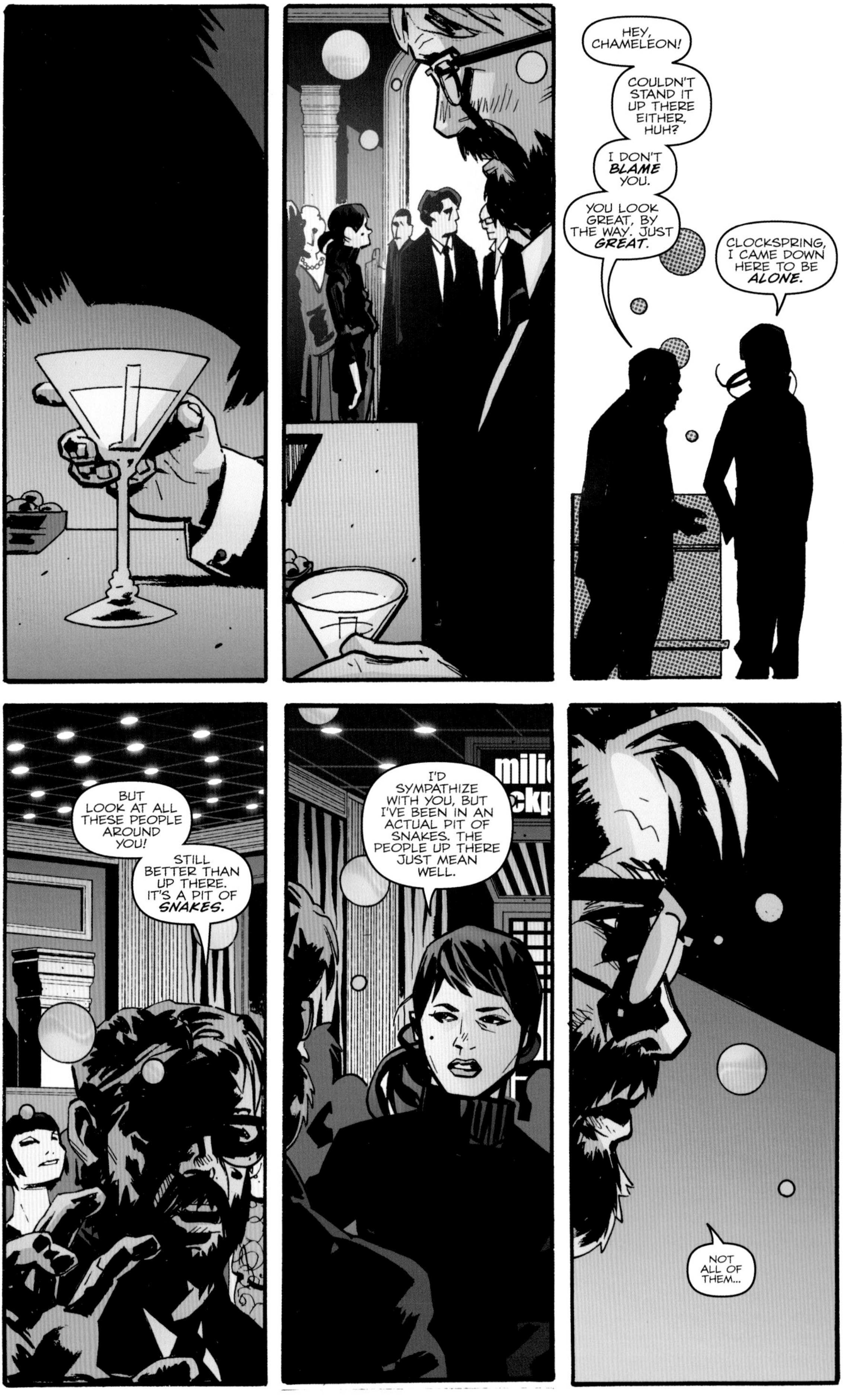
HEY, CHAMELEON!
COULDN'T STAND IT UP THERE EITHER, HUH?
I DON'T BLAME YOU.
YOU LOOK GREAT, BY THE WAY. JUST GREAT.
CLOCKSPRING, I CAME DOWN HERE TO BE ALONE.
BUT LOOK AT ALL THESE PEOPLE AROUND YOU!
STILL BETTER THAN UP THERE. IT'S A PIT OF SNAKES.
I'D SYMPATHIZE WITH YOU, BUT I'VE BEEN IN AN ACTUAL PIT OF SNAKES. THE PEOPLE UP THERE JUST MEAN WELL.
NOT ALL OF THEM...

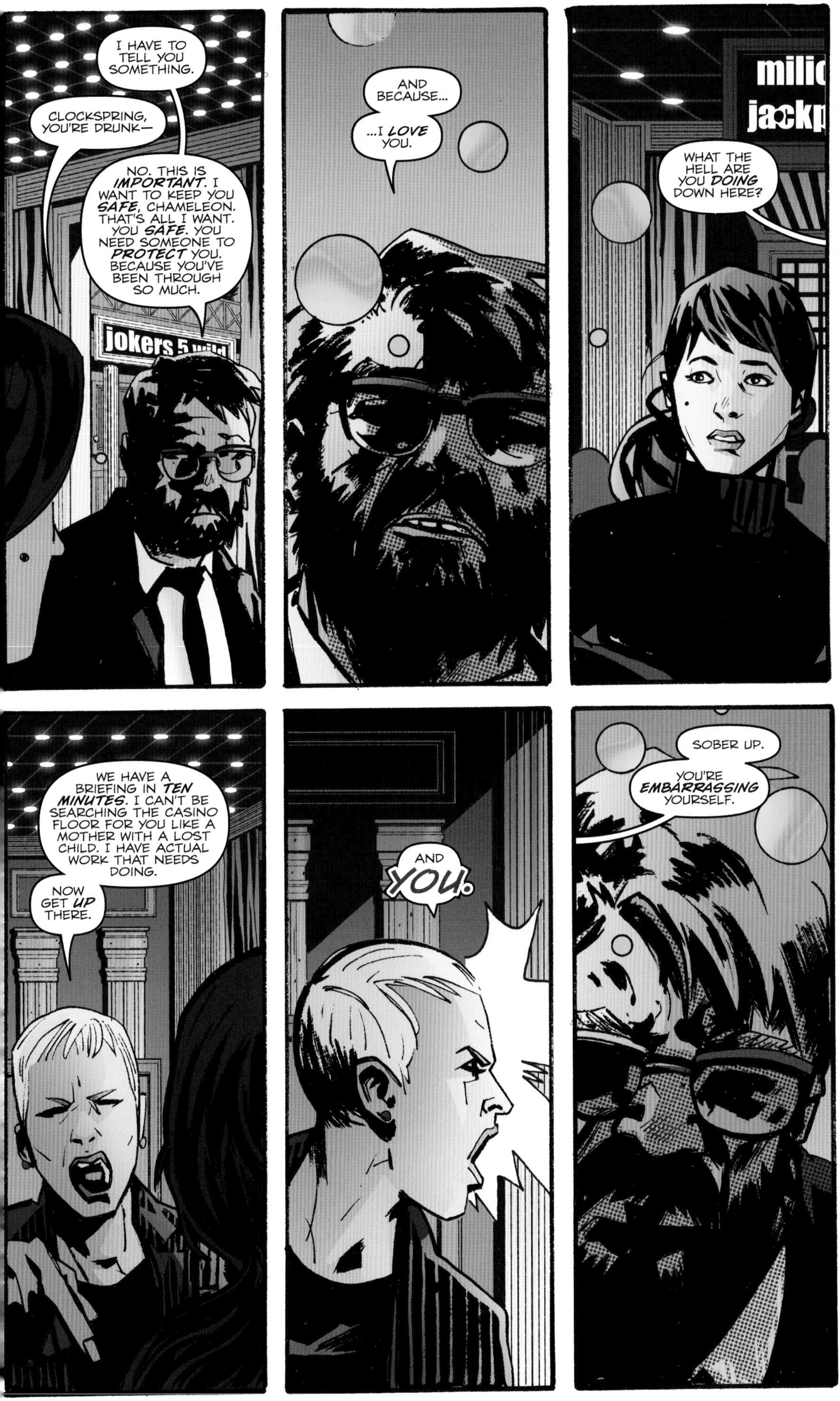

I HAVE TO TELL YOU SOMETHING.
CLOCKSPRING, YOU'RE DRUNK—
NO. THIS IS IMPORTANT. I WANT TO KEEP YOU SAFE, CHAMELEON. THAT'S ALL I WANT. YOU SAFE. YOU NEED SOMEONE TO PROTECT YOU. BECAUSE YOU'VE BEEN THROUGH SO MUCH.
jokers 5 wild
AND BECAUSE...
...I LOVE YOU.
milic
jackp
WHAT THE HELL ARE YOU DOING DOWN HERE?
WE HAVE A BRIEFING IN TEN MINUTES. I CAN'T BE SEARCHING THE CASINO FLOOR FOR YOU LIKE A MOTHER WITH A LOST CHILD. I HAVE ACTUAL WORK THAT NEEDS DOING.
NOW GET UP THERE.
AND YOU.
SOBER UP.
YOU'RE EMBARRASSING YOURSELF.

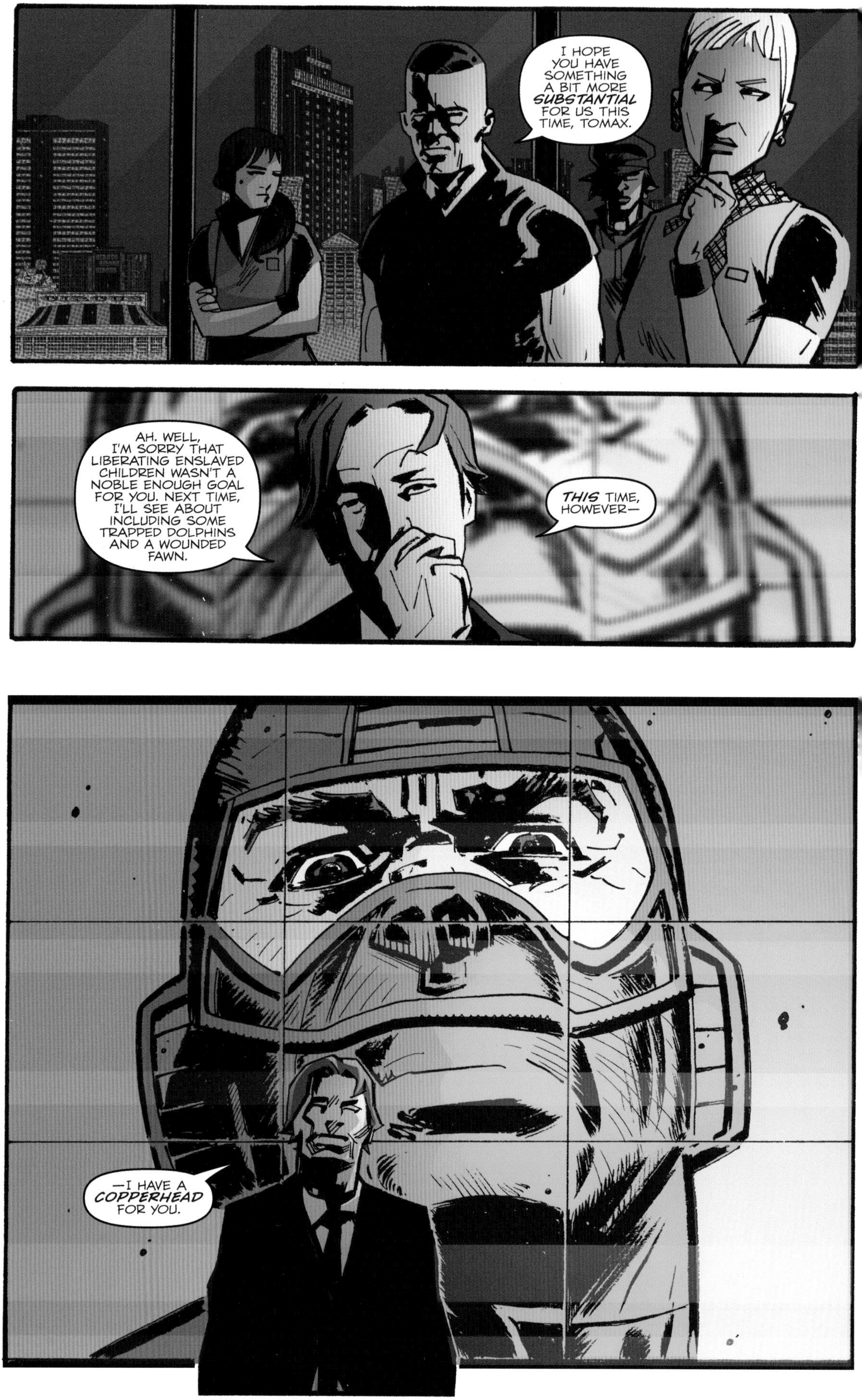
I HOPE YOU HAVE SOMETHING A BIT MORE SUBSTANTIAL FOR US THIS TIME, TOMAX.
AH. WELL, I'M SORRY THAT LIBERATING ENSLAVED CHILDREN WASN'T A NOBLE ENOUGH GOAL FOR YOU. NEXT TIME, I'LL SEE ABOUT INCLUDING SOME TRAPPED DOLPHINS AND A WOUNDED FAWN.
THIS TIME, HOWEVER—
—I HAVE A COPPERHEAD FOR YOU.

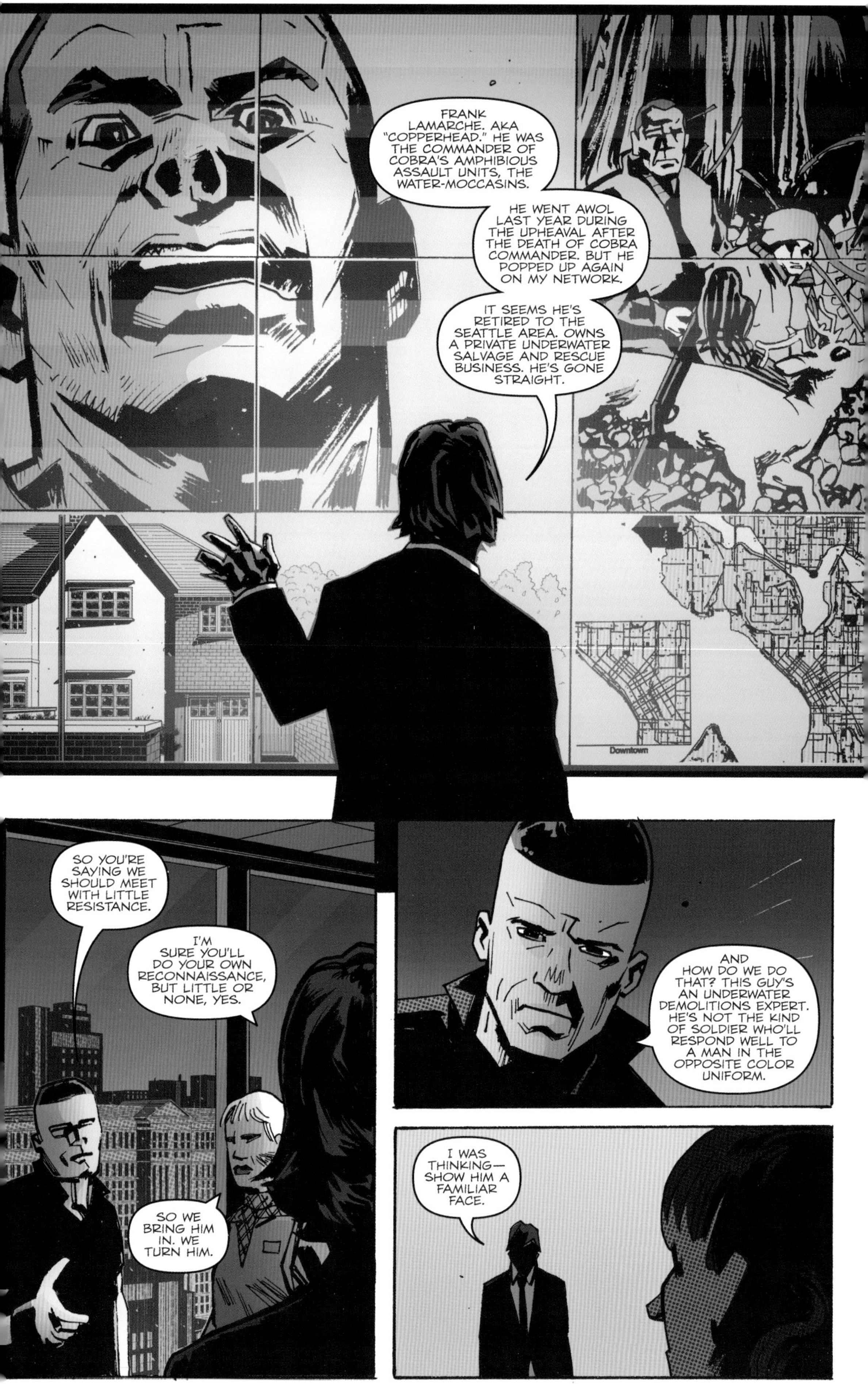

FRANK LAMARCHE. AKA "COPPERHEAD." HE WAS THE COMMANDER OF COBRA'S AMPHIBIOUS ASSAULT UNITS, THE WATER-MOCCASINS.
HE WENT AWOL LAST YEAR DURING THE UPHEAVAL AFTER THE DEATH OF COBRA COMMANDER. BUT HE POPPED UP AGAIN ON MY NETWORK.
IT SEEMS HE'S RETIRED TO THE SEATTLE AREA. OWNS A PRIVATE UNDERWATER SALVAGE AND RESCUE BUSINESS. HE'S GONE STRAIGHT.
Downtown
SO YOU'RE SAYING WE SHOULD MEET WITH LITTLE RESISTANCE.
I'M SURE YOU'LL DO YOUR OWN RECONNAISSANCE, BUT LITTLE OR NONE, YES.
SO WE BRING HIM IN. WE TURN HIM.
AND HOW DO WE DO THAT? THIS GUY'S AN UNDERWATER DEMOLITIONS EXPERT. HE'S NOT THE KIND OF SOLDIER WHO'LL RESPOND WELL TO A MAN IN THE OPPOSITE COLOR UNIFORM.
I WAS THINKING— SHOW HIM A FAMILIAR FACE.

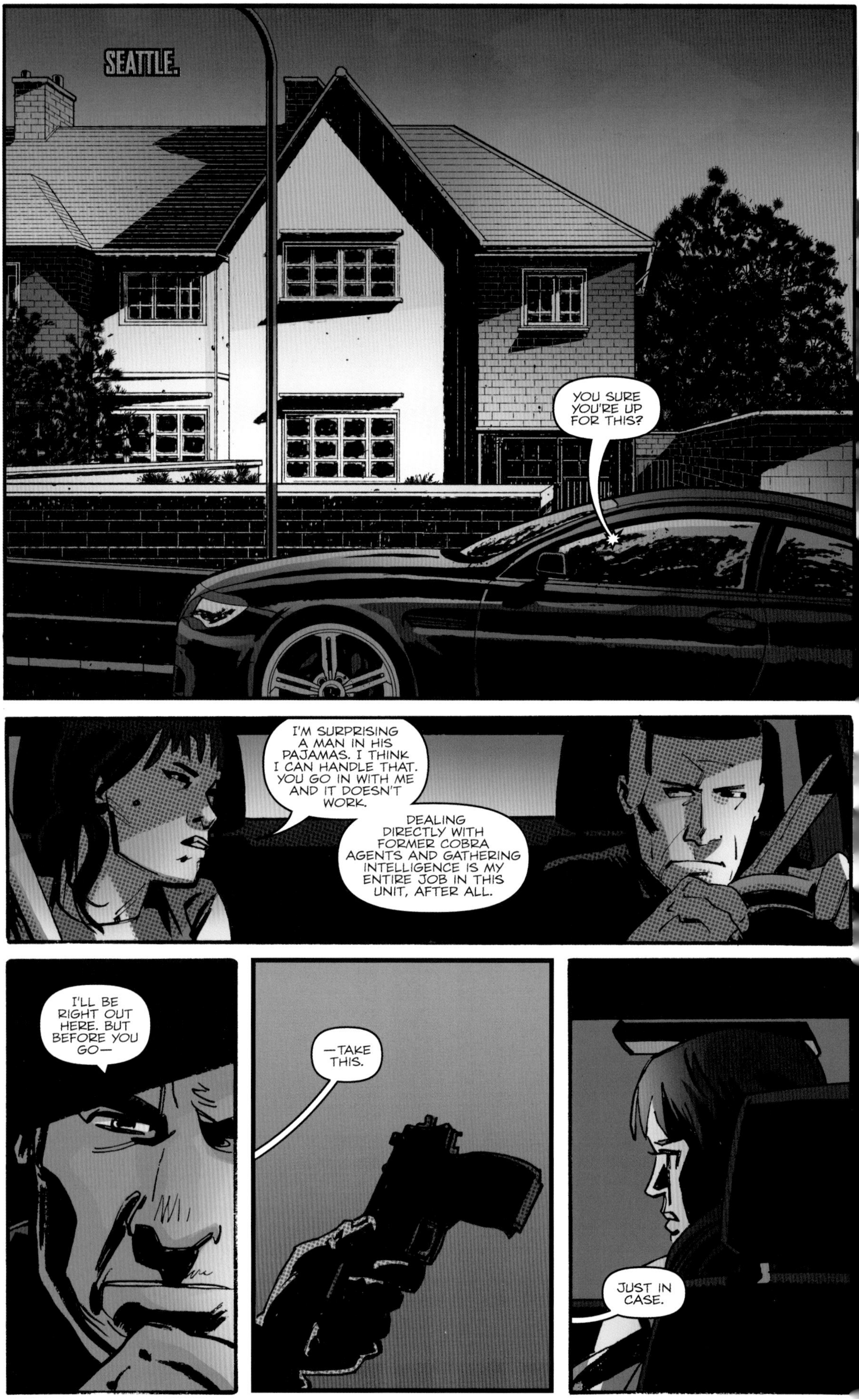
SEATTLE.
YOU SURE YOU'RE UP FOR THIS?
I'M SURPRISING A MAN IN HIS PAJAMAS. I THINK I CAN HANDLE THAT. YOU GO IN WITH ME AND IT DOESN'T WORK.
DEALING DIRECTLY WITH FORMER COBRA AGENTS AND GATHERING INTELLIGENCE IS MY ENTIRE JOB IN THIS UNIT, AFTER ALL.
I'LL BE RIGHT OUT HERE. BUT BEFORE YOU GO—
—TAKE THIS.
JUST IN CASE.

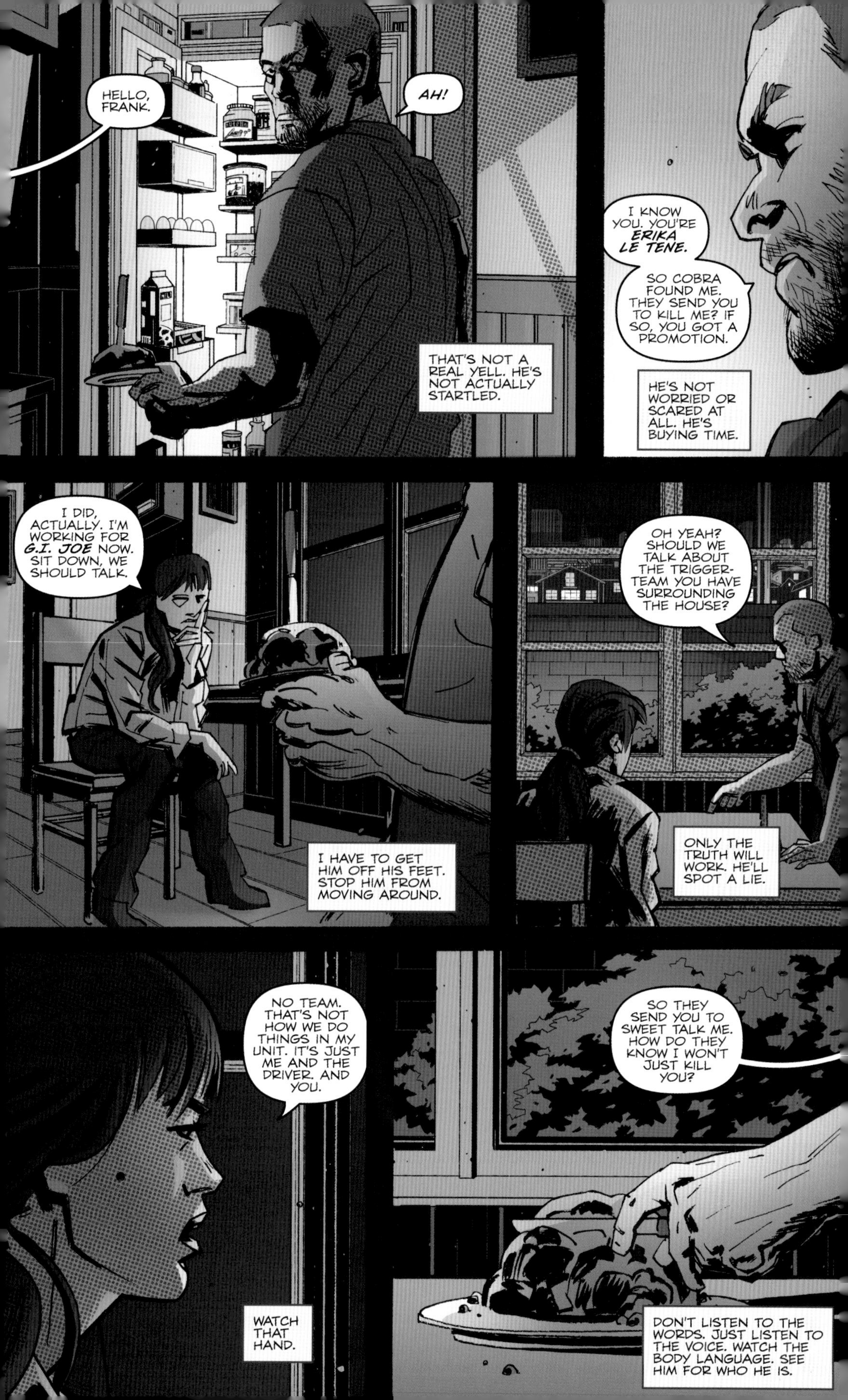
HELLO, FRANK.
AH!
THAT'S NOT A REAL YELL. HE'S NOT ACTUALLY STARTLED.
I KNOW YOU. YOU'RE ERIKA LE TENE.
SO COBRA FOUND ME. THEY SEND YOU TO KILL ME? IF SO, YOU GOT A PROMOTION.
HE'S NOT WORRIED OR SCARED AT ALL. HE'S BUYING TIME.
I DID, ACTUALLY. I'M WORKING FOR G.I. JOE NOW. SIT DOWN, WE SHOULD TALK.
I HAVE TO GET HIM OFF HIS FEET. STOP HIM FROM MOVING AROUND.
OH YEAH? SHOULD WE TALK ABOUT THE TRIGGER-TEAM YOU HAVE SURROUNDING THE HOUSE?
ONLY THE TRUTH WILL WORK. HE'LL SPOT A LIE.
NO TEAM. THAT'S NOT HOW WE DO THINGS IN MY UNIT. IT'S JUST ME AND THE DRIVER. AND YOU.
WATCH THAT HAND.
SO THEY SEND YOU TO SWEET TALK ME. HOW DO THEY KNOW I WON'T JUST KILL YOU?
DON'T LISTEN TO THE WORDS. JUST LISTEN TO THE VOICE. WATCH THE BODY LANGUAGE. SEE HIM FOR WHO HE IS.

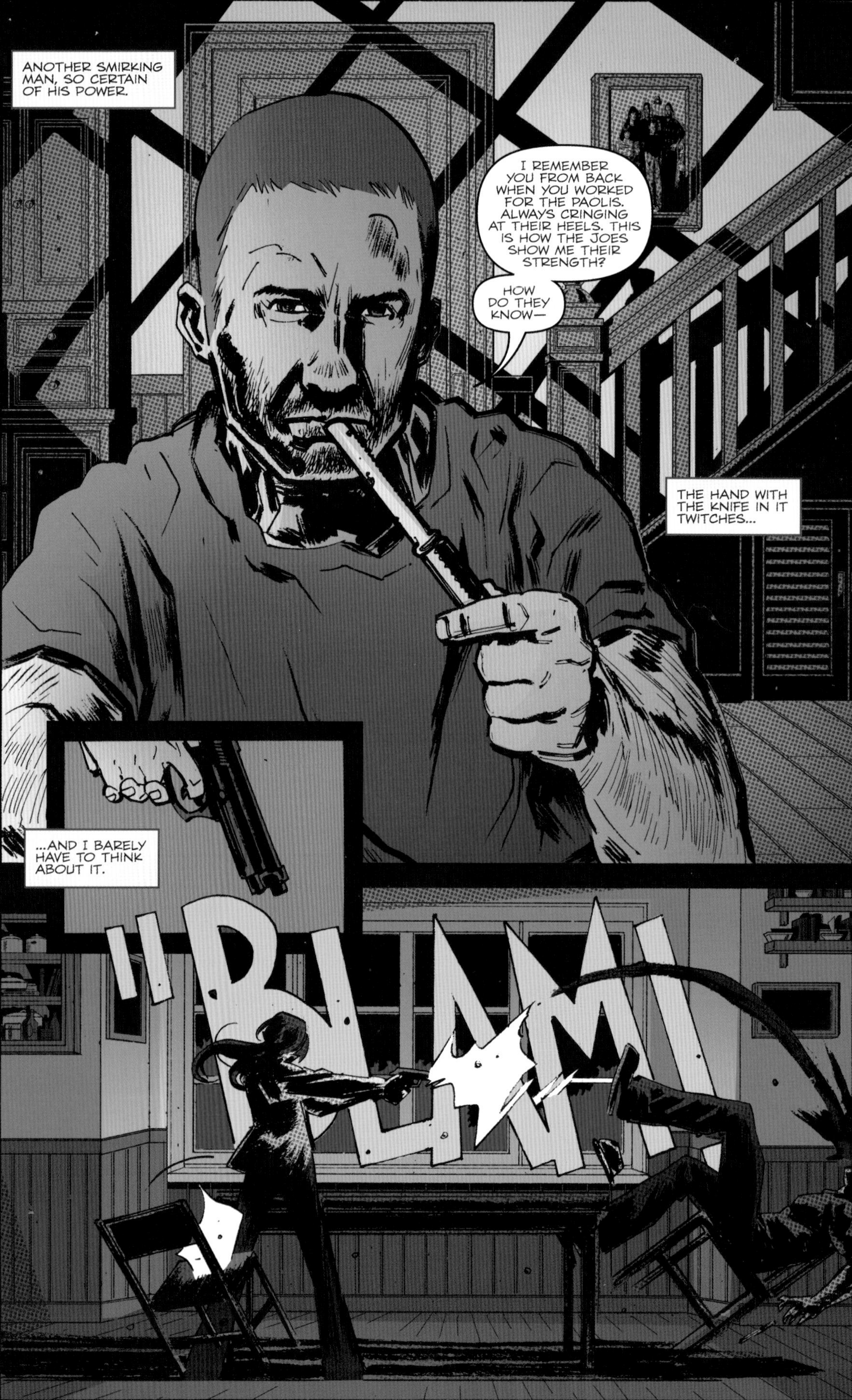
ANOTHER SMIRKING MAN, SO CERTAIN OF HIS POWER.
I REMEMBER YOU FROM BACK WHEN YOU WORKED FOR THE PAOLIS. ALWAYS CRINGING AT THEIR HEELS. THIS IS HOW THE JOES SHOW ME THEIR STRENGTH?
HOW DO THEY KNOW—
THE HAND WITH THE KNIFE IN IT TWITCHES...
...AND I BARELY HAVE TO THINK ABOUT IT.
BLAM!!

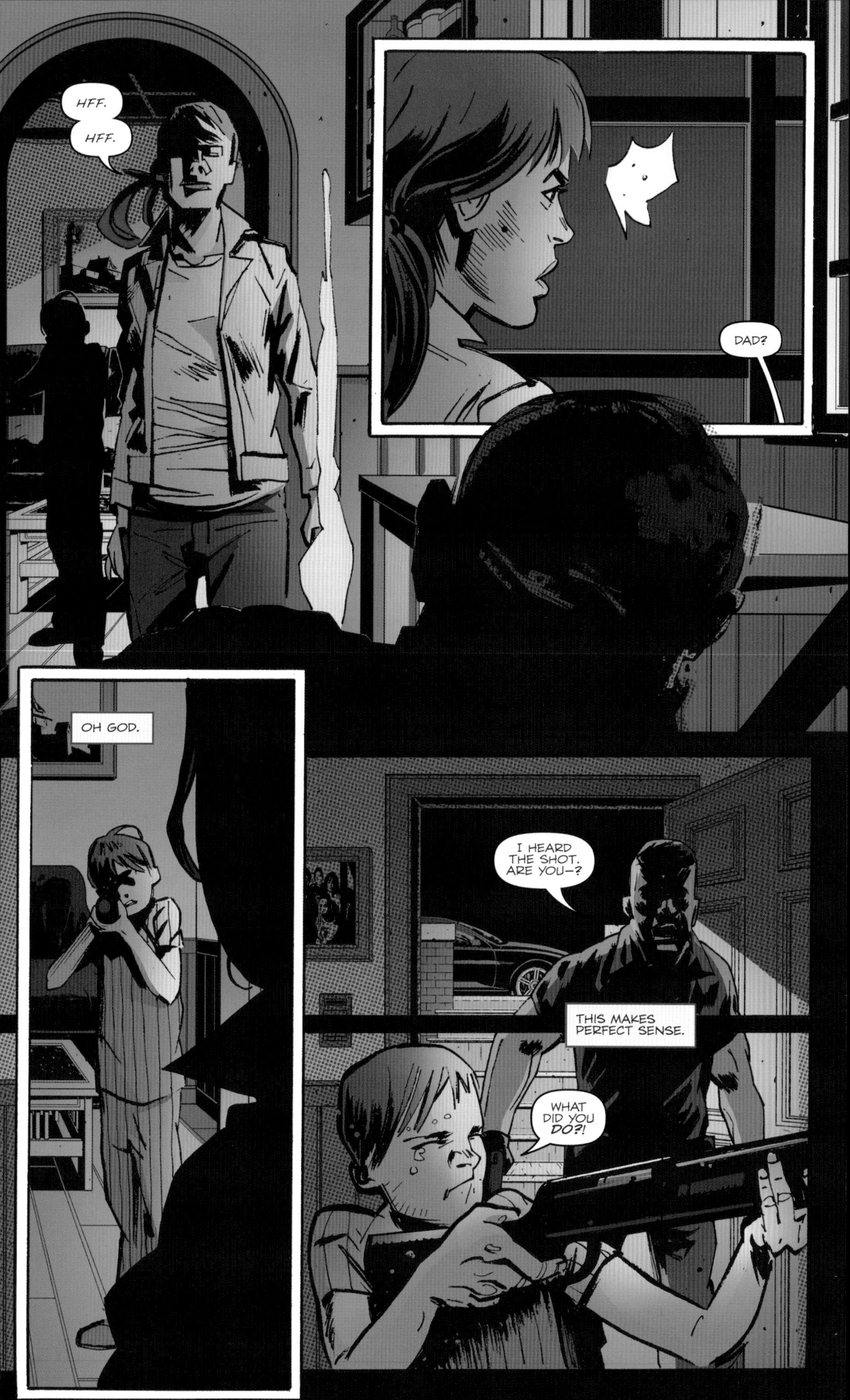
HFF.
HFF.
DAD?
OH GOD.
I HEARD THE SHOT. ARE YOU--?
THIS MAKES PERFECT SENSE.
WHAT DID YOU *DO?!*

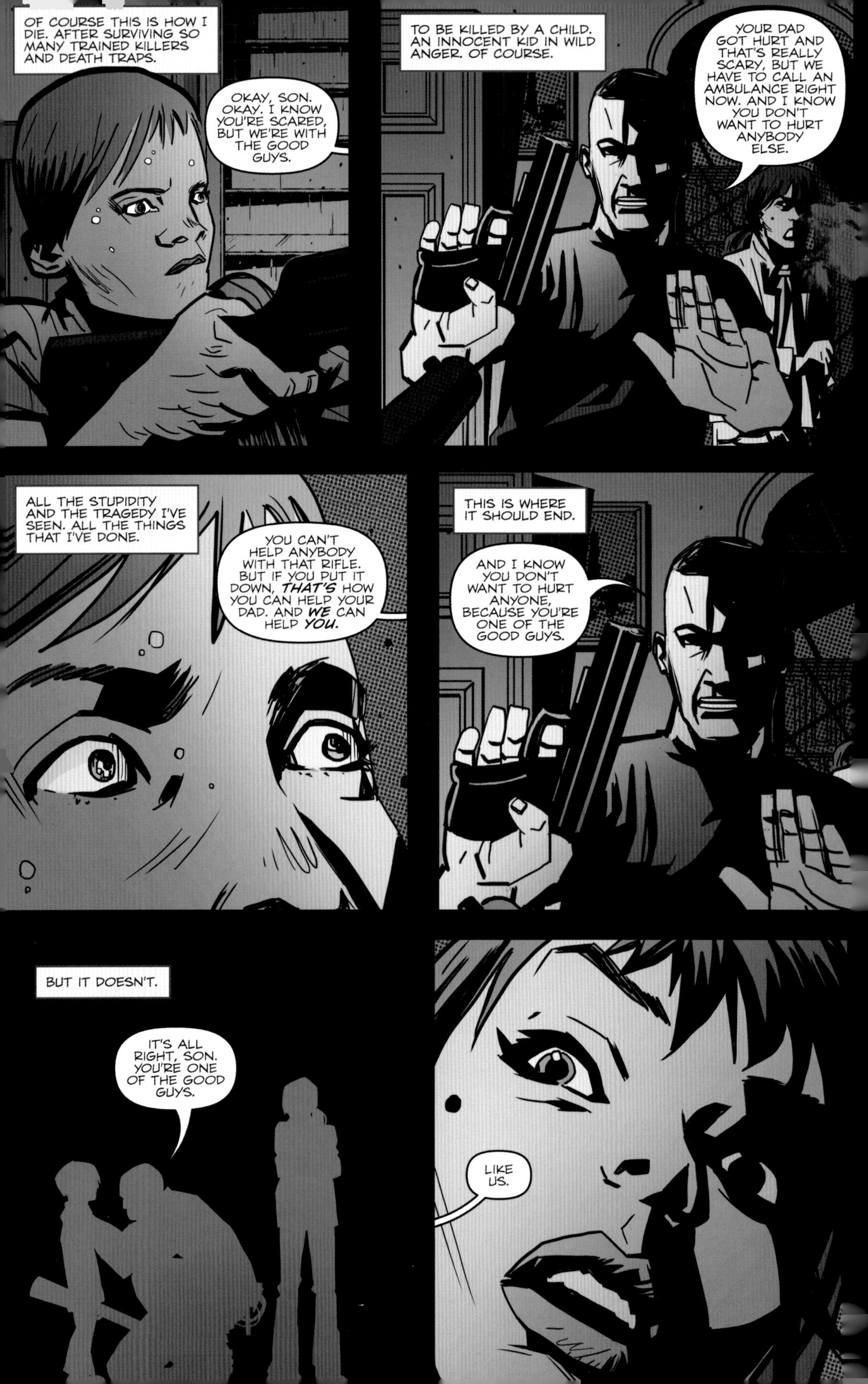
OF COURSE THIS IS HOW I DIE. AFTER SURVIVING SO MANY TRAINED KILLERS AND DEATH TRAPS.
OKAY, SON. OKAY. I KNOW YOU'RE SCARED, BUT WE'RE WITH THE GOOD GUYS.
TO BE KILLED BY A CHILD. AN INNOCENT KID IN WILD ANGER. OF COURSE.
YOUR DAD GOT HURT AND THAT'S REALLY SCARY, BUT WE HAVE TO CALL AN AMBULANCE RIGHT NOW. AND I KNOW YOU DON'T WANT TO HURT ANYBODY ELSE.
ALL THE STUPIDITY AND THE TRAGEDY I'VE SEEN. ALL THE THINGS THAT I'VE DONE.
YOU CAN'T HELP ANYBODY WITH THAT RIFLE. BUT IF YOU PUT IT DOWN, THAT'S HOW YOU CAN HELP YOUR DAD. AND WE CAN HELP YOU.
THIS IS WHERE IT SHOULD END.
AND I KNOW YOU DON'T WANT TO HURT ANYONE, BECAUSE YOU'RE ONE OF THE GOOD GUYS.
BUT IT DOESN'T.
IT'S ALL RIGHT, SON. YOU'RE ONE OF THE GOOD GUYS.
LIKE US.

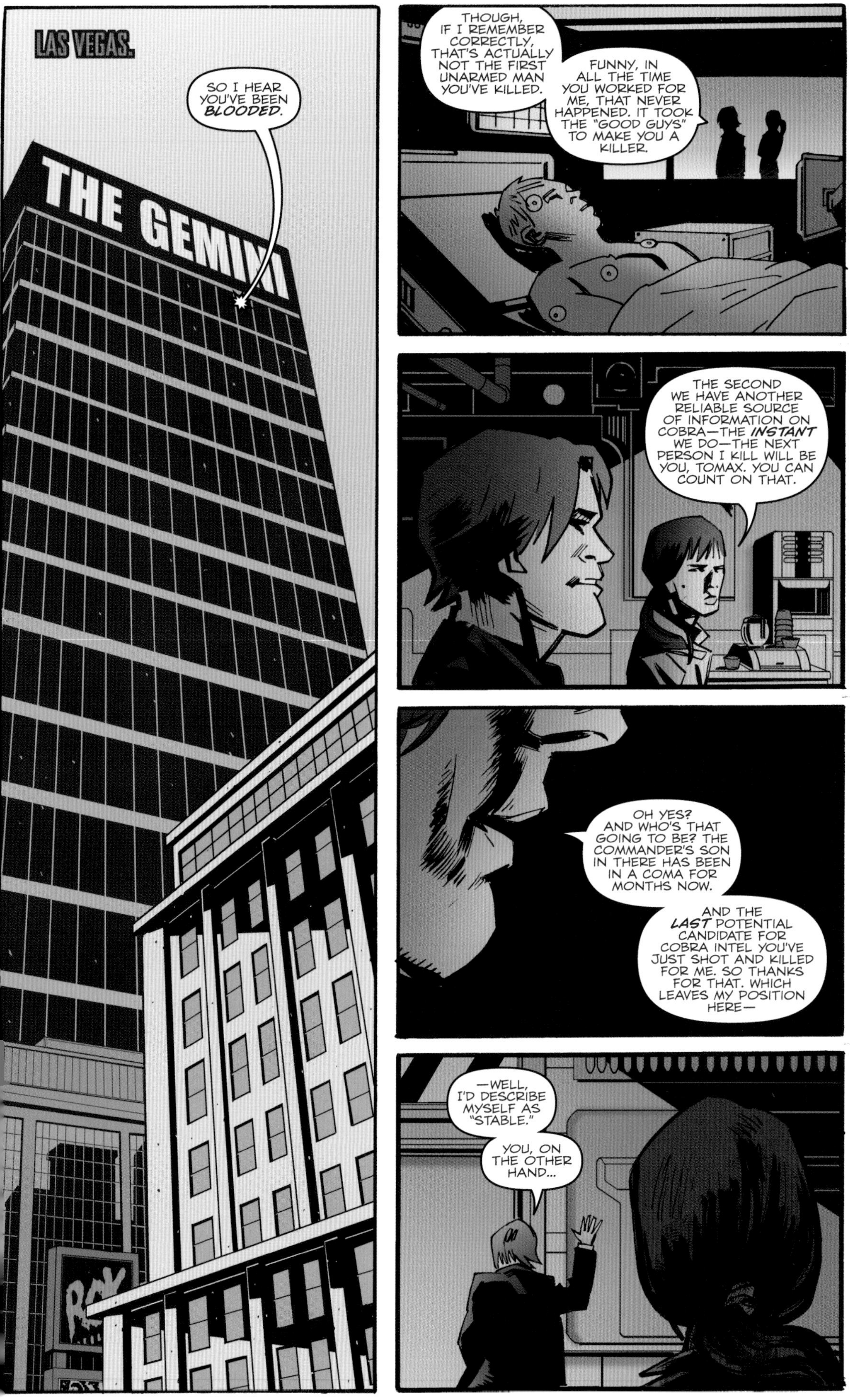
LAS VEGAS.
SO I HEAR YOU'VE BEEN *BLOODED*.
THE GEMINI
THOUGH, IF I REMEMBER CORRECTLY, THAT'S ACTUALLY NOT THE FIRST UNARMED MAN YOU'VE KILLED.
FUNNY, IN ALL THE TIME YOU WORKED FOR ME, THAT NEVER HAPPENED. IT TOOK THE "GOOD GUYS" TO MAKE YOU A KILLER.
THE SECOND WE HAVE ANOTHER RELIABLE SOURCE OF INFORMATION ON COBRA—THE *INSTANT* WE DO—THE NEXT PERSON I KILL WILL BE YOU, TOMAX. YOU CAN COUNT ON THAT.
OH YES? AND WHO'S THAT GOING TO BE? THE COMMANDER'S SON IN THERE HAS BEEN IN A COMA FOR MONTHS NOW.
AND THE *LAST* POTENTIAL CANDIDATE FOR COBRA INTEL YOU'VE JUST SHOT AND KILLED FOR ME. SO THANKS FOR THAT. WHICH LEAVES MY POSITION HERE—
—WELL, I'D DESCRIBE MYSELF AS "STABLE."
YOU, ON THE OTHER HAND...

DON'T LISTEN TO HIM. EVERYTHING HE SAYS IS POISON.

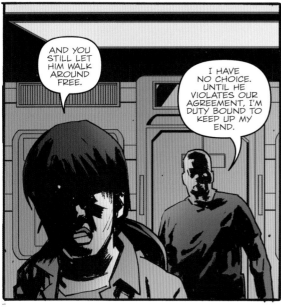

AND YOU STILL LET HIM WALK AROUND FREE.

I HAVE NO CHOICE. UNTIL HE VIOLATES OUR AGREEMENT, I'M DUTY BOUND TO KEEP UP MY END.

YOU'RE A GOOD MAN, AREN'T YOU?

I'M A SOLDIER. THAT'S ALL.

NO. THAT'S NOT ALL. YOU STEPPED RIGHT IN FRONT OF A BULLET FOR ME IN THAT KITCHEN. YOU DIDN'T EVEN THINK ABOUT IT.

AND THE WAY YOU TALKED THAT KID DOWN AFTER I...

DON'T LET YOURSELF BE HAUNTED BY GHOSTS. YOU DID WHAT YOU HAD TO DO. YOU'RE STRONG AND CAPABLE AND YOU PROVED IT IN THERE.

I WOULD HAVE DONE THE SAME THING.

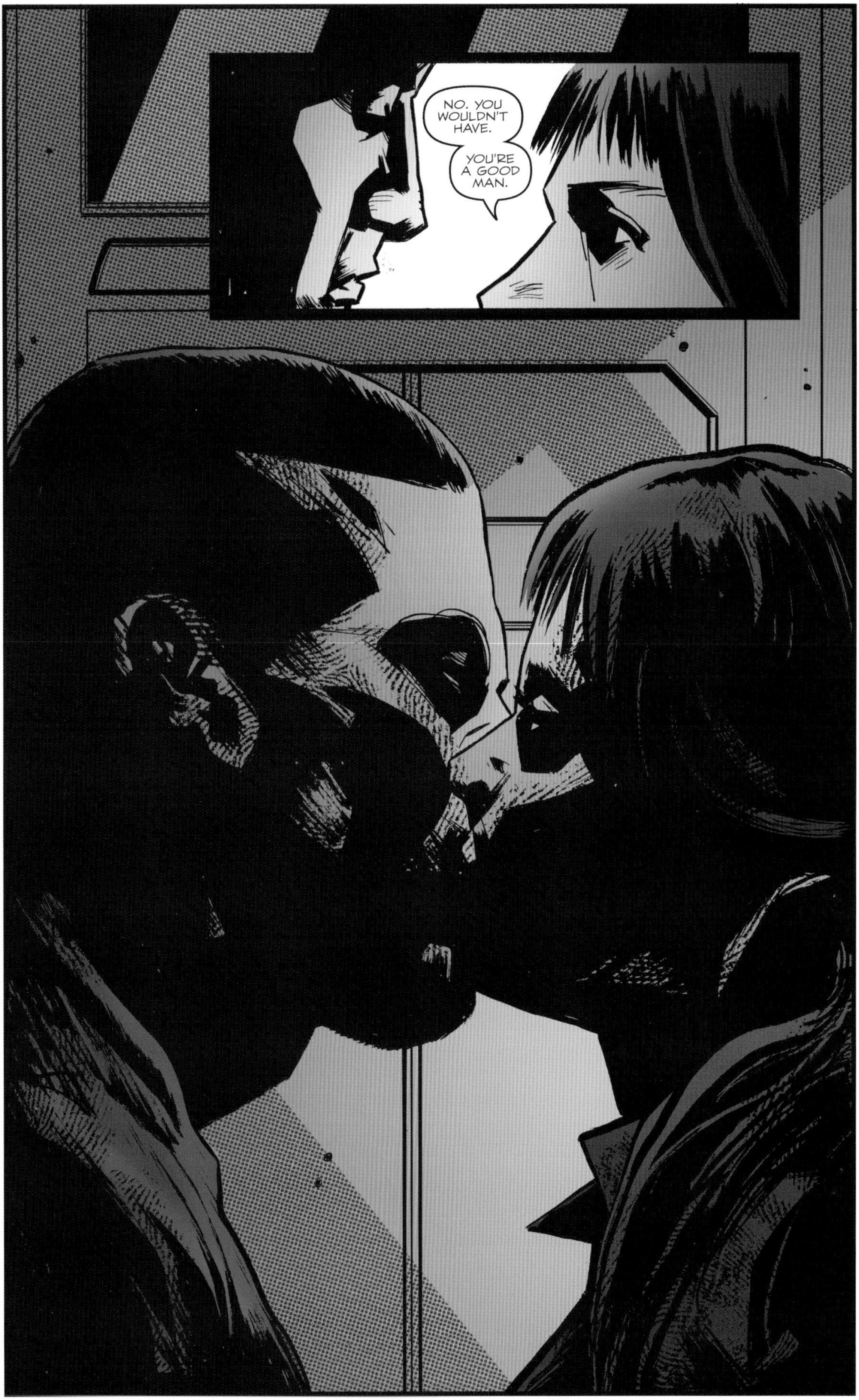
NO. YOU WOULDN'T HAVE.
YOU'RE A GOOD MAN.

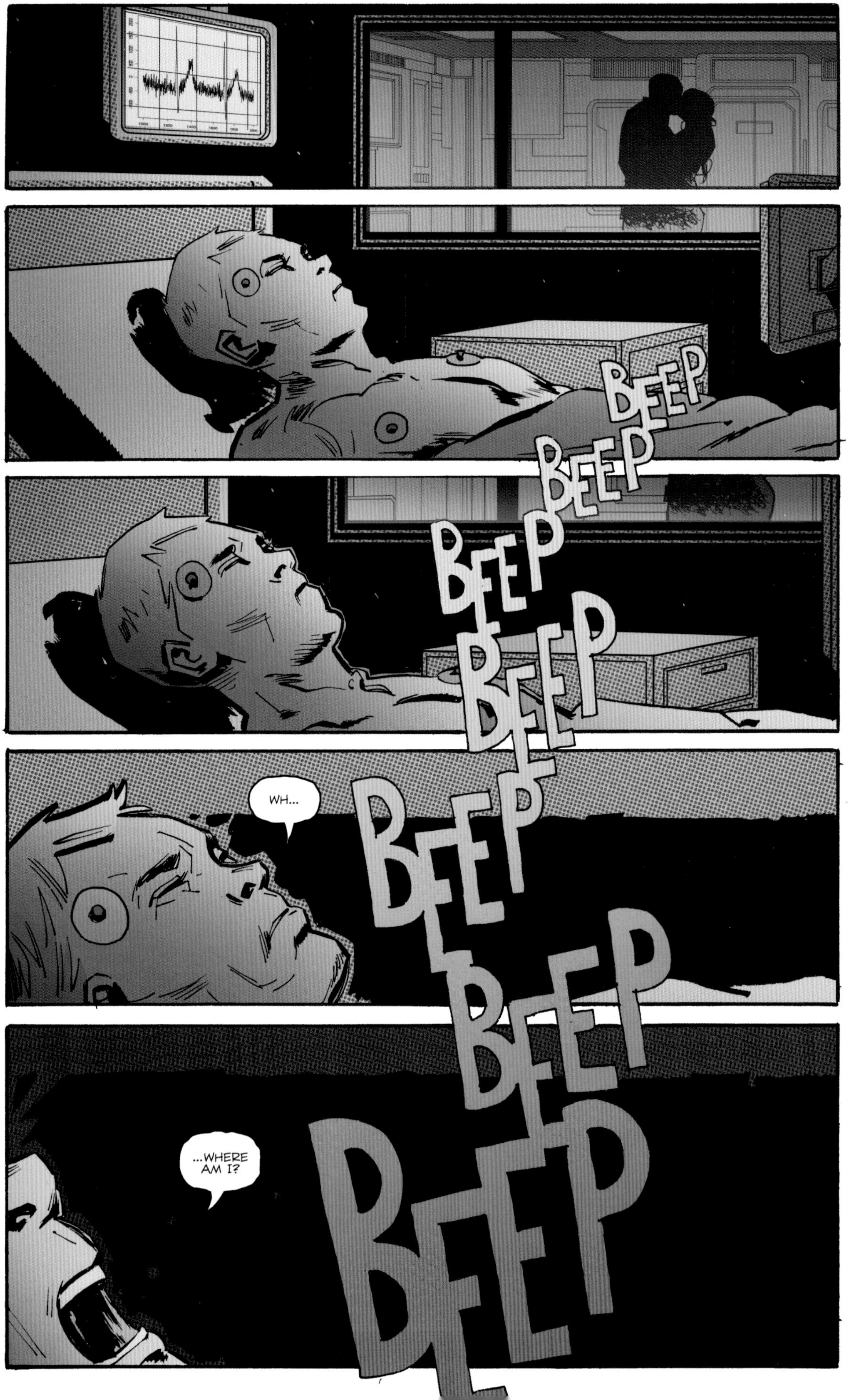
BEEP
BEEP
BEEP
BEEP
WH...
BEEP
BEEP
BEEP
...WHERE AM I?
BEEP

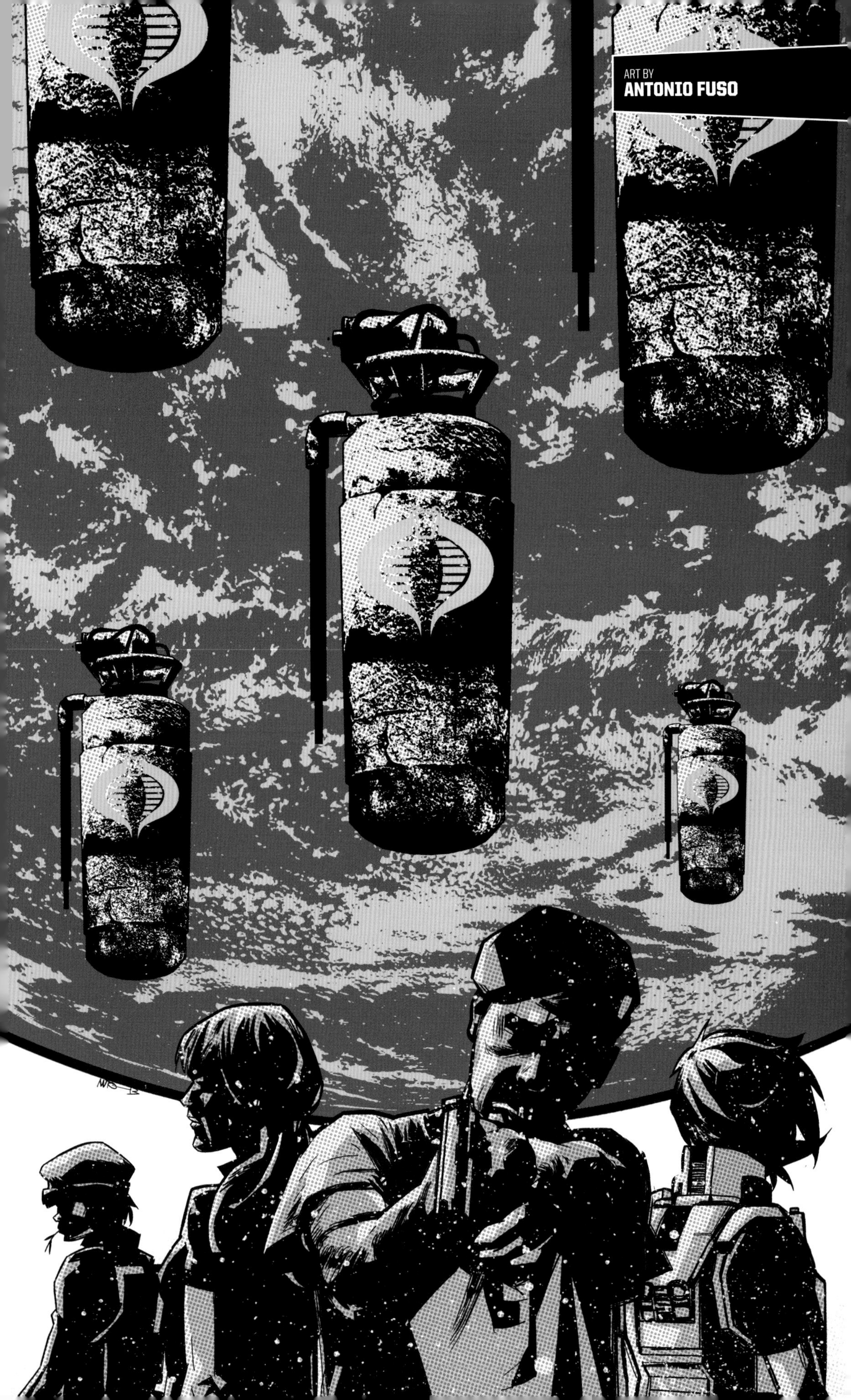

ART BY
**ANTONIO FUSO**

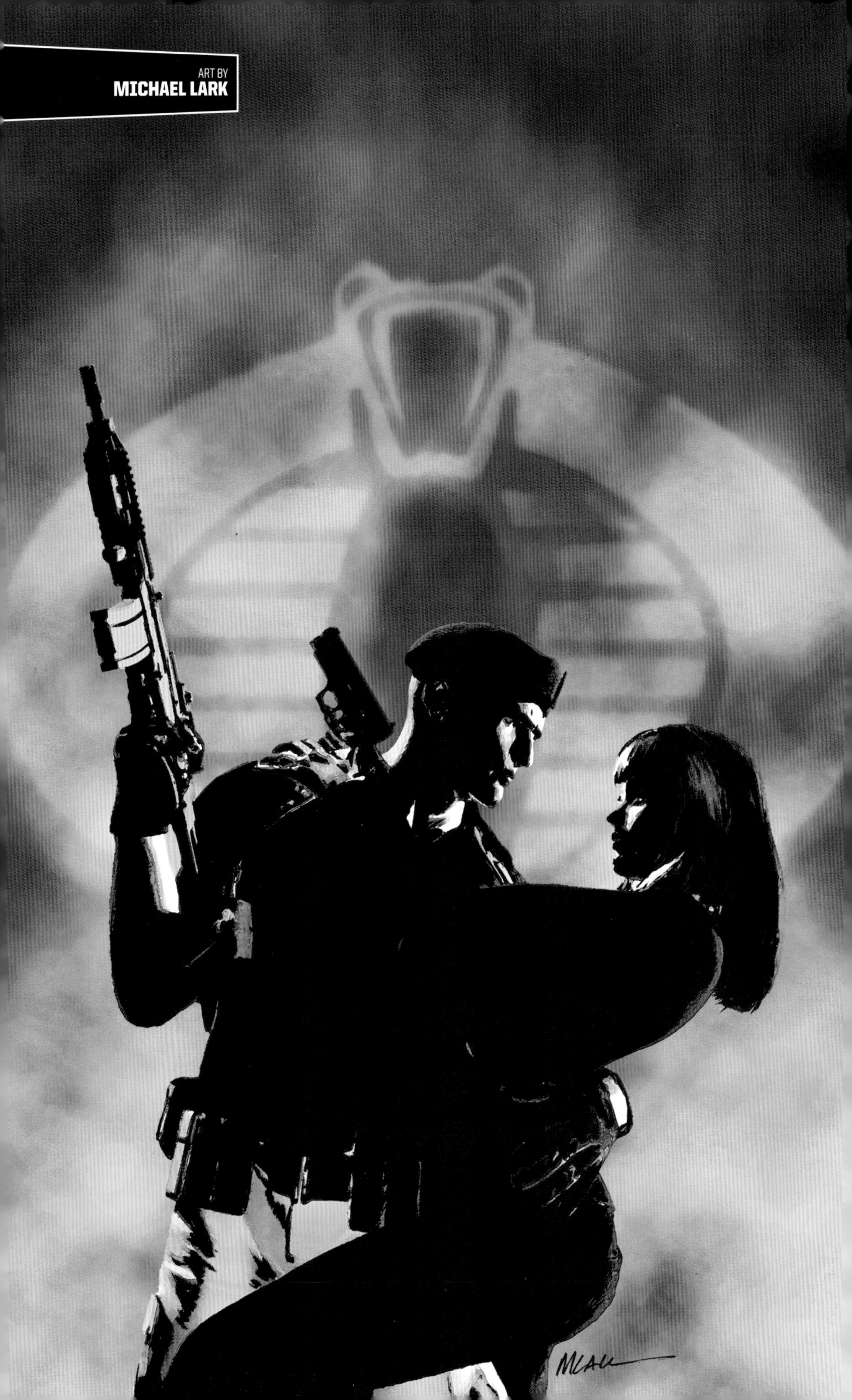

ART BY
**MICHAEL LARK**

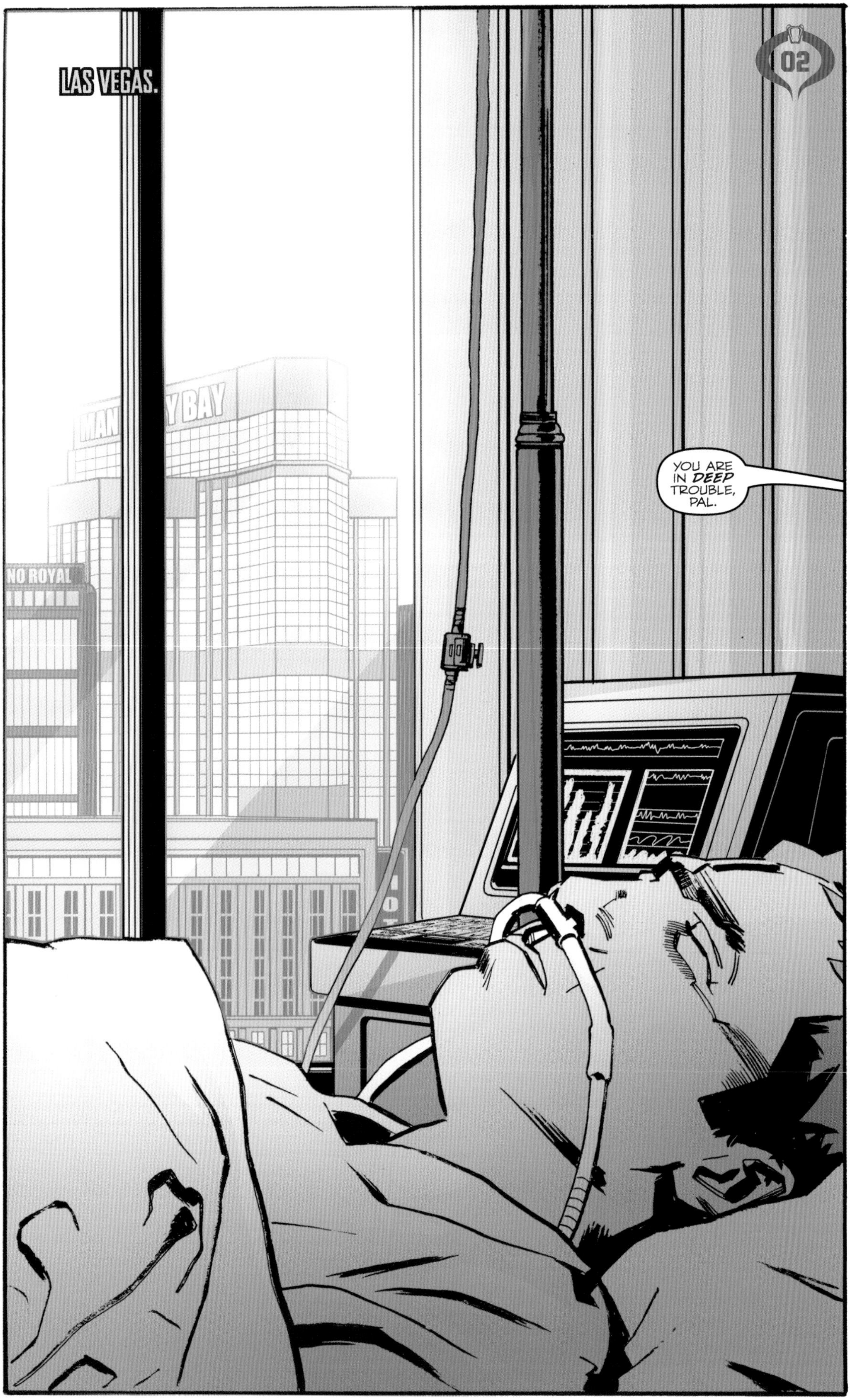
LAS VEGAS.
02
MAN BAY BAY
NO ROYAL
YOU ARE IN DEEP TROUBLE, PAL.

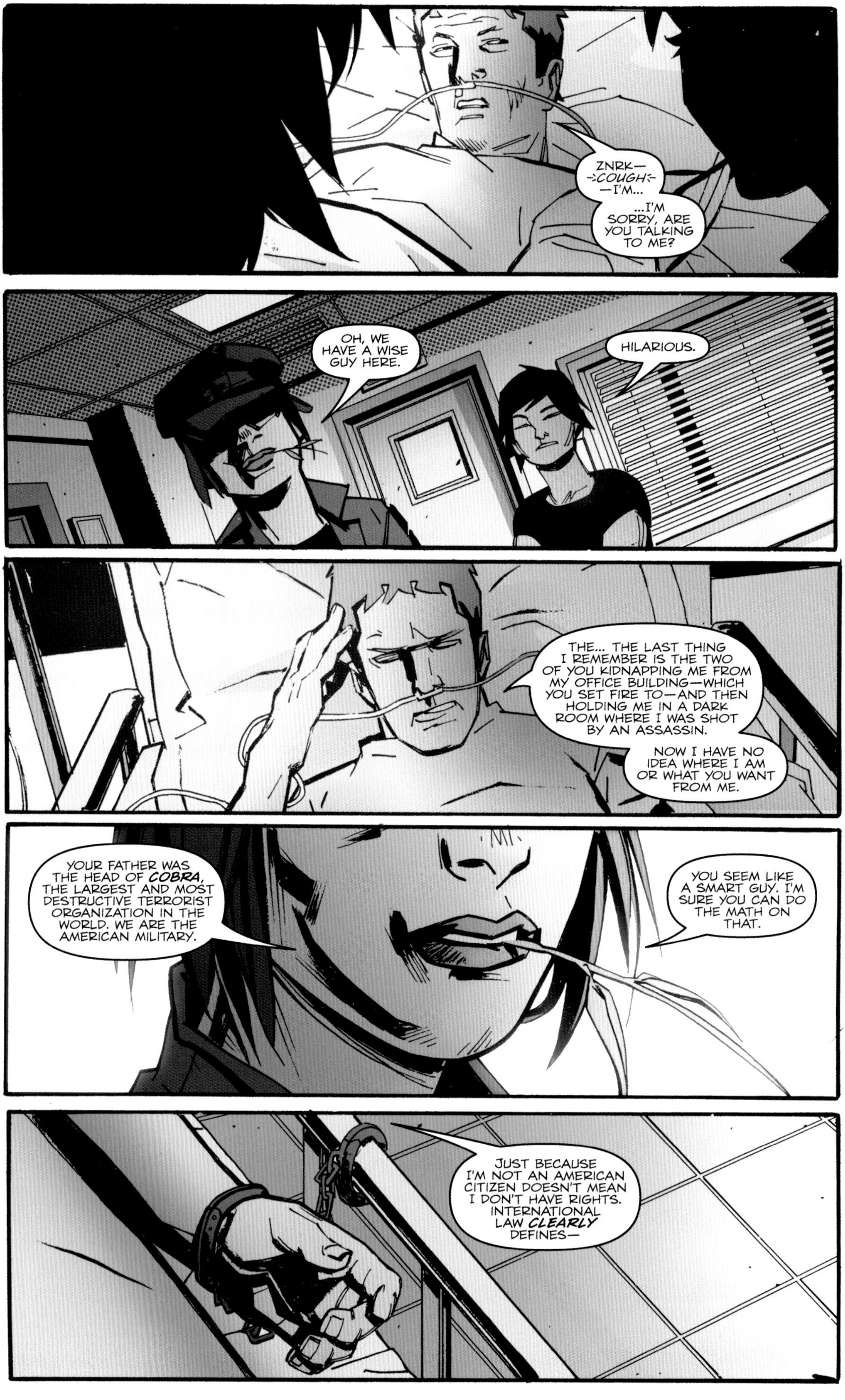
ZNRK—
-COUGH-
—I'M...
...I'M SORRY, ARE YOU TALKING TO ME?
OH, WE HAVE A WISE GUY HERE.
HILARIOUS.
THE... THE LAST THING I REMEMBER IS THE TWO OF YOU KIDNAPPING ME FROM MY OFFICE BUILDING—WHICH YOU SET FIRE TO—AND THEN HOLDING ME IN A DARK ROOM WHERE I WAS SHOT BY AN ASSASSIN.
NOW I HAVE NO IDEA WHERE I AM OR WHAT YOU WANT FROM ME.
YOUR FATHER WAS THE HEAD OF ***COBRA***, THE LARGEST AND MOST DESTRUCTIVE TERRORIST ORGANIZATION IN THE WORLD. WE ARE THE AMERICAN MILITARY.
YOU SEEM LIKE A SMART GUY. I'M SURE YOU CAN DO THE MATH ON THAT.
JUST BECAUSE I'M NOT AN AMERICAN CITIZEN DOESN'T MEAN I DON'T HAVE RIGHTS. INTERNATIONAL LAW ***CLEARLY*** DEFINES—

"INTERNATIONAL LAW"? THE OUTFIT YOU'RE CURRENTLY A PRISONER OF DOESN'T EVEN OFFICIALLY EXIST.
YOU SEE THIS WOMAN? SHE KILLS PEOPLE WITH A SWORD. YOU THINK EITHER ONE OF US IS CLUTCHING OUR PEARLS ABOUT "INTERNATIONAL LAW"?
LISTEN, WHAT IS THIS? I SAVED YOUR LIFE.
SO, WHAT? WE'RE SUPPOSED TO FALL IN LOVE NOW? AS FAR AS I KNOW, YOU JUMPED IN FRONT OF THOSE BULLETS SO WE WOULDN'T GET INFORMATION OUT OF YOU LATER.
BECAUSE WE WILL GET IT OUT OF YOU.
I DON'T KNOW ANYTHING.
PLEASE. HE KEPT ALL THIS FROM ME. I WAS AWAY IN PRIVATE SCHOOLS.
PLEASE—
YOU TWO.
OUTSIDE.

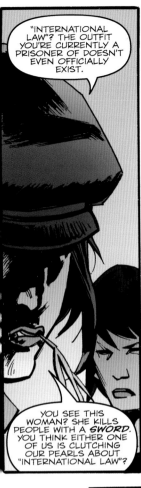

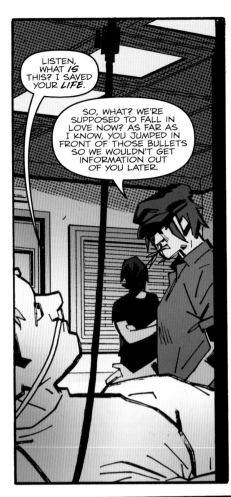

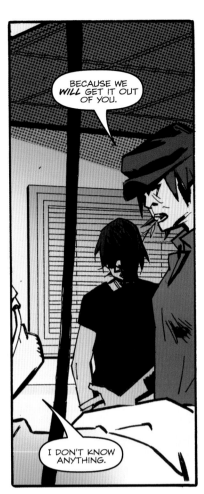

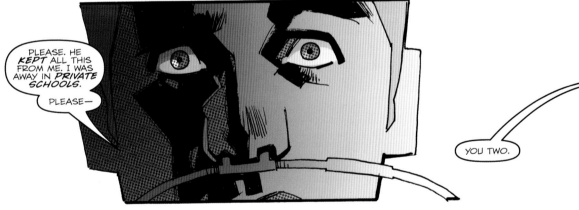

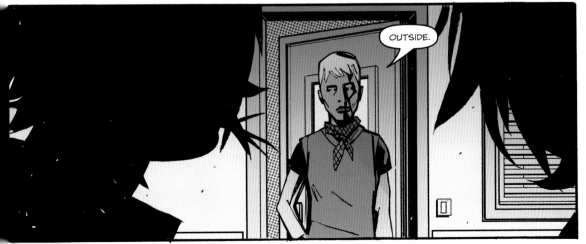

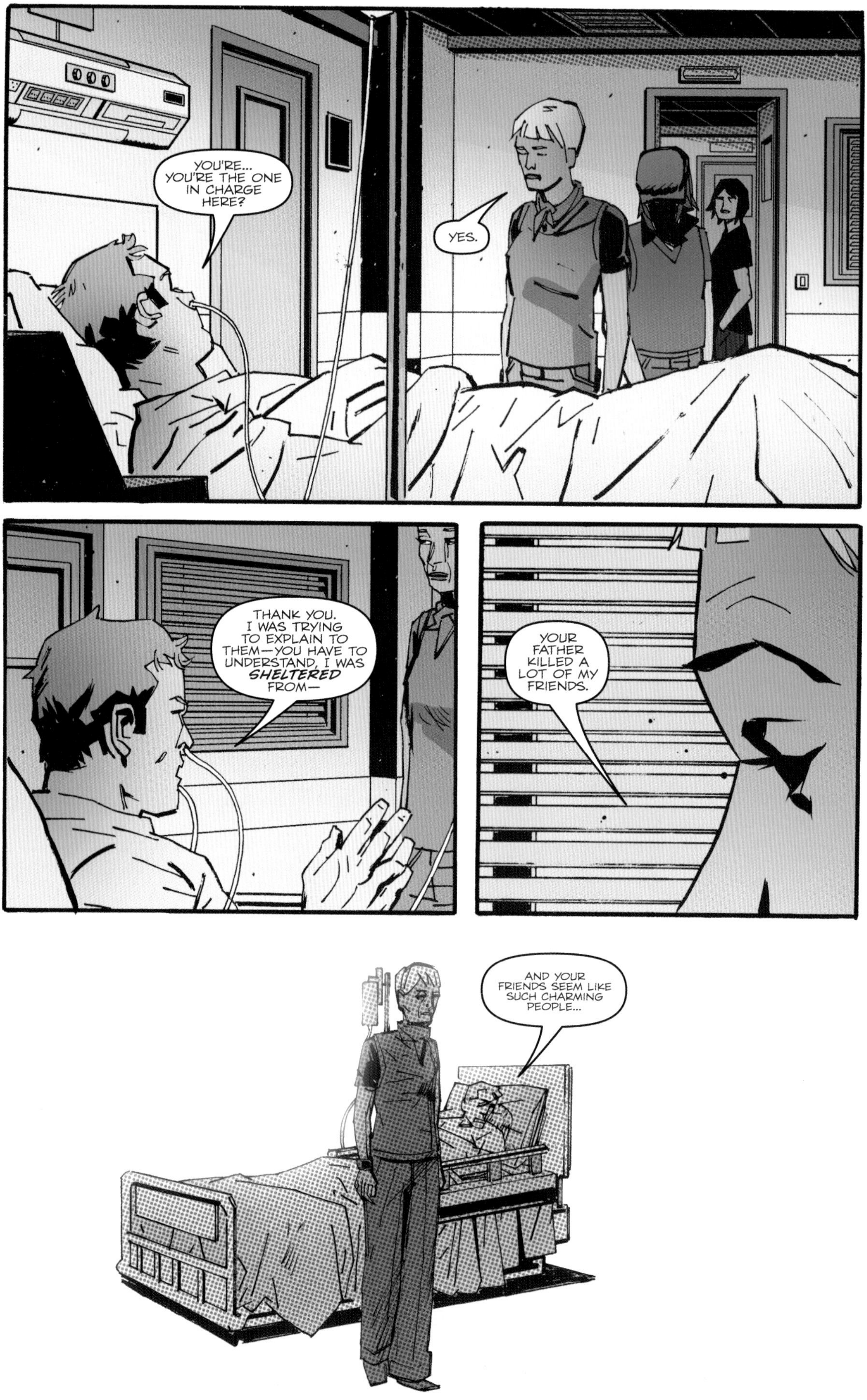
YOU'RE... YOU'RE THE ONE IN CHARGE HERE?
YES.
THANK YOU. I WAS TRYING TO EXPLAIN TO THEM—YOU HAVE TO UNDERSTAND, I WAS *SHELTERED* FROM—
YOUR FATHER KILLED A LOT OF MY FRIENDS.
AND YOUR FRIENDS SEEM LIKE SUCH CHARMING PEOPLE...

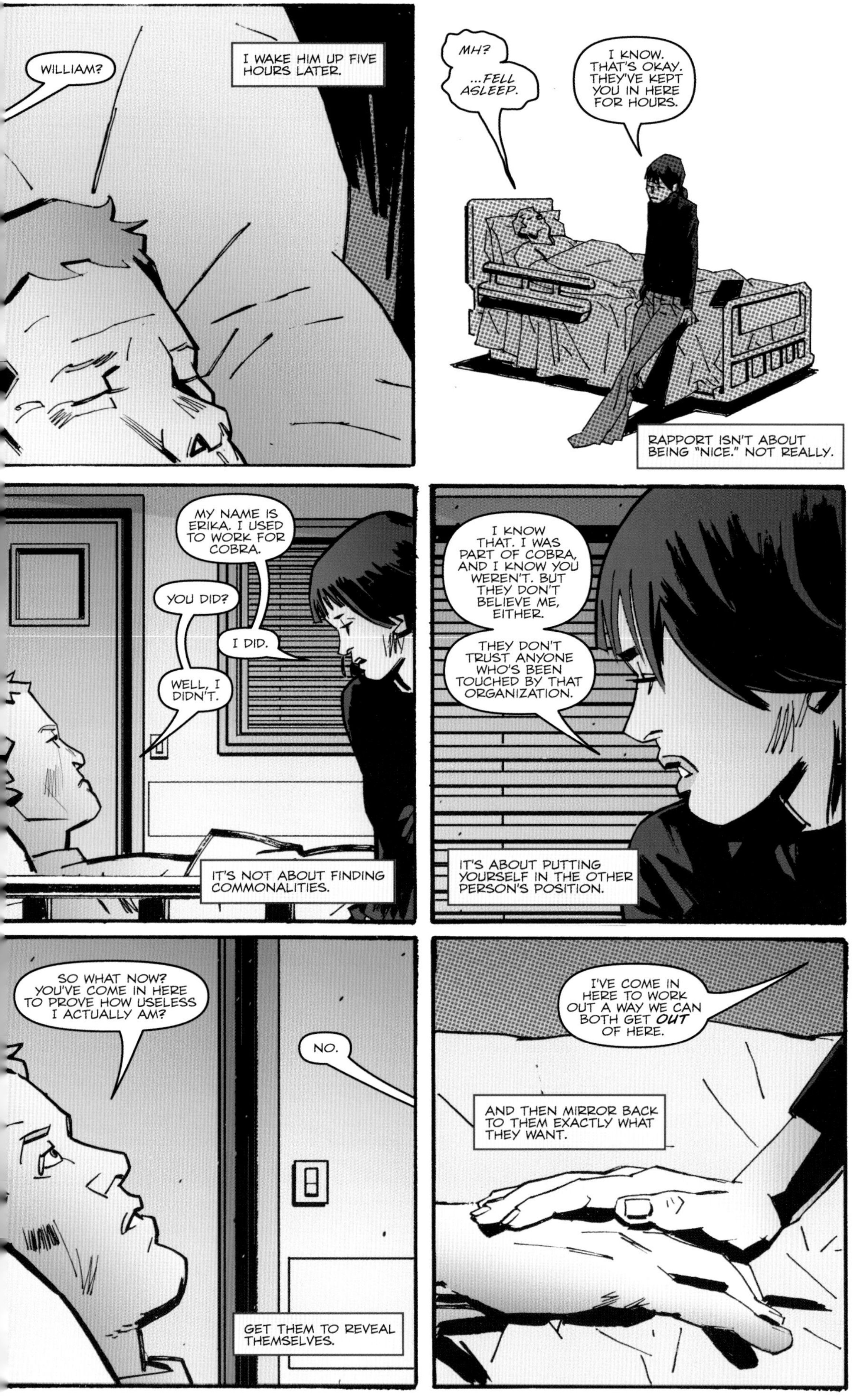
WILLIAM?
I WAKE HIM UP FIVE HOURS LATER.
MH?
...FELL ASLEEP.
I KNOW. THAT'S OKAY. THEY'VE KEPT YOU IN HERE FOR HOURS.
RAPPORT ISN'T ABOUT BEING "NICE." NOT REALLY.
MY NAME IS ERIKA. I USED TO WORK FOR COBRA.
YOU DID?
I DID.
WELL, I DIDN'T.
IT'S NOT ABOUT FINDING COMMONALITIES.
I KNOW THAT. I WAS PART OF COBRA, AND I KNOW YOU WEREN'T. BUT THEY DON'T BELIEVE ME, EITHER.
THEY DON'T TRUST ANYONE WHO'S BEEN TOUCHED BY THAT ORGANIZATION.
IT'S ABOUT PUTTING YOURSELF IN THE OTHER PERSON'S POSITION.
SO WHAT NOW? YOU'VE COME IN HERE TO PROVE HOW USELESS I ACTUALLY AM?
NO.
GET THEM TO REVEAL THEMSELVES.
I'VE COME IN HERE TO WORK OUT A WAY WE CAN BOTH GET OUT OF HERE.
AND THEN MIRROR BACK TO THEM EXACTLY WHAT THEY WANT.

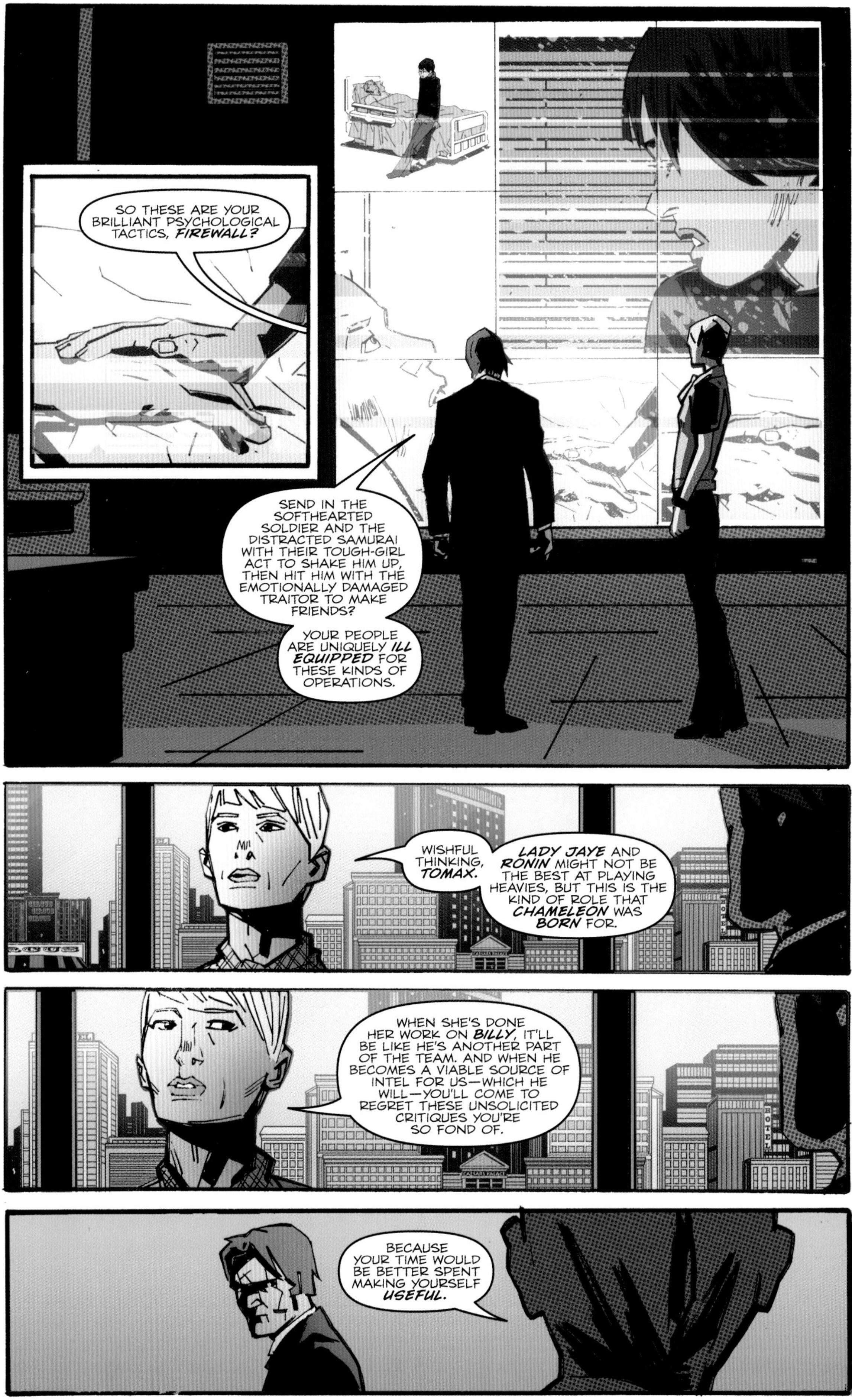
SO THESE ARE YOUR BRILLIANT PSYCHOLOGICAL TACTICS, FIREWALL?
SEND IN THE SOFTHEARTED SOLDIER AND THE DISTRACTED SAMURAI WITH THEIR TOUGH-GIRL ACT TO SHAKE HIM UP, THEN HIT HIM WITH THE EMOTIONALLY DAMAGED TRAITOR TO MAKE FRIENDS?
YOUR PEOPLE ARE UNIQUELY ILL EQUIPPED FOR THESE KINDS OF OPERATIONS.
WISHFUL THINKING, TOMAX.
LADY JAYE AND RONIN MIGHT NOT BE THE BEST AT PLAYING HEAVIES, BUT THIS IS THE KIND OF ROLE THAT CHAMELEON WAS BORN FOR.
WHEN SHE'S DONE HER WORK ON BILLY, IT'LL BE LIKE HE'S ANOTHER PART OF THE TEAM. AND WHEN HE BECOMES A VIABLE SOURCE OF INTEL FOR US—WHICH HE WILL—YOU'LL COME TO REGRET THESE UNSOLICITED CRITIQUES YOU'RE SO FOND OF.
BECAUSE YOUR TIME WOULD BE BETTER SPENT MAKING YOURSELF USEFUL.

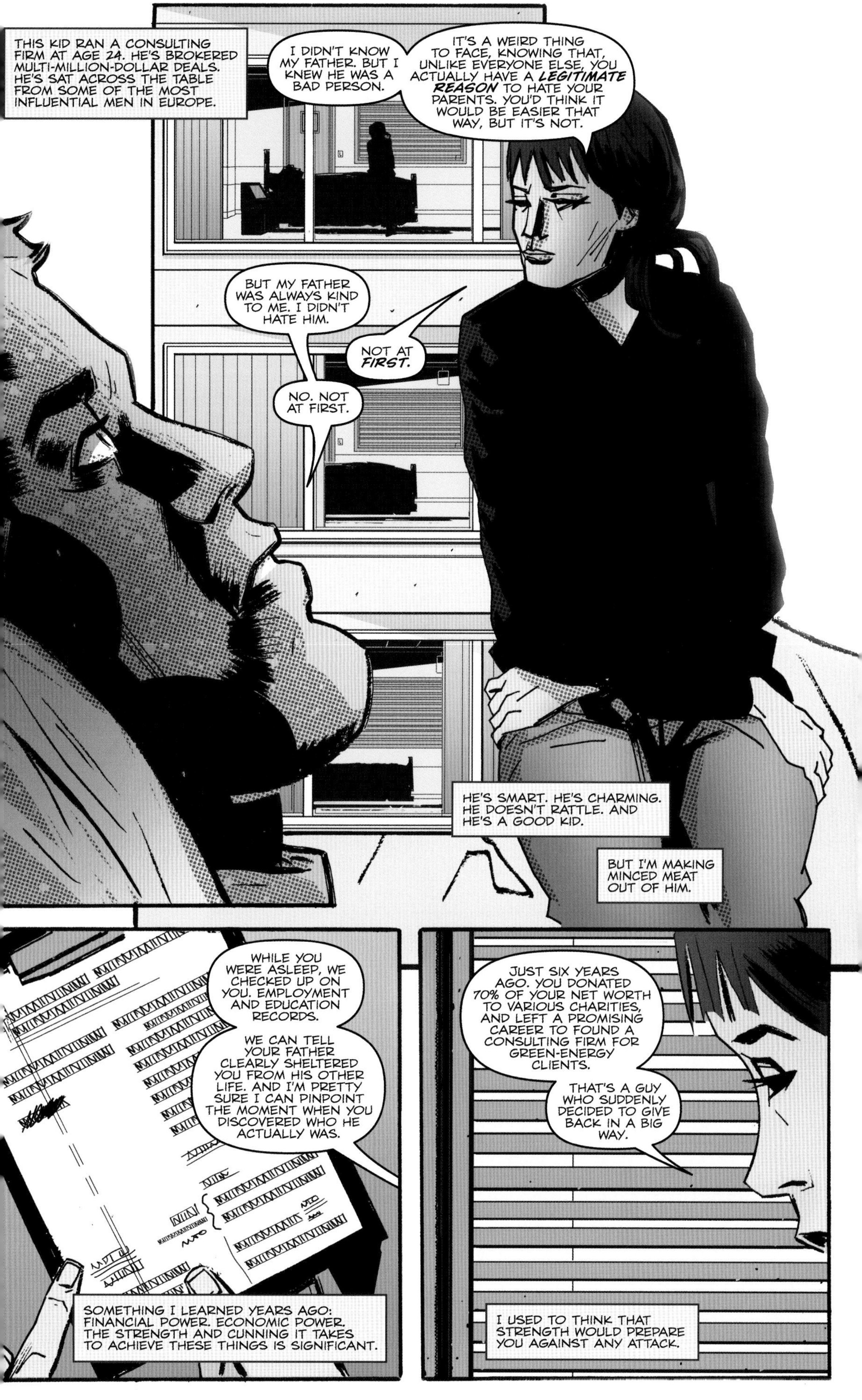

THIS KID RAN A CONSULTING FIRM AT AGE 24. HE'S BROKERED MULTI-MILLION-DOLLAR DEALS. HE'S SAT ACROSS THE TABLE FROM SOME OF THE MOST INFLUENTIAL MEN IN EUROPE.
I DIDN'T KNOW MY FATHER. BUT I KNEW HE WAS A BAD PERSON.
IT'S A WEIRD THING TO FACE, KNOWING THAT, UNLIKE EVERYONE ELSE, YOU ACTUALLY HAVE A ***LEGITIMATE REASON*** TO HATE YOUR PARENTS. YOU'D THINK IT WOULD BE EASIER THAT WAY, BUT IT'S NOT.
BUT MY FATHER WAS ALWAYS KIND TO ME. I DIDN'T HATE HIM.
NOT AT ***FIRST.***
NO. NOT AT FIRST.
HE'S SMART. HE'S CHARMING. HE DOESN'T RATTLE. AND HE'S A GOOD KID.
BUT I'M MAKING MINCED MEAT OUT OF HIM.
WHILE YOU WERE ASLEEP, WE CHECKED UP ON YOU. EMPLOYMENT AND EDUCATION RECORDS.
WE CAN TELL YOUR FATHER CLEARLY SHELTERED YOU FROM HIS OTHER LIFE. AND I'M PRETTY SURE I CAN PINPOINT THE MOMENT WHEN YOU DISCOVERED WHO HE ACTUALLY WAS.
SOMETHING I LEARNED YEARS AGO: FINANCIAL POWER. ECONOMIC POWER. THE STRENGTH AND CUNNING IT TAKES TO ACHIEVE THESE THINGS IS SIGNIFICANT.
JUST SIX YEARS AGO. YOU DONATED 70% OF YOUR NET WORTH TO VARIOUS CHARITIES, AND LEFT A PROMISING CAREER TO FOUND A CONSULTING FIRM FOR GREEN-ENERGY CLIENTS.
THAT'S A GUY WHO SUDDENLY DECIDED TO GIVE BACK IN A BIG WAY.
I USED TO THINK THAT STRENGTH WOULD PREPARE YOU AGAINST ANY ATTACK.

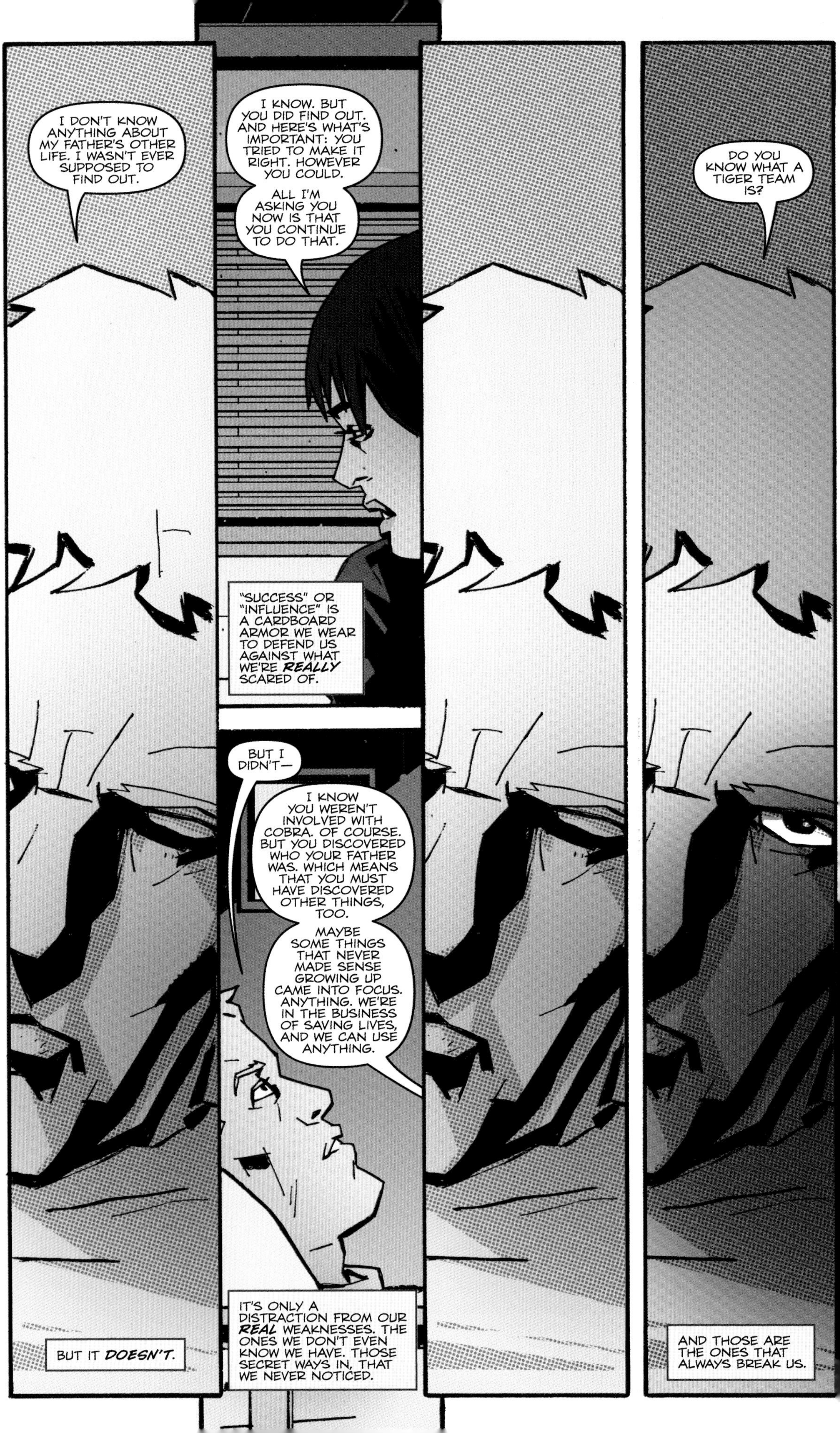
I DON'T KNOW ANYTHING ABOUT MY FATHER'S OTHER LIFE. I WASN'T EVER SUPPOSED TO FIND OUT.
BUT IT *DOESN'T*.
I KNOW. BUT YOU DID FIND OUT. AND HERE'S WHAT'S IMPORTANT: YOU TRIED TO MAKE IT RIGHT. HOWEVER YOU COULD.
ALL I'M ASKING YOU NOW IS THAT YOU CONTINUE TO DO THAT.
"SUCCESS" OR "INFLUENCE" IS A CARDBOARD ARMOR WE WEAR TO DEFEND US AGAINST WHAT WE'RE *REALLY* SCARED OF.
BUT I DIDN'T—
I KNOW YOU WEREN'T INVOLVED WITH COBRA. OF COURSE. BUT YOU DISCOVERED WHO YOUR FATHER WAS. WHICH MEANS THAT YOU MUST HAVE DISCOVERED OTHER THINGS, TOO.
MAYBE SOME THINGS THAT NEVER MADE SENSE GROWING UP CAME INTO FOCUS. ANYTHING. WE'RE IN THE BUSINESS OF SAVING LIVES, AND WE CAN USE ANYTHING.
IT'S ONLY A DISTRACTION FROM OUR *REAL* WEAKNESSES. THE ONES WE DON'T EVEN KNOW WE HAVE. THOSE SECRET WAYS IN, THAT WE NEVER NOTICED.
DO YOU KNOW WHAT A TIGER TEAM IS?
AND THOSE ARE THE ONES THAT ALWAYS BREAK US.

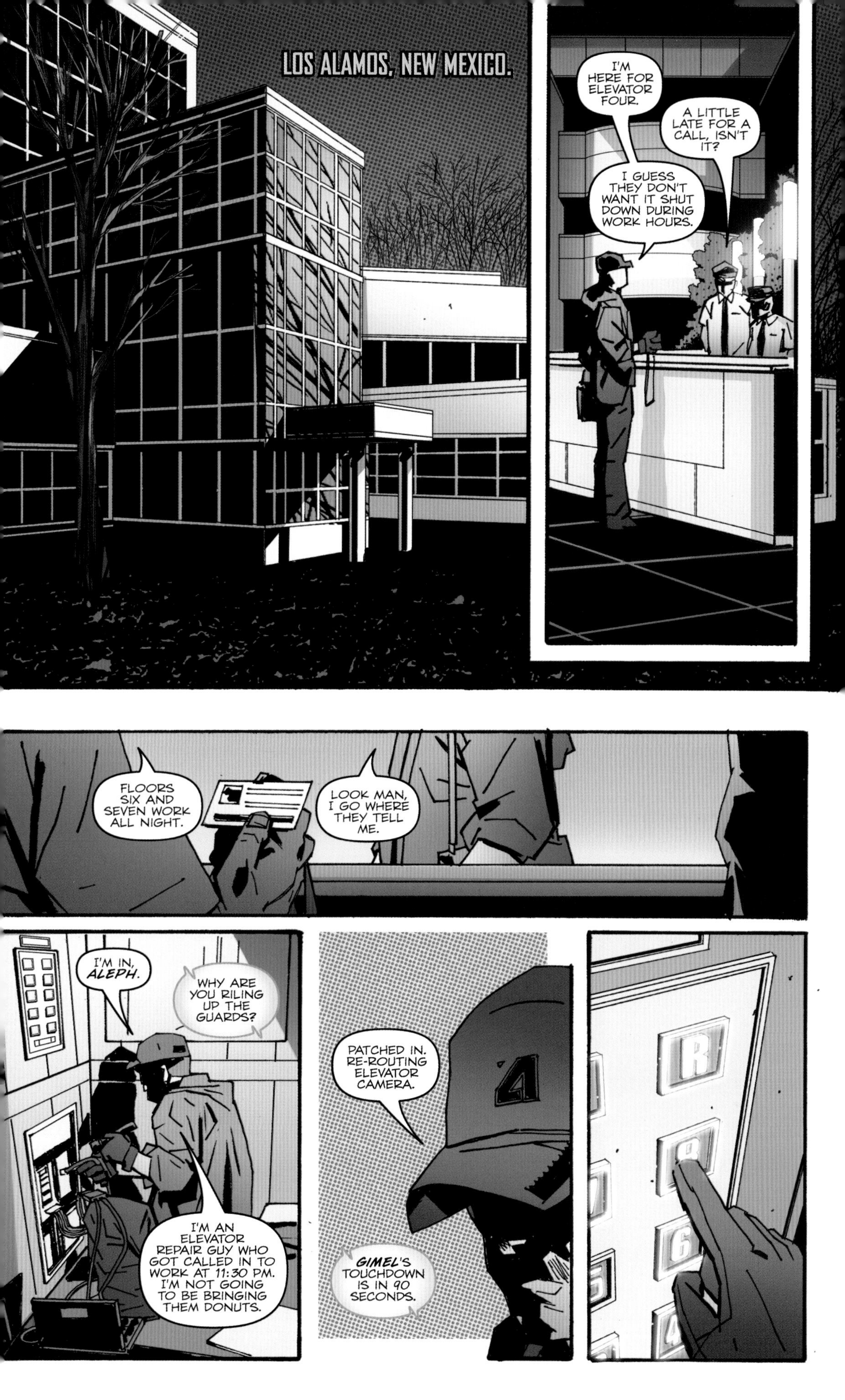

LOS ALAMOS, NEW MEXICO.
I'M HERE FOR ELEVATOR FOUR.
A LITTLE LATE FOR A CALL, ISN'T IT?
I GUESS THEY DON'T WANT IT SHUT DOWN DURING WORK HOURS.
FLOORS SIX AND SEVEN WORK ALL NIGHT.
LOOK MAN, I GO WHERE THEY TELL ME.
I'M IN, ALEPH.
WHY ARE YOU RILING UP THE GUARDS?
I'M AN ELEVATOR REPAIR GUY WHO GOT CALLED IN TO WORK AT 11:30 PM. I'M NOT GOING TO BE BRINGING THEM DONUTS.
PATCHED IN. RE-ROUTING ELEVATOR CAMERA.
GIMEL'S TOUCHDOWN IS IN 90 SECONDS.

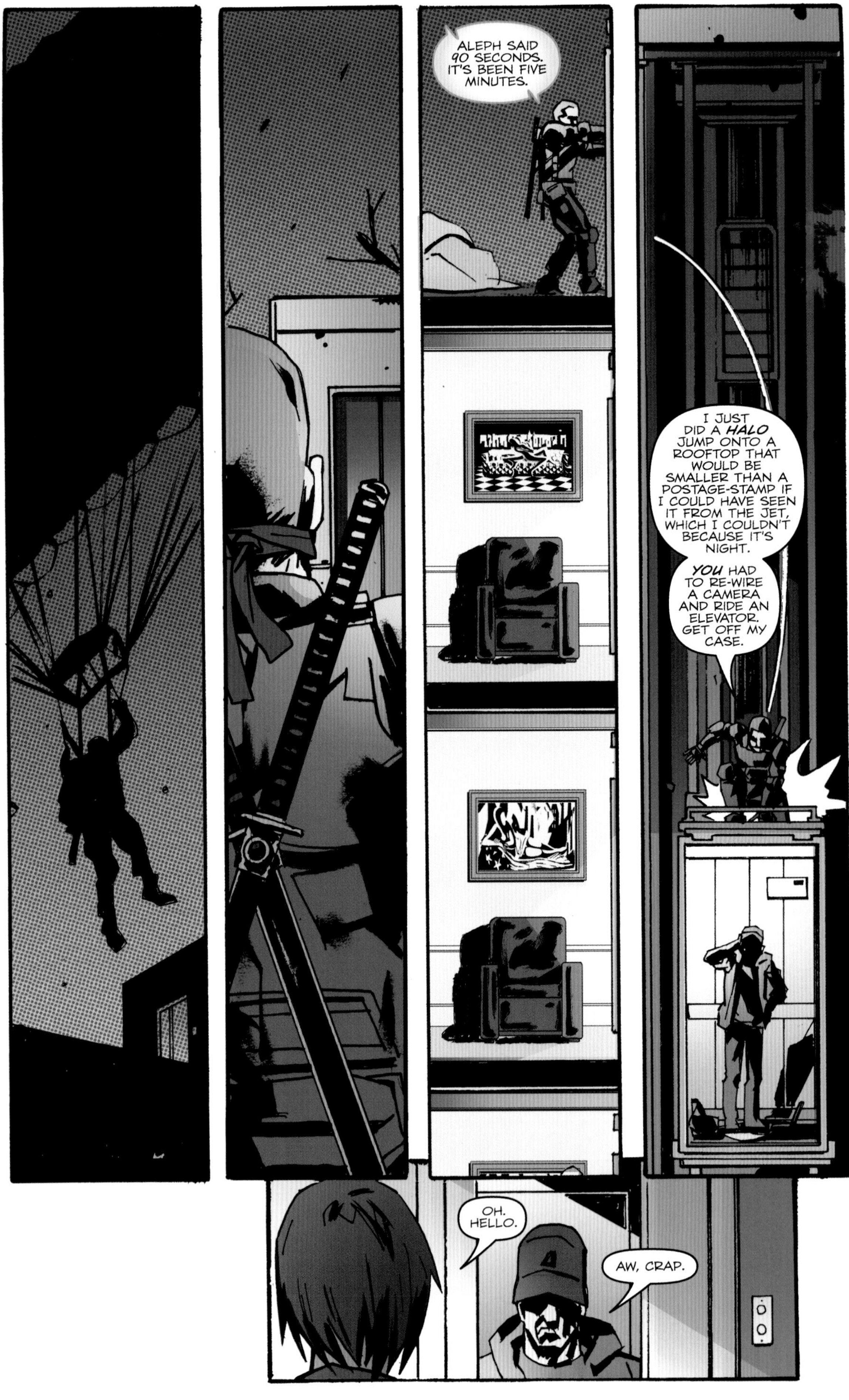
ALEPH SAID 90 SECONDS. IT'S BEEN FIVE MINUTES.
I JUST DID A HALO JUMP ONTO A ROOFTOP THAT WOULD BE SMALLER THAN A POSTAGE-STAMP IF I COULD HAVE SEEN IT FROM THE JET, WHICH I COULDN'T BECAUSE IT'S NIGHT.
YOU HAD TO RE-WIRE A CAMERA AND RIDE AN ELEVATOR. GET OFF MY CASE.
OH. HELLO.
AW, CRAP.

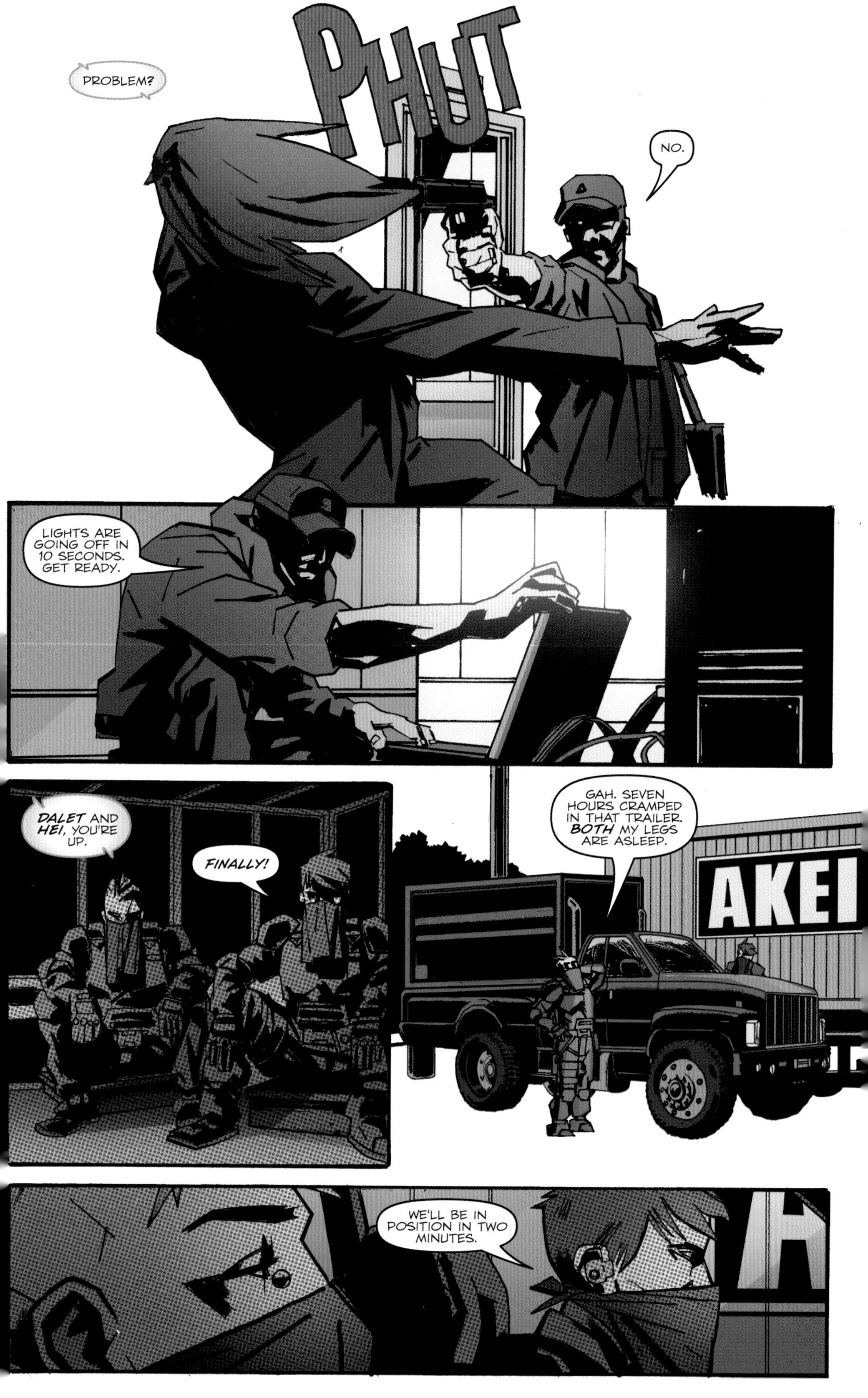
PHUT
PROBLEM?
NO.
LIGHTS ARE GOING OFF IN 10 SECONDS. GET READY.
*DALET* AND *HEI*, YOU'RE UP.
*FINALLY!*
GAH. SEVEN HOURS CRAMPED IN THAT TRAILER. *BOTH* MY LEGS ARE ASLEEP.
AKEI
WE'LL BE IN POSITION IN TWO MINUTES.

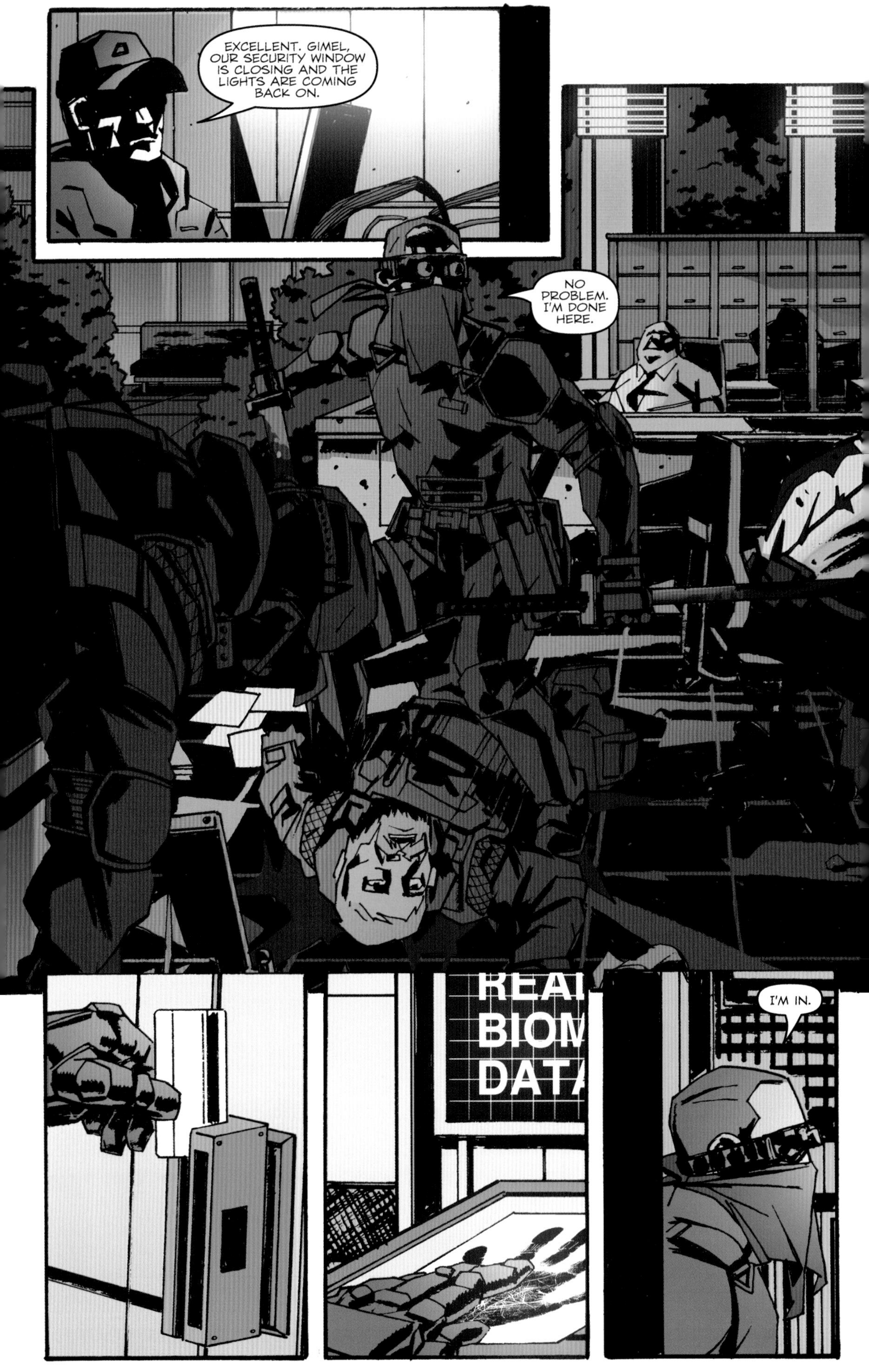
EXCELLENT. GIMEL, OUR SECURITY WINDOW IS CLOSING AND THE LIGHTS ARE COMING BACK ON.
NO PROBLEM. I'M DONE HERE.
REA
BIOM
DATA
I'M IN.

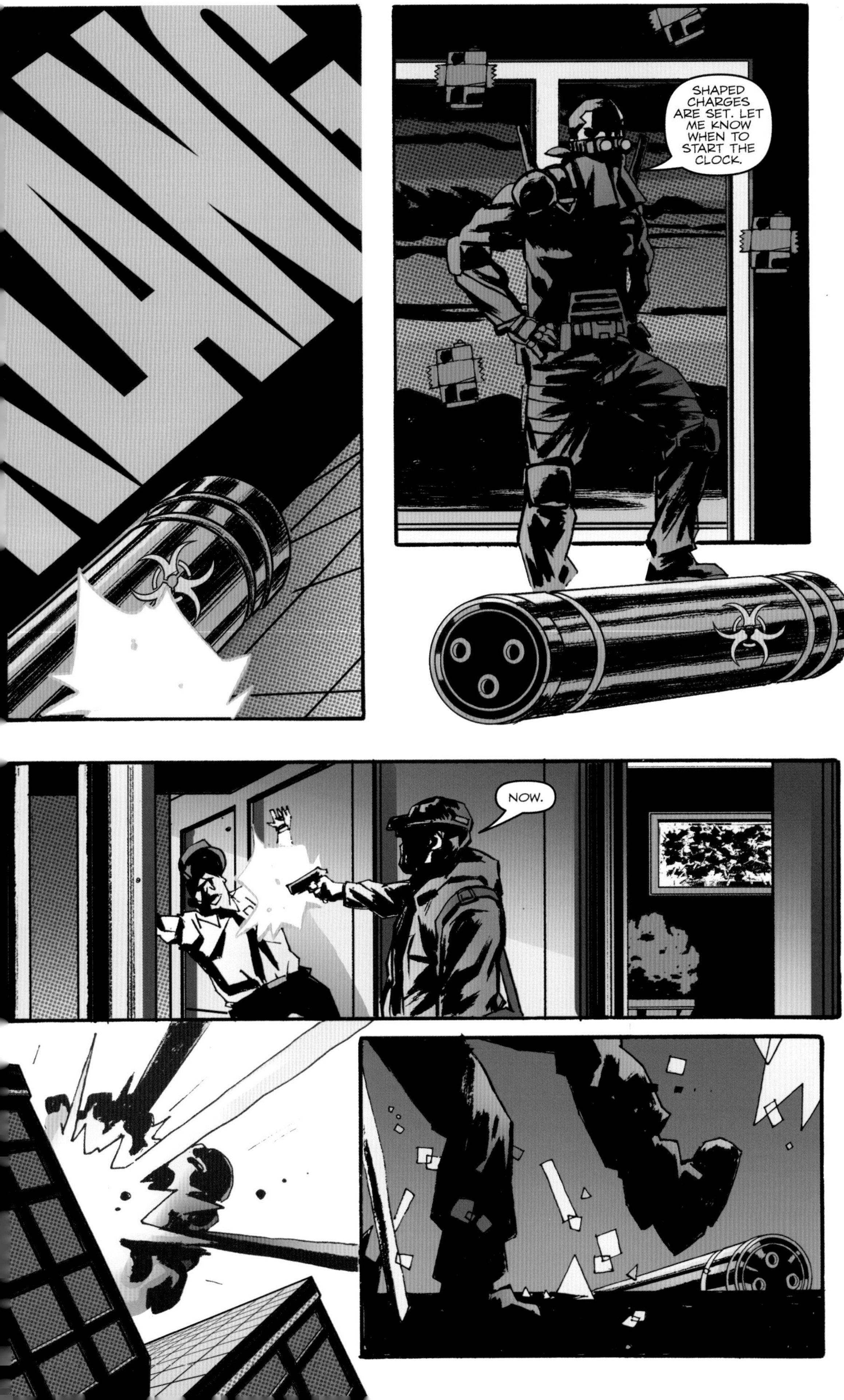
SHAPED CHARGES ARE SET. LET ME KNOW WHEN TO START THE CLOCK.
NOW.

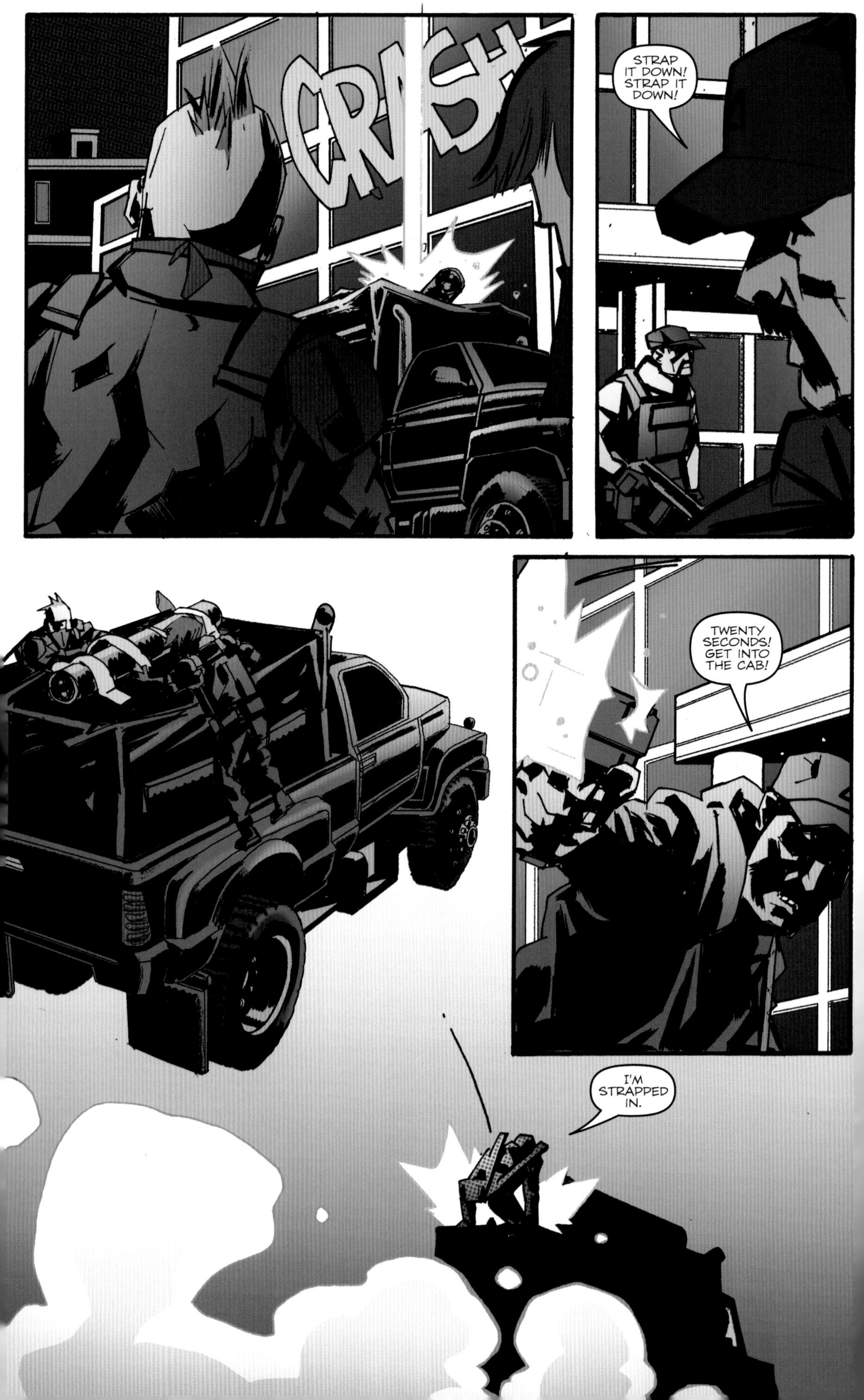
CRASH
STRAP IT DOWN! STRAP IT DOWN!
TWENTY SECONDS! GET INTO THE CAB!
I'M STRAPPED IN.

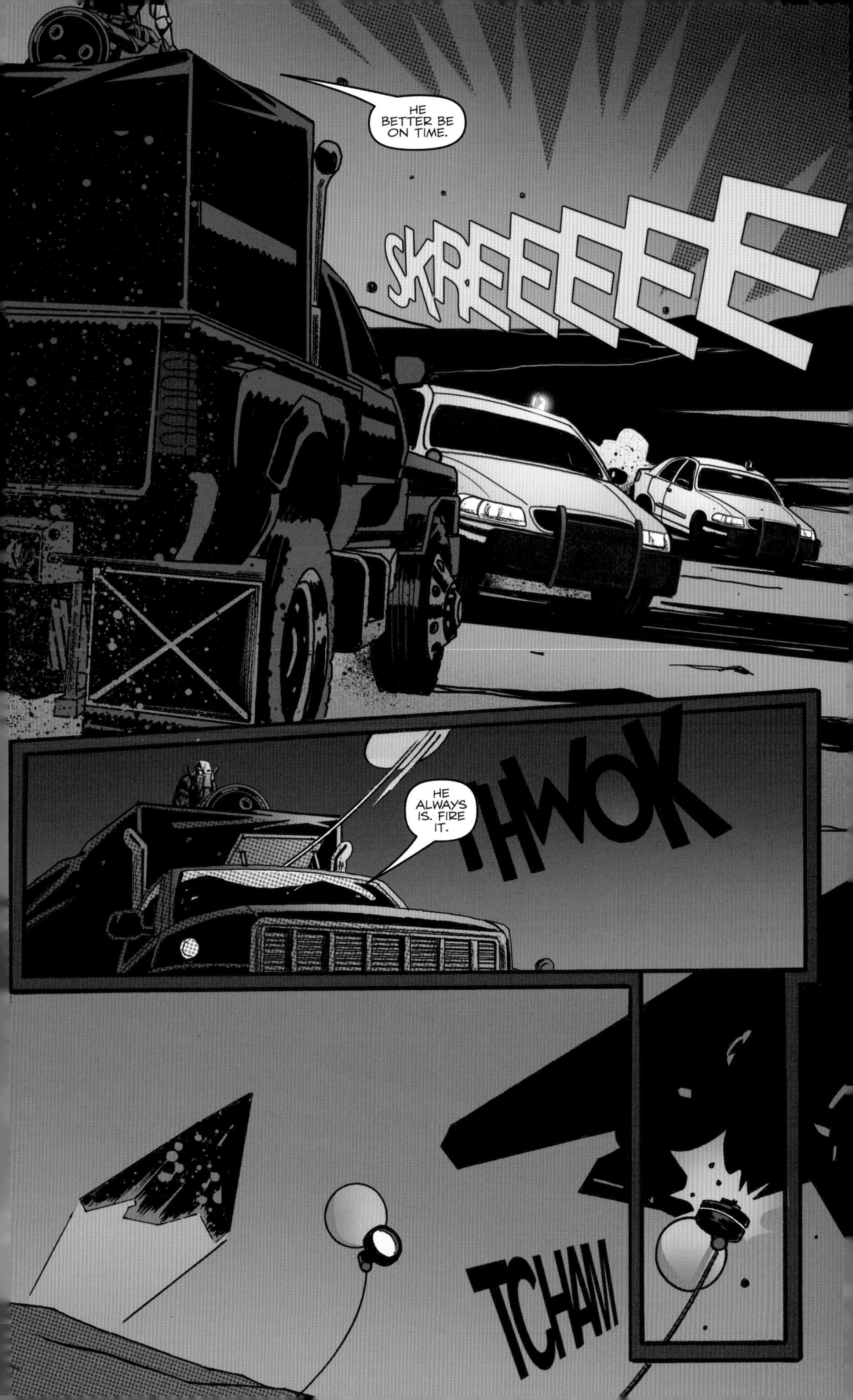
HE BETTER BE ON TIME.
SKREEEEEEE
HE ALWAYS IS. FIRE IT.
THWOK
TCHAM

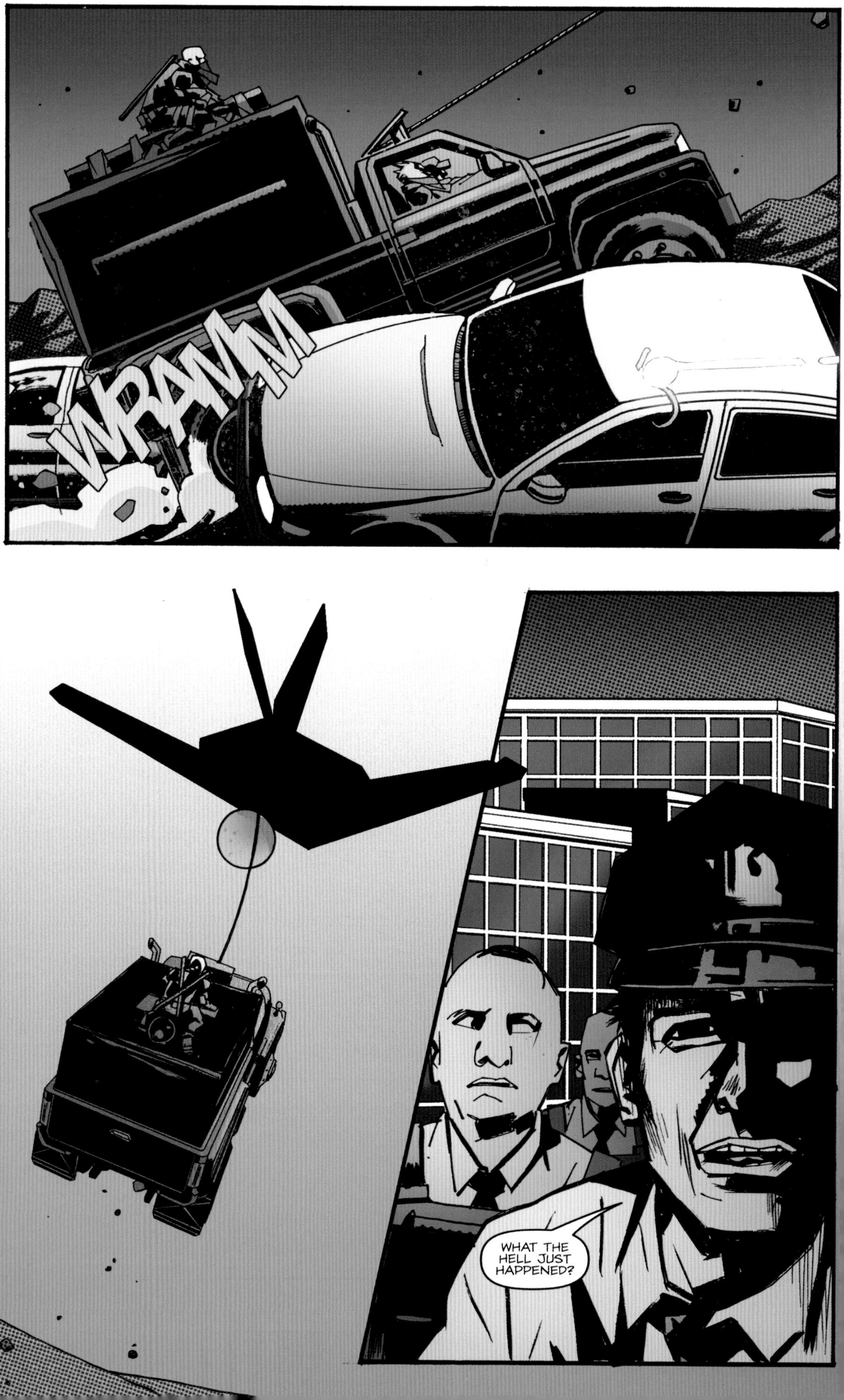
WRAMM
WHAT THE HELL JUST HAPPENED?

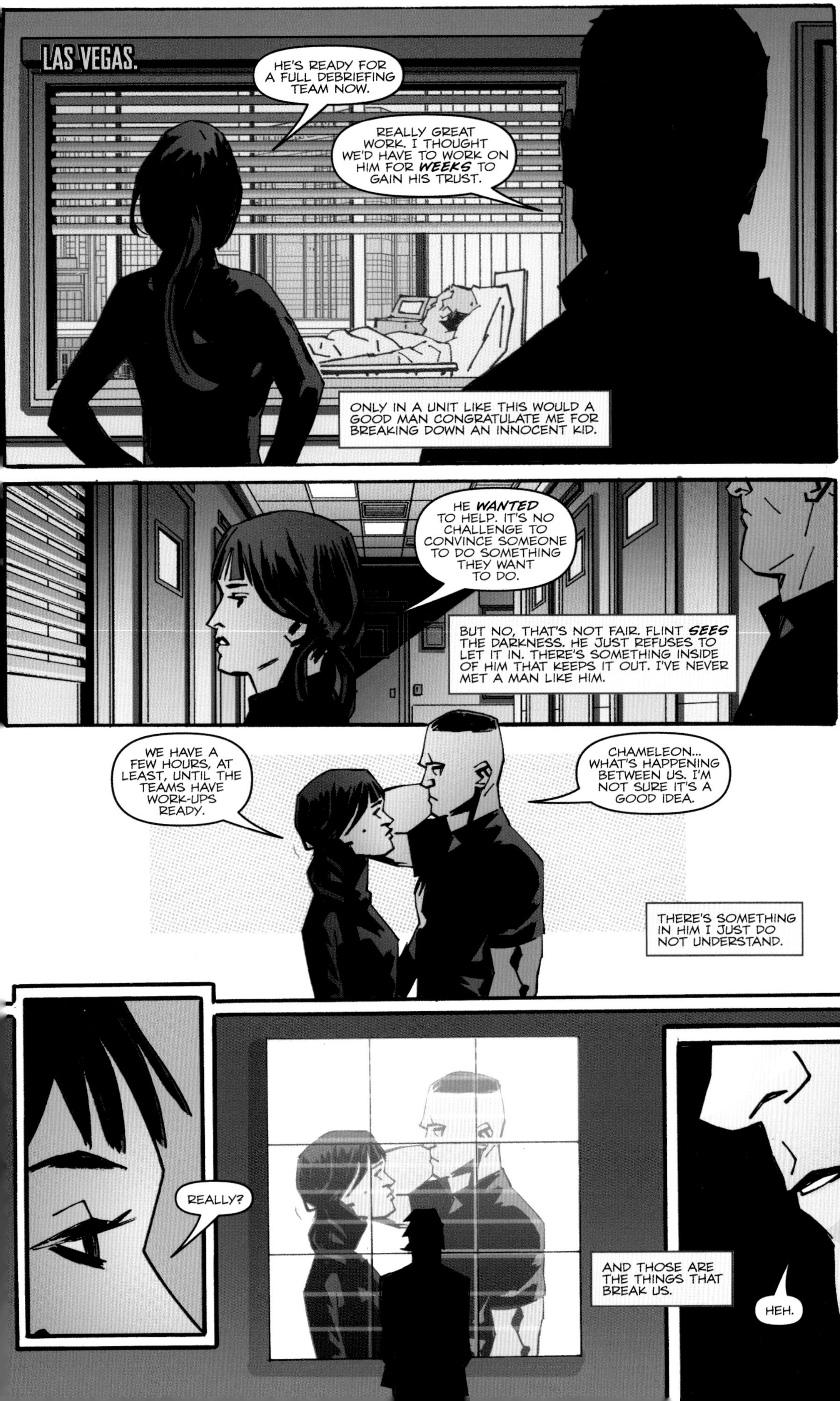
LAS VEGAS.
HE'S READY FOR A FULL DEBRIEFING TEAM NOW.
REALLY GREAT WORK. I THOUGHT WE'D HAVE TO WORK ON HIM FOR WEEKS TO GAIN HIS TRUST.
ONLY IN A UNIT LIKE THIS WOULD A GOOD MAN CONGRATULATE ME FOR BREAKING DOWN AN INNOCENT KID.
HE WANTED TO HELP. IT'S NO CHALLENGE TO CONVINCE SOMEONE TO DO SOMETHING THEY WANT TO DO.
BUT NO, THAT'S NOT FAIR. FLINT SEES THE DARKNESS. HE JUST REFUSES TO LET IT IN. THERE'S SOMETHING INSIDE OF HIM THAT KEEPS IT OUT. I'VE NEVER MET A MAN LIKE HIM.
WE HAVE A FEW HOURS, AT LEAST, UNTIL THE TEAMS HAVE WORK-UPS READY.
CHAMELEON... WHAT'S HAPPENING BETWEEN US. I'M NOT SURE IT'S A GOOD IDEA.
THERE'S SOMETHING IN HIM I JUST DO NOT UNDERSTAND.
REALLY?
AND THOSE ARE THE THINGS THAT BREAK US.
HEH.

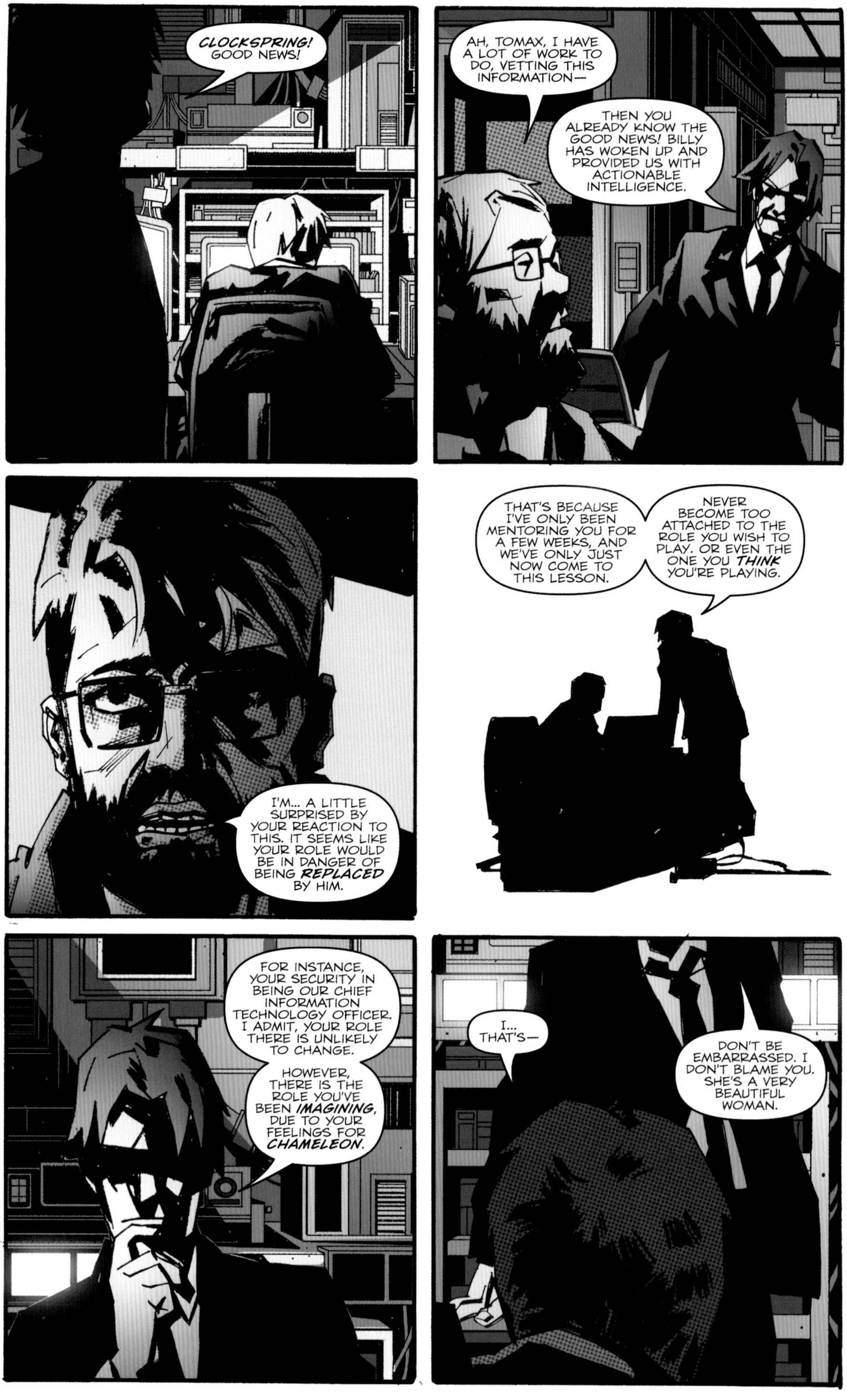
CLOCKSPRING! GOOD NEWS!
AH, TOMAX, I HAVE A LOT OF WORK TO DO, VETTING THIS INFORMATION—
THEN YOU ALREADY KNOW THE GOOD NEWS! BILLY HAS WOKEN UP AND PROVIDED US WITH ACTIONABLE INTELLIGENCE.
I'M... A LITTLE SURPRISED BY YOUR REACTION TO THIS. IT SEEMS LIKE YOUR ROLE WOULD BE IN DANGER OF BEING REPLACED BY HIM.
THAT'S BECAUSE I'VE ONLY BEEN MENTORING YOU FOR A FEW WEEKS, AND WE'VE ONLY JUST NOW COME TO THIS LESSON.
NEVER BECOME TOO ATTACHED TO THE ROLE YOU WISH TO PLAY. OR EVEN THE ONE YOU THINK YOU'RE PLAYING.
FOR INSTANCE, YOUR SECURITY IN BEING OUR CHIEF INFORMATION TECHNOLOGY OFFICER. I ADMIT, YOUR ROLE THERE IS UNLIKELY TO CHANGE.
HOWEVER, THERE IS THE ROLE YOU'VE BEEN IMAGINING, DUE TO YOUR FEELINGS FOR CHAMELEON.
I... THAT'S—
DON'T BE EMBARRASSED. I DON'T BLAME YOU. SHE'S A VERY BEAUTIFUL WOMAN.

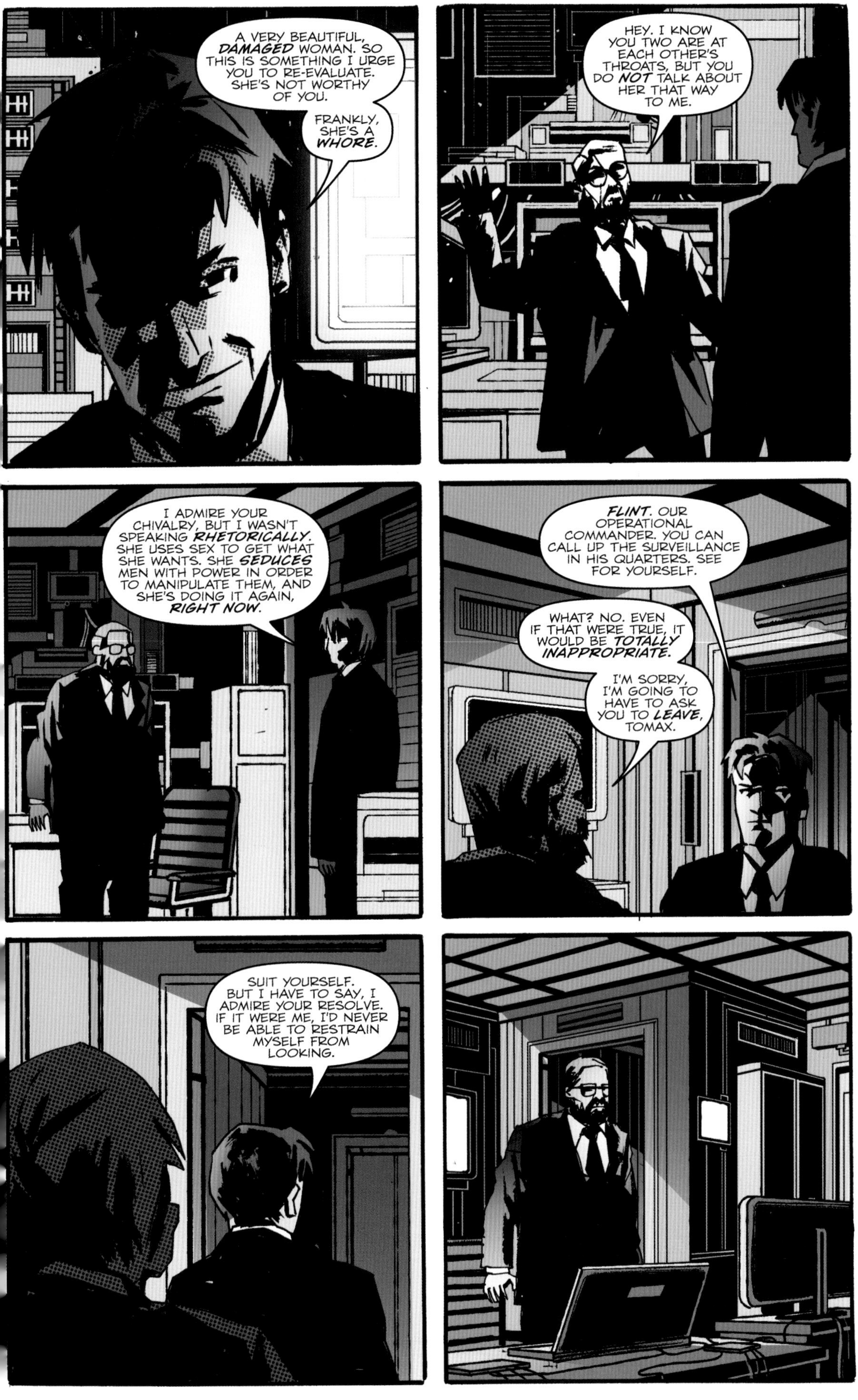
A VERY BEAUTIFUL, DAMAGED WOMAN. SO THIS IS SOMETHING I URGE YOU TO RE-EVALUATE. SHE'S NOT WORTHY OF YOU.
FRANKLY, SHE'S A WHORE.
HEY. I KNOW YOU TWO ARE AT EACH OTHER'S THROATS, BUT YOU DO NOT TALK ABOUT HER THAT WAY TO ME.
I ADMIRE YOUR CHIVALRY, BUT I WASN'T SPEAKING RHETORICALLY. SHE USES SEX TO GET WHAT SHE WANTS. SHE SEDUCES MEN WITH POWER IN ORDER TO MANIPULATE THEM, AND SHE'S DOING IT AGAIN, RIGHT NOW.
FLINT. OUR OPERATIONAL COMMANDER. YOU CAN CALL UP THE SURVEILLANCE IN HIS QUARTERS. SEE FOR YOURSELF.
WHAT? NO. EVEN IF THAT WERE TRUE, IT WOULD BE TOTALLY INAPPROPRIATE.
I'M SORRY, I'M GOING TO HAVE TO ASK YOU TO LEAVE, TOMAX.
SUIT YOURSELF. BUT I HAVE TO SAY, I ADMIRE YOUR RESOLVE. IF IT WERE ME, I'D NEVER BE ABLE TO RESTRAIN MYSELF FROM LOOKING.

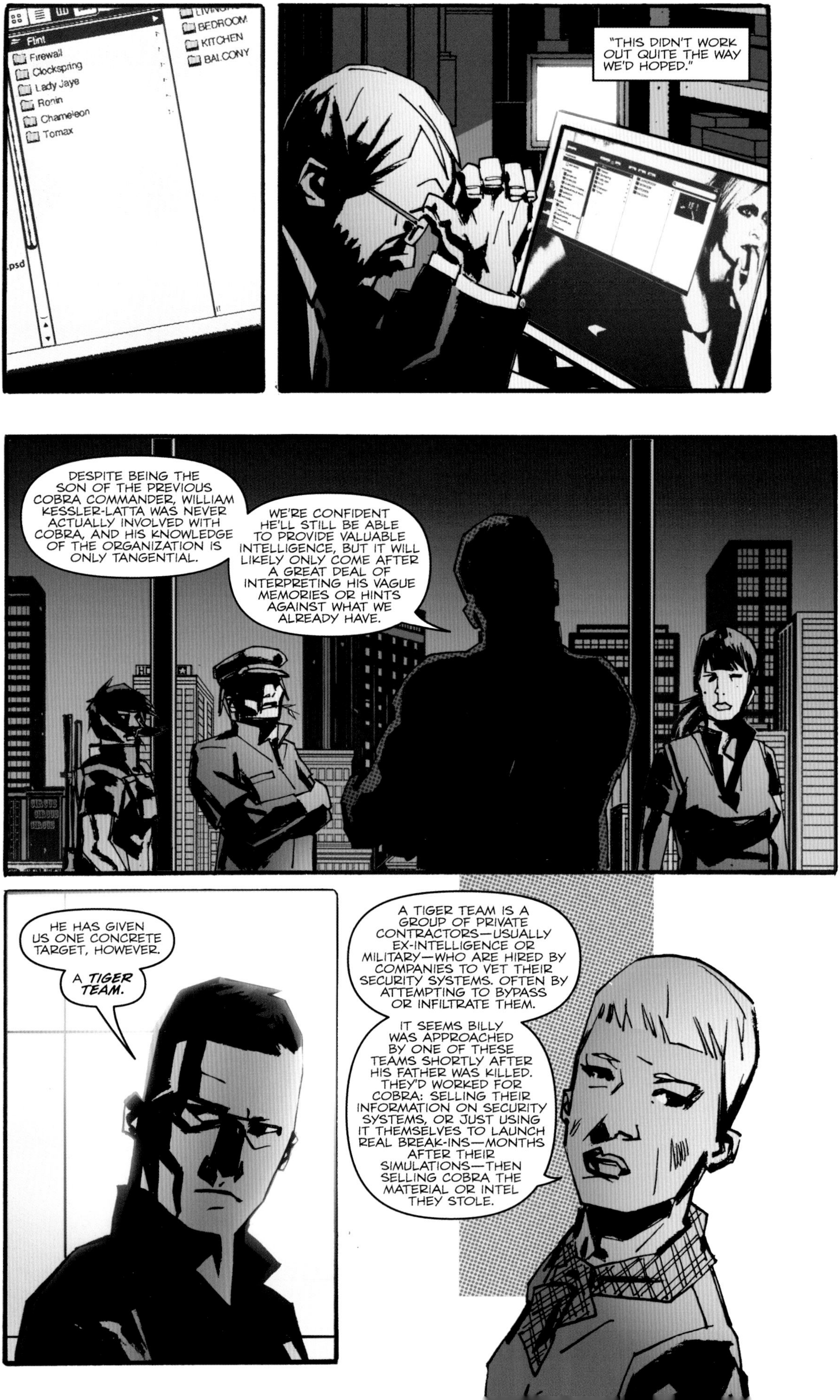
Flint
Firewall
Clockspring
Lady Jaye
Ronin
Chameleon
Tomax
BEDROOM
KITCHEN
BALCONY
"THIS DIDN'T WORK OUT QUITE THE WAY WE'D HOPED."
DESPITE BEING THE SON OF THE PREVIOUS COBRA COMMANDER, WILLIAM KESSLER-LATTA WAS NEVER ACTUALLY INVOLVED WITH COBRA, AND HIS KNOWLEDGE OF THE ORGANIZATION IS ONLY TANGENTIAL.
WE'RE CONFIDENT HE'LL STILL BE ABLE TO PROVIDE VALUABLE INTELLIGENCE, BUT IT WILL LIKELY ONLY COME AFTER A GREAT DEAL OF INTERPRETING HIS VAGUE MEMORIES OR HINTS AGAINST WHAT WE ALREADY HAVE.
HE HAS GIVEN US ONE CONCRETE TARGET, HOWEVER.
A *TIGER TEAM.*
A TIGER TEAM IS A GROUP OF PRIVATE CONTRACTORS—USUALLY EX-INTELLIGENCE OR MILITARY—WHO ARE HIRED BY COMPANIES TO VET THEIR SECURITY SYSTEMS. OFTEN BY ATTEMPTING TO BYPASS OR INFILTRATE THEM.
IT SEEMS BILLY WAS APPROACHED BY ONE OF THESE TEAMS SHORTLY AFTER HIS FATHER WAS KILLED. THEY'D WORKED FOR COBRA: SELLING THEIR INFORMATION ON SECURITY SYSTEMS, OR JUST USING IT THEMSELVES TO LAUNCH REAL BREAK-INS—MONTHS AFTER THEIR SIMULATIONS—THEN SELLING COBRA THE MATERIAL OR INTEL THEY STOLE.

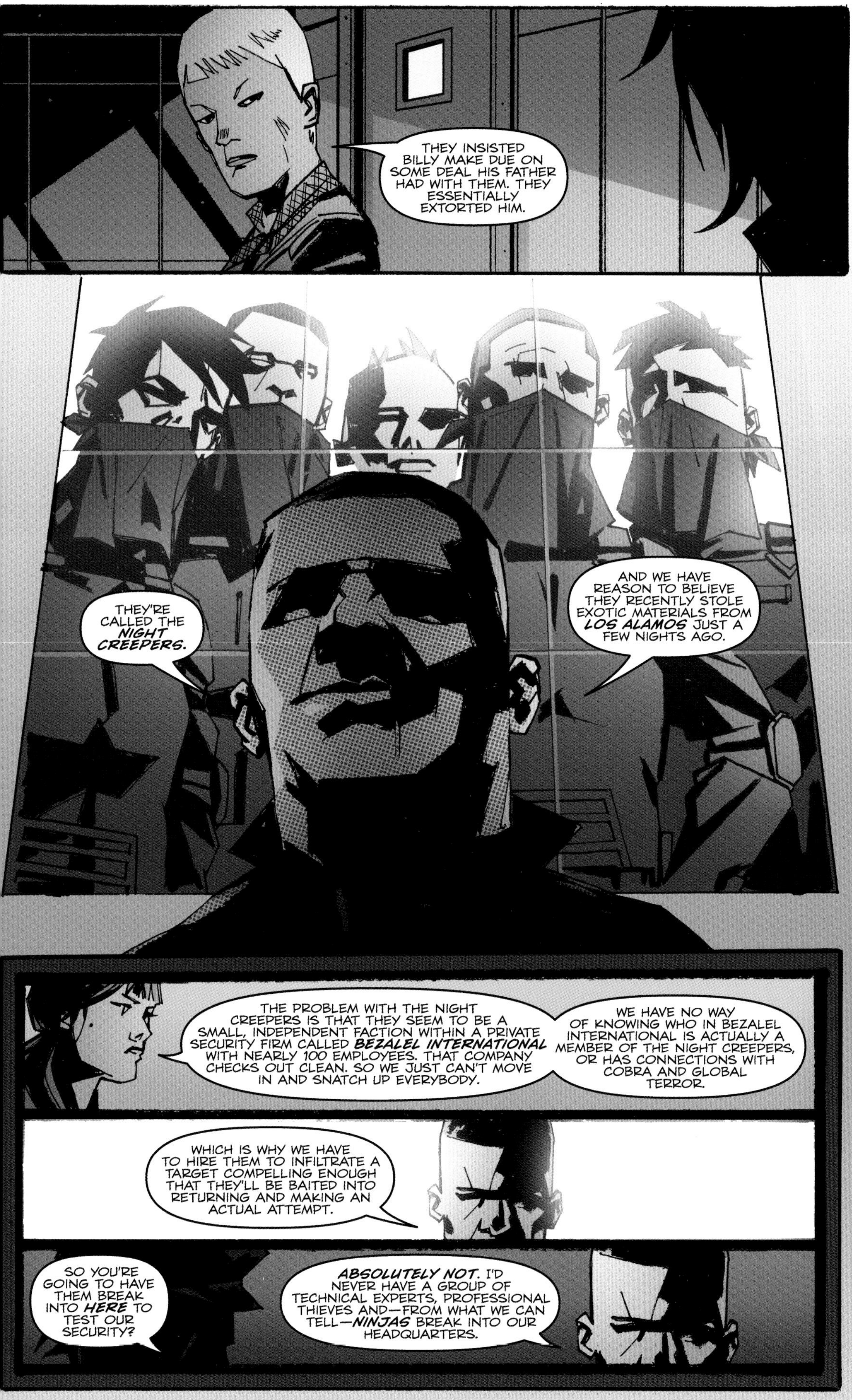
THEY INSISTED BILLY MAKE DUE ON SOME DEAL HIS FATHER HAD WITH THEM. THEY ESSENTIALLY EXTORTED HIM.
THEY'RE CALLED THE NIGHT CREEPERS.
AND WE HAVE REASON TO BELIEVE THEY RECENTLY STOLE EXOTIC MATERIALS FROM LOS ALAMOS JUST A FEW NIGHTS AGO.
THE PROBLEM WITH THE NIGHT CREEPERS IS THAT THEY SEEM TO BE A SMALL, INDEPENDENT FACTION WITHIN A PRIVATE SECURITY FIRM CALLED BEZALEL INTERNATIONAL WITH NEARLY 100 EMPLOYEES. THAT COMPANY CHECKS OUT CLEAN. SO WE JUST CAN'T MOVE IN AND SNATCH UP EVERYBODY.
WE HAVE NO WAY OF KNOWING WHO IN BEZALEL INTERNATIONAL IS ACTUALLY A MEMBER OF THE NIGHT CREEPERS, OR HAS CONNECTIONS WITH COBRA AND GLOBAL TERROR.
WHICH IS WHY WE HAVE TO HIRE THEM TO INFILTRATE A TARGET COMPELLING ENOUGH THAT THEY'LL BE BAITED INTO RETURNING AND MAKING AN ACTUAL ATTEMPT.
SO YOU'RE GOING TO HAVE THEM BREAK INTO HERE TO TEST OUR SECURITY?
ABSOLUTELY NOT. I'D NEVER HAVE A GROUP OF TECHNICAL EXPERTS, PROFESSIONAL THIEVES AND—FROM WHAT WE CAN TELL—NINJAS BREAK INTO OUR HEADQUARTERS.

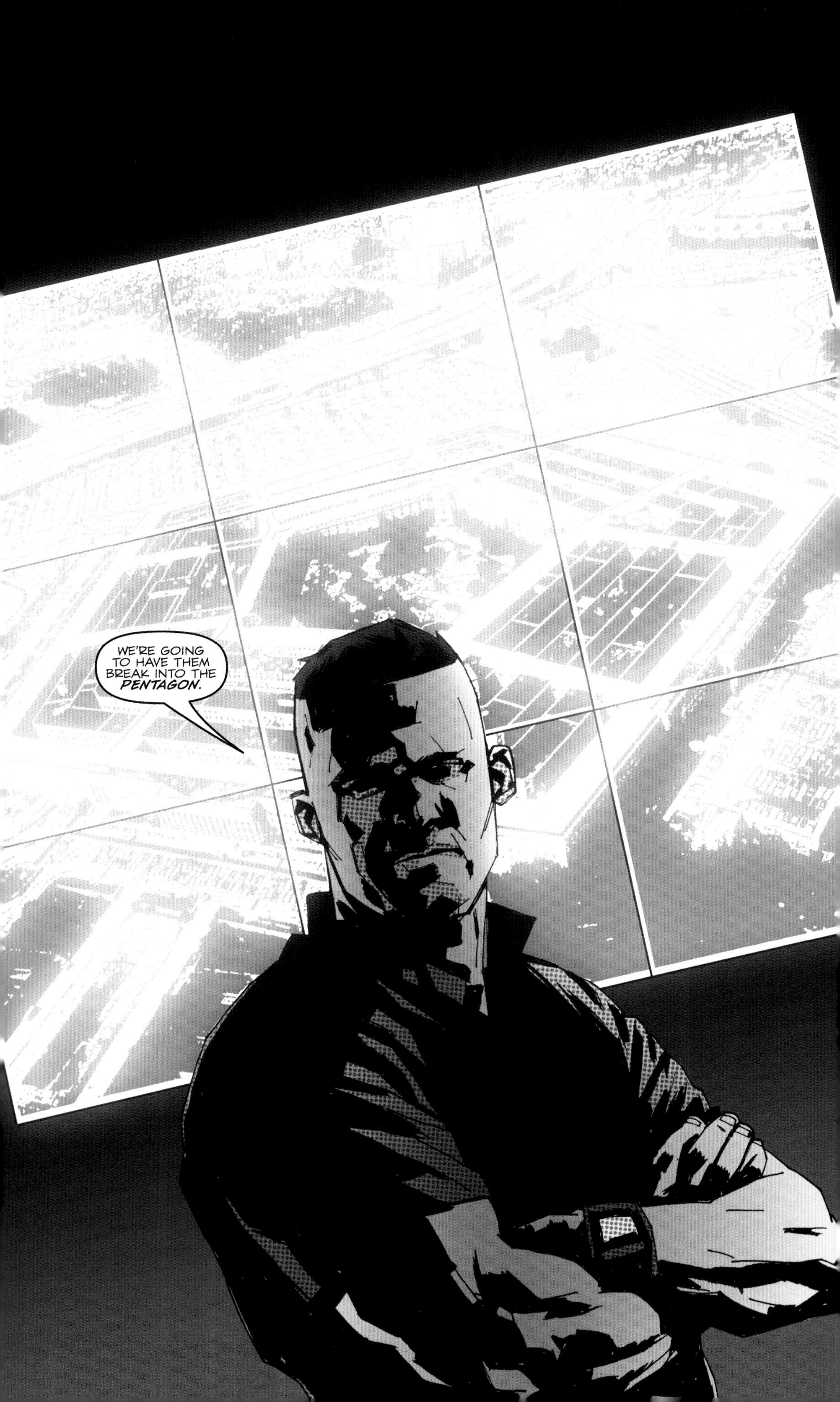
WE'RE GOING TO HAVE THEM BREAK INTO THE *PENTAGON*.

ART BY
**ANTONIO FUSO**

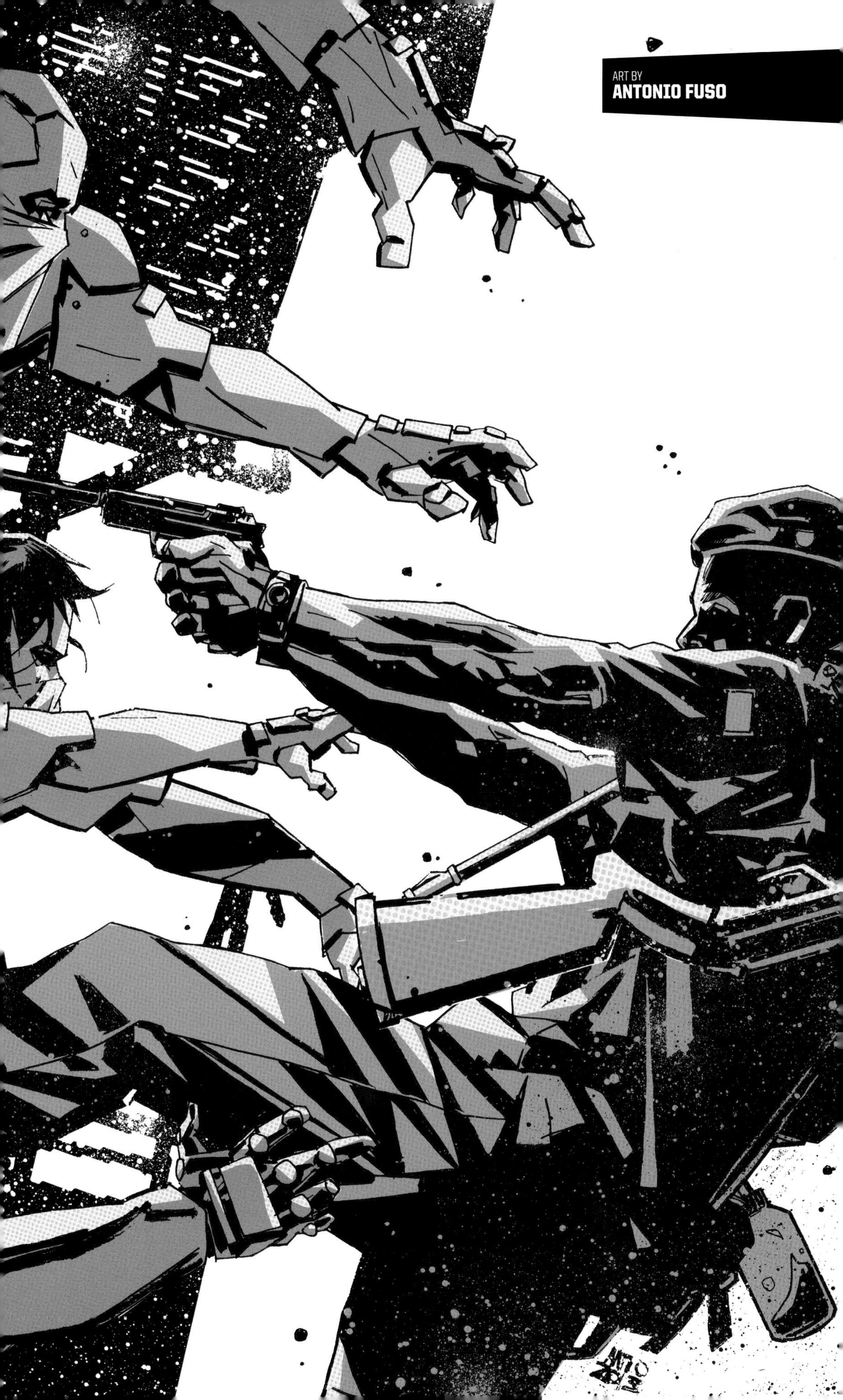

ART BY
**MICHAEL LARK**

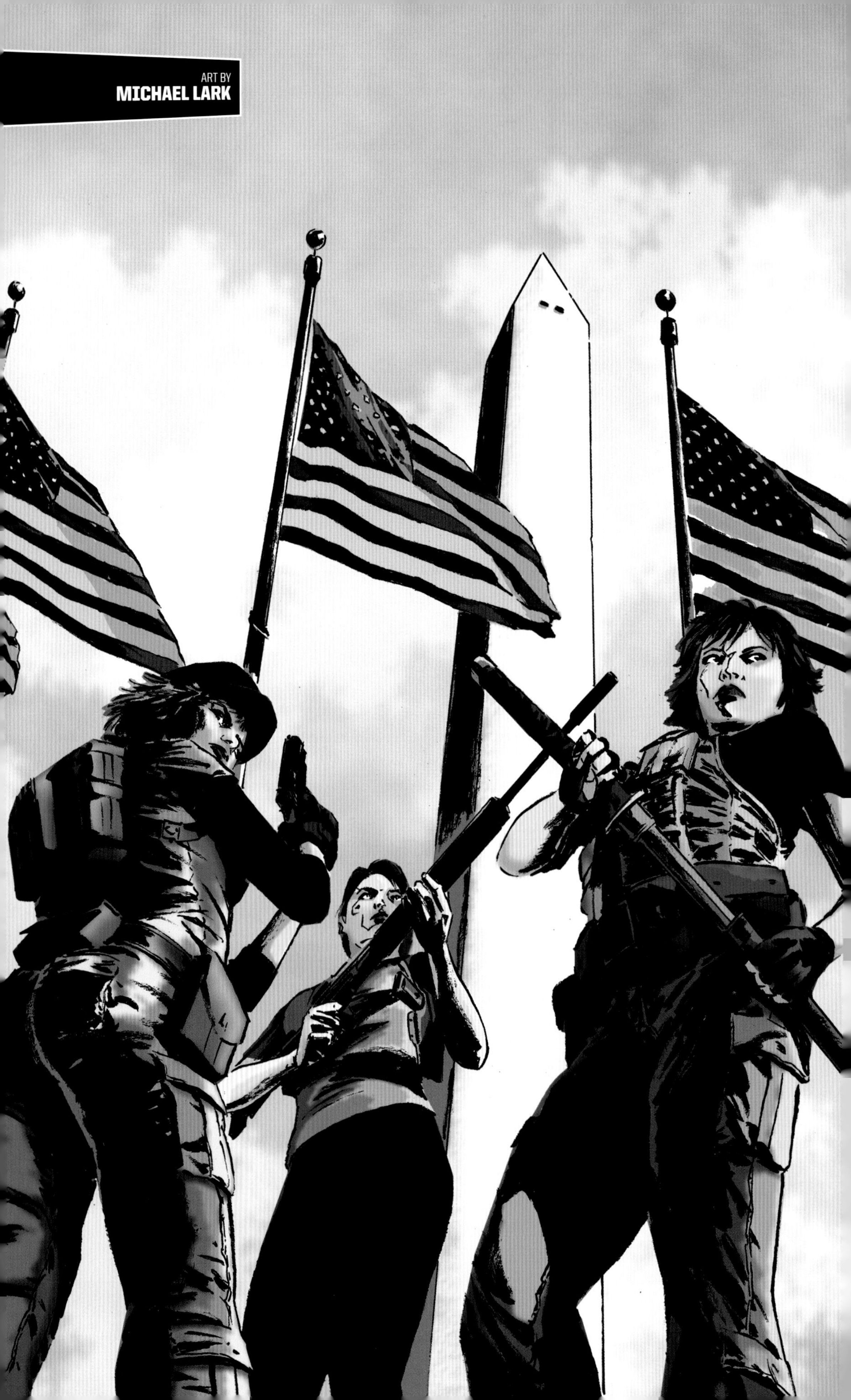

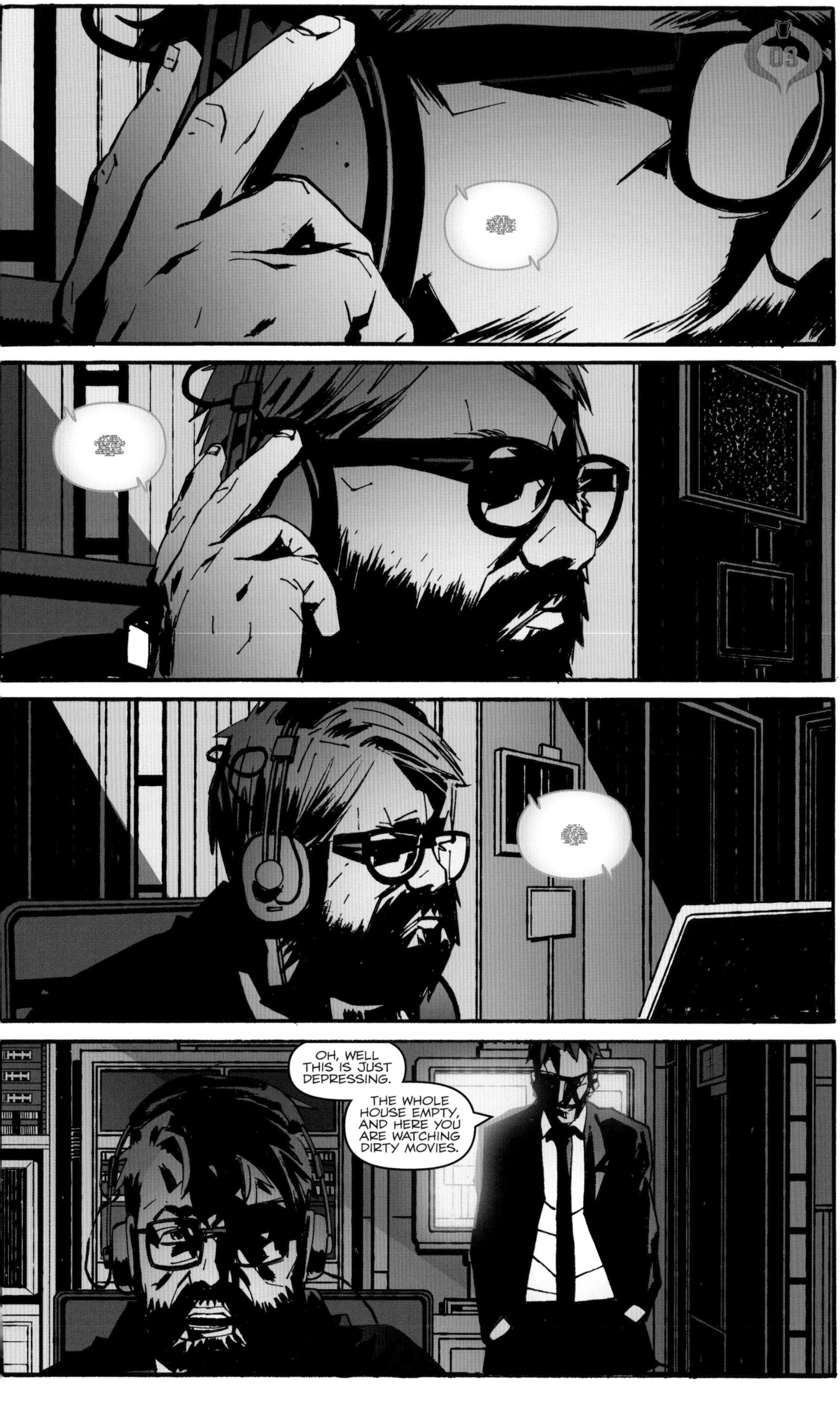
OH, WELL THIS IS JUST DEPRESSING.
THE WHOLE HOUSE EMPTY, AND HERE YOU ARE WATCHING DIRTY MOVIES.

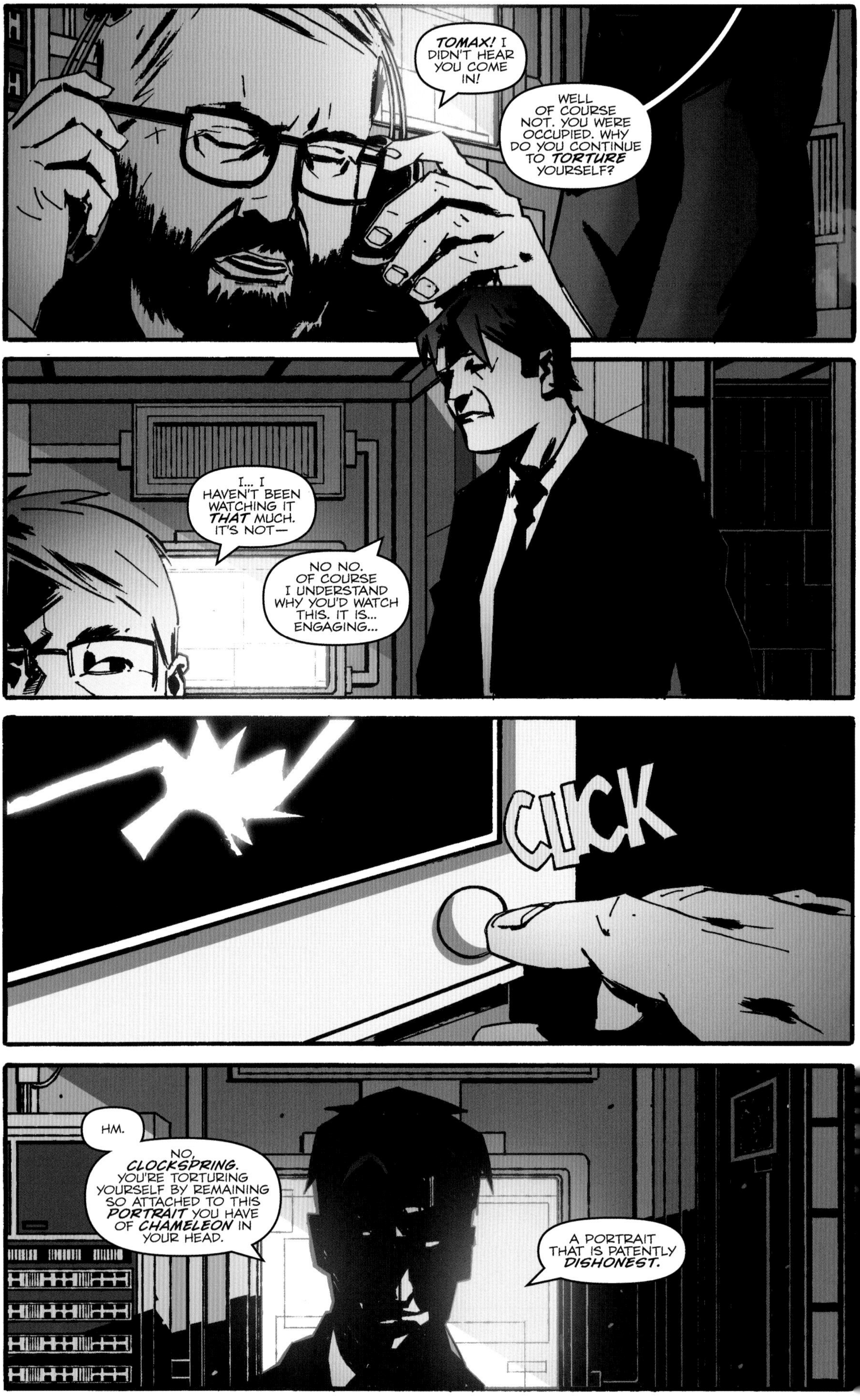
TOMAX! I DIDN'T HEAR YOU COME IN!
WELL OF COURSE NOT. YOU WERE OCCUPIED. WHY DO YOU CONTINUE TO TORTURE YOURSELF?
I... I HAVEN'T BEEN WATCHING IT THAT MUCH. IT'S NOT—
NO NO. OF COURSE I UNDERSTAND WHY YOU'D WATCH THIS. IT IS... ENGAGING...
CLICK
HM.
NO, CLOCKSPRING. YOU'RE TORTURING YOURSELF BY REMAINING SO ATTACHED TO THIS PORTRAIT YOU HAVE OF CHAMELEON IN YOUR HEAD.
A PORTRAIT THAT IS PATENTLY DISHONEST.

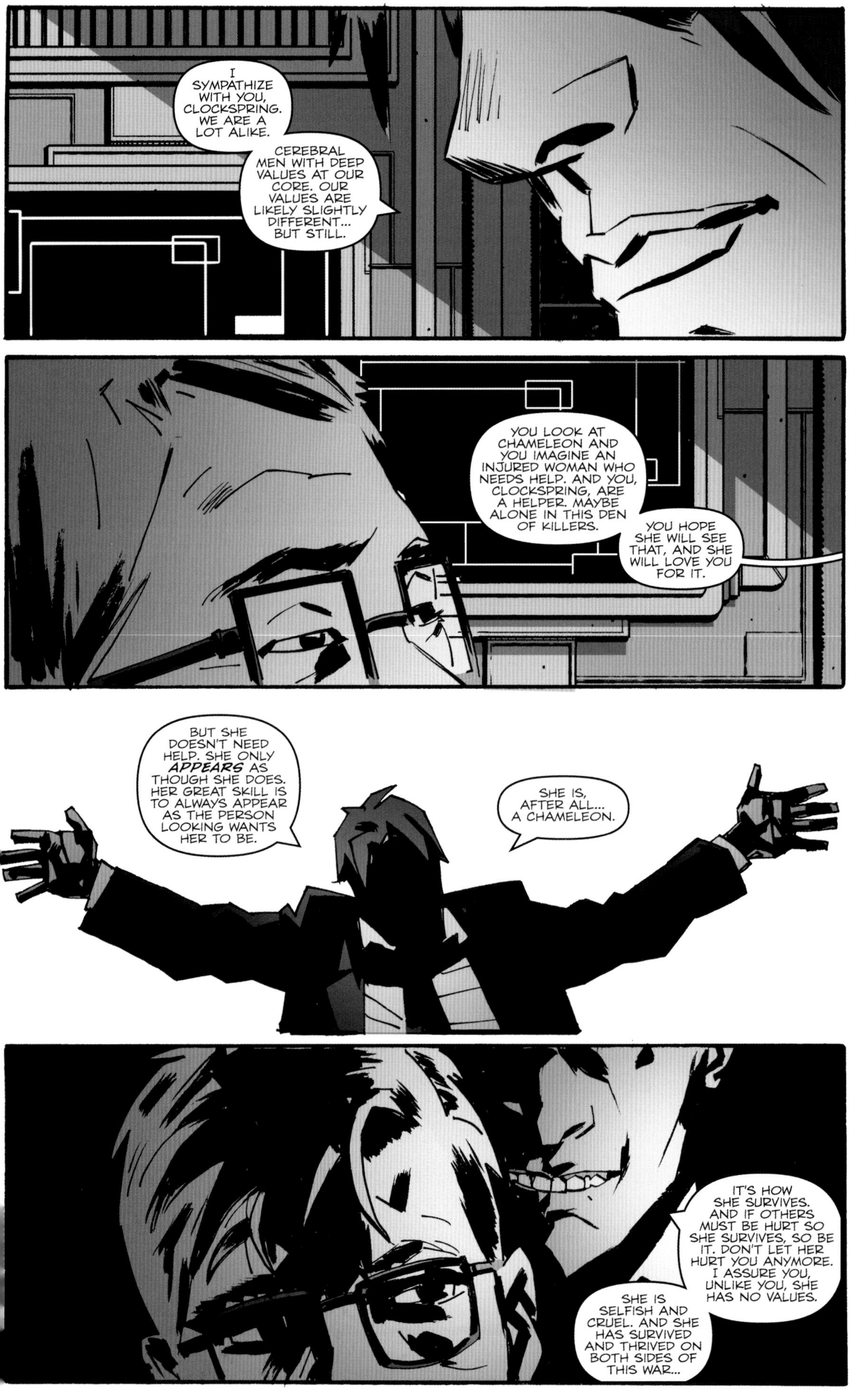

I SYMPATHIZE WITH YOU, CLOCKSPRING. WE ARE A LOT ALIKE.
CEREBRAL MEN WITH DEEP VALUES AT OUR CORE. OUR VALUES ARE LIKELY SLIGHTLY DIFFERENT... BUT STILL.
YOU LOOK AT CHAMELEON AND YOU IMAGINE AN INJURED WOMAN WHO NEEDS HELP. AND YOU, CLOCKSPRING, ARE A HELPER. MAYBE ALONE IN THIS DEN OF KILLERS.
YOU HOPE SHE WILL SEE THAT, AND SHE WILL LOVE YOU FOR IT.
BUT SHE DOESN'T NEED HELP. SHE ONLY *APPEARS* AS THOUGH SHE DOES. HER GREAT SKILL IS TO ALWAYS APPEAR AS THE PERSON LOOKING WANTS HER TO BE.
SHE IS, AFTER ALL... A CHAMELEON.
IT'S HOW SHE SURVIVES. AND IF OTHERS MUST BE HURT SO SHE SURVIVES, SO BE IT. DON'T LET HER HURT YOU ANYMORE. I ASSURE YOU, UNLIKE YOU, SHE HAS NO VALUES.
SHE IS SELFISH AND CRUEL. AND SHE HAS SURVIVED AND THRIVED ON BOTH SIDES OF THIS WAR...

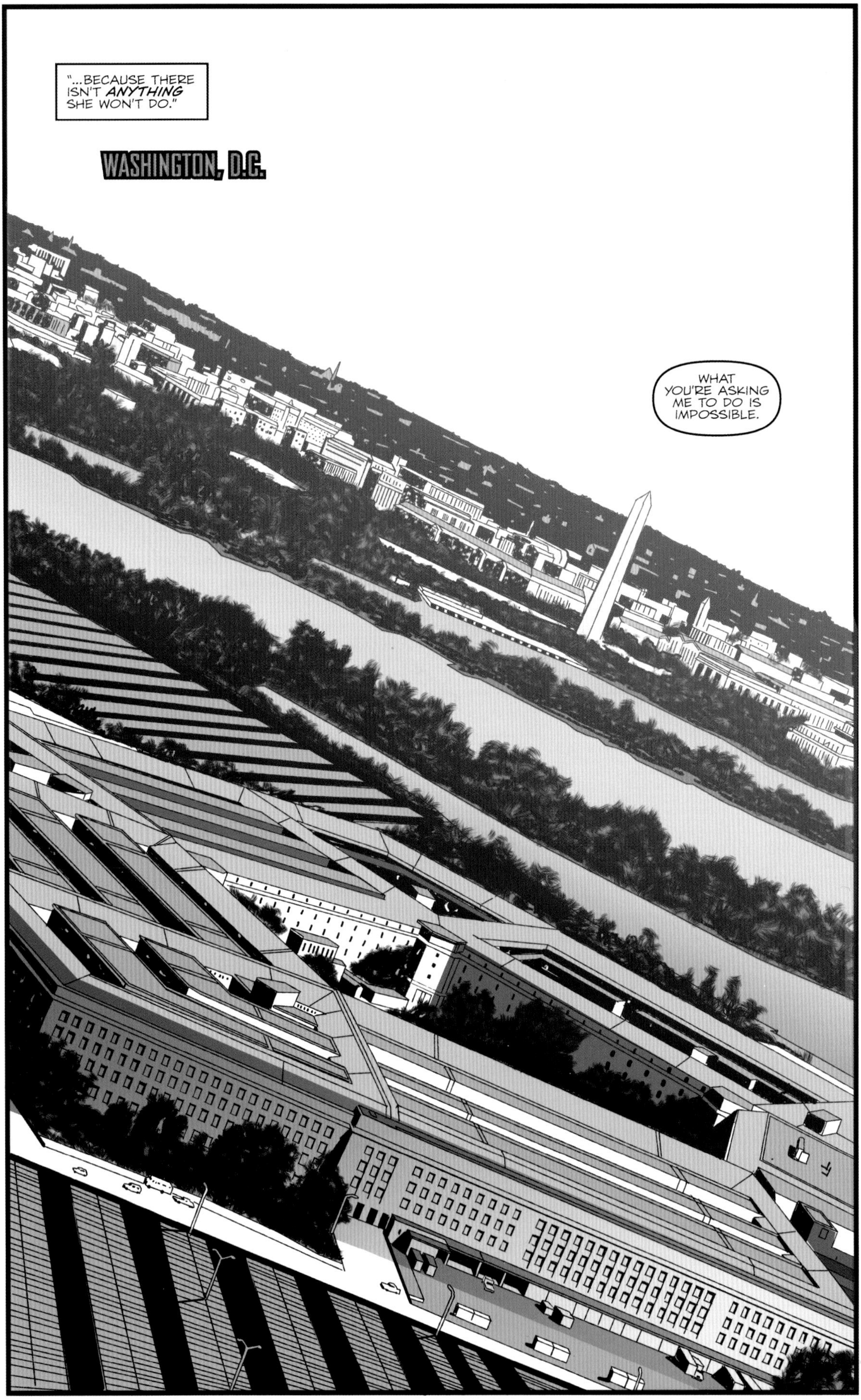
"...BECAUSE THERE ISN'T ANYTHING SHE WON'T DO."
WASHINGTON, D.C.
WHAT YOU'RE ASKING ME TO DO IS IMPOSSIBLE.

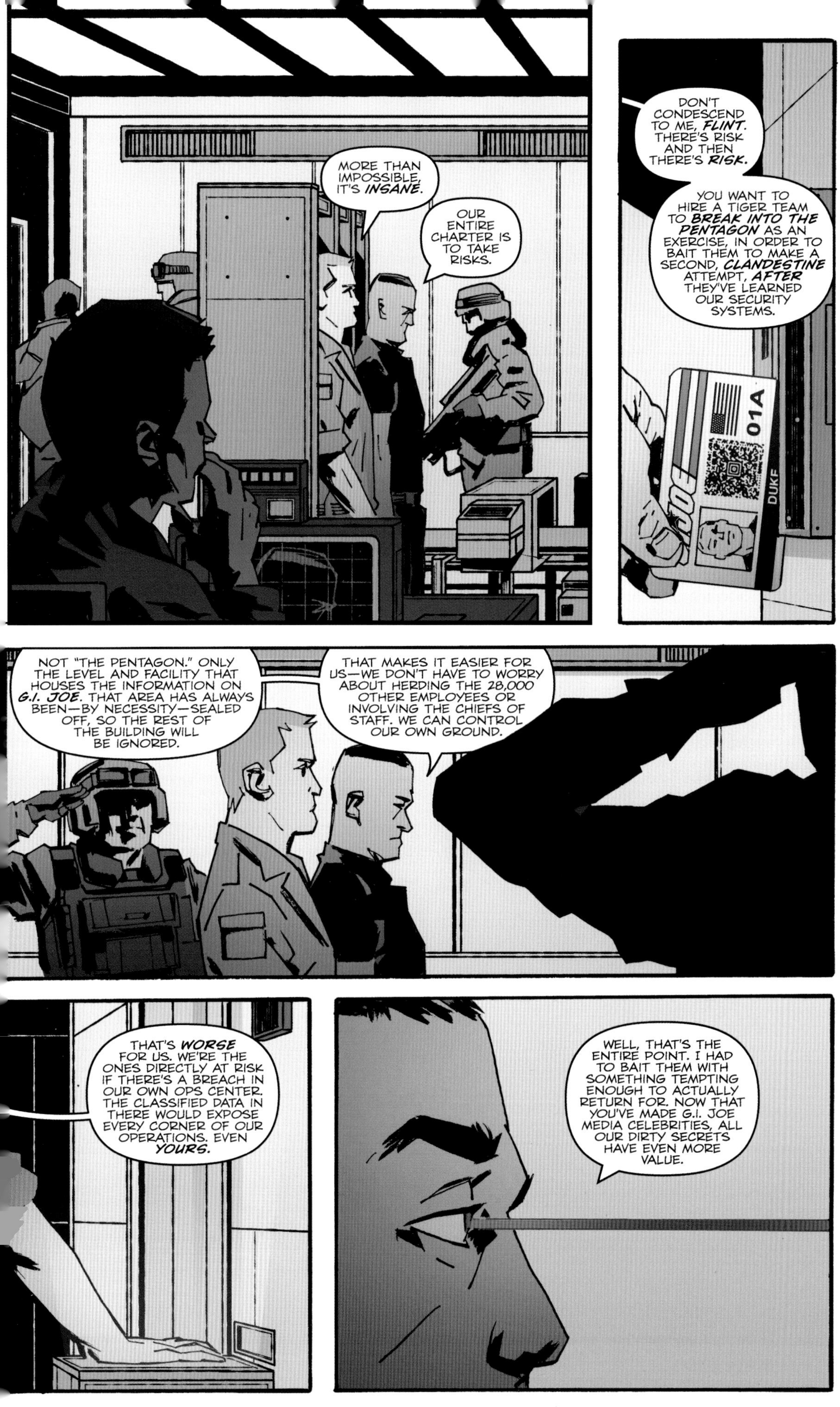

MORE THAN IMPOSSIBLE, IT'S *INSANE*.
OUR ENTIRE CHARTER IS TO TAKE RISKS.
DON'T CONDESCEND TO ME, *FLINT*. THERE'S RISK AND THEN THERE'S *RISK*.
YOU WANT TO HIRE A TIGER TEAM TO *BREAK INTO THE PENTAGON* AS AN EXERCISE, IN ORDER TO BAIT THEM TO MAKE A SECOND, *CLANDESTINE* ATTEMPT, *AFTER* THEY'VE LEARNED OUR SECURITY SYSTEMS.
01A
DUKF
NOT "THE PENTAGON." ONLY THE LEVEL AND FACILITY THAT HOUSES THE INFORMATION ON *G.I. JOE*. THAT AREA HAS ALWAYS BEEN—BY NECESSITY—SEALED OFF, SO THE REST OF THE BUILDING WILL BE IGNORED.
THAT MAKES IT EASIER FOR US—WE DON'T HAVE TO WORRY ABOUT HERDING THE 28,000 OTHER EMPLOYEES OR INVOLVING THE CHIEFS OF STAFF. WE CAN CONTROL OUR OWN GROUND.
THAT'S *WORSE* FOR US. WE'RE THE ONES DIRECTLY AT RISK IF THERE'S A BREACH IN OUR OWN OPS CENTER. THE CLASSIFIED DATA IN THERE WOULD EXPOSE EVERY CORNER OF OUR OPERATIONS. EVEN *YOURS*.
WELL, THAT'S THE ENTIRE POINT. I HAD TO BAIT THEM WITH SOMETHING TEMPTING ENOUGH TO ACTUALLY RETURN FOR. NOW THAT YOU'VE MADE G.I. JOE MEDIA CELEBRITIES, ALL OUR DIRTY SECRETS HAVE EVEN MORE VALUE.

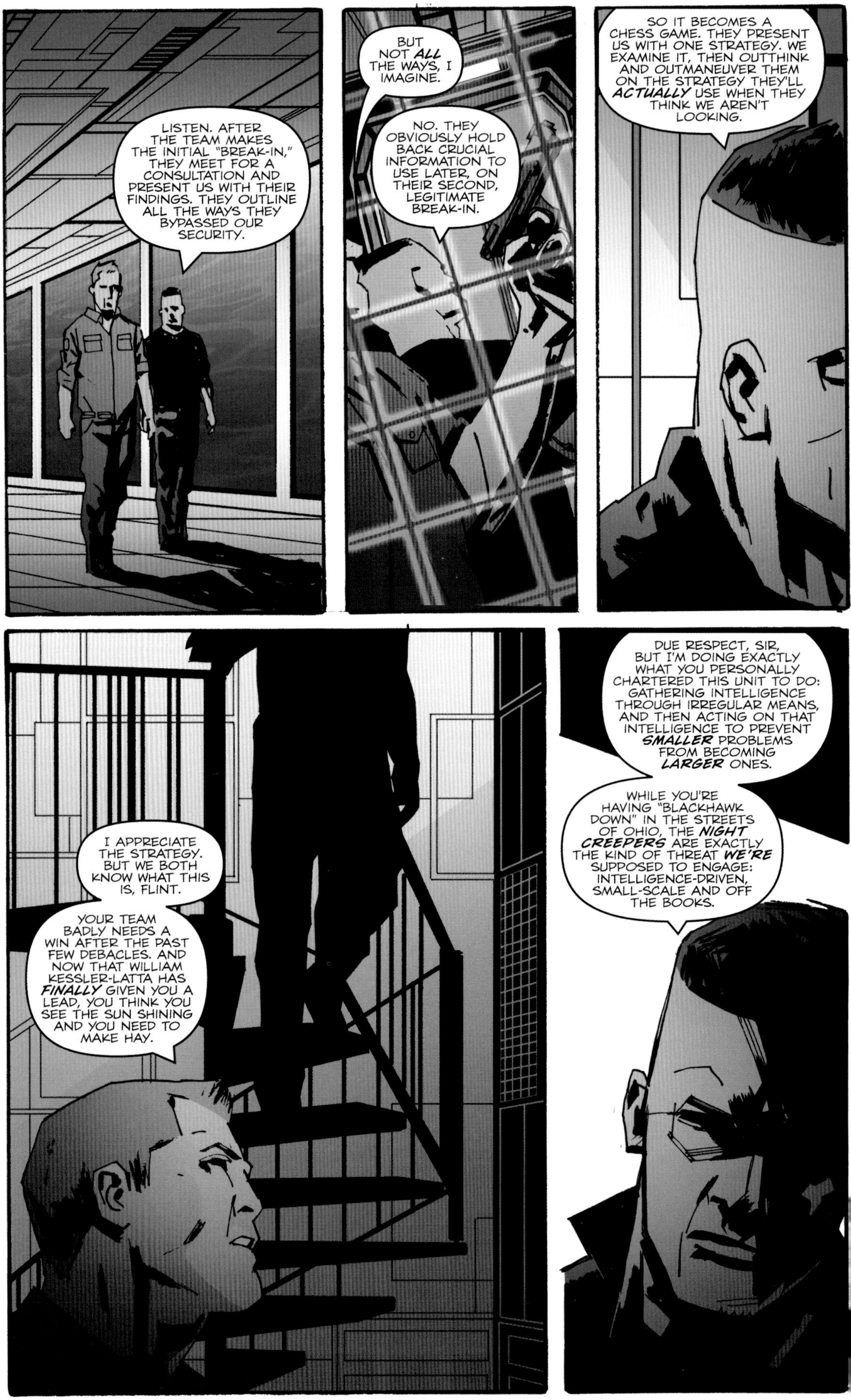
LISTEN. AFTER THE TEAM MAKES THE INITIAL "BREAK-IN," THEY MEET FOR A CONSULTATION AND PRESENT US WITH THEIR FINDINGS. THEY OUTLINE ALL THE WAYS THEY BYPASSED OUR SECURITY.
BUT NOT ALL THE WAYS, I IMAGINE.
NO. THEY OBVIOUSLY HOLD BACK CRUCIAL INFORMATION TO USE LATER, ON THEIR SECOND, LEGITIMATE BREAK-IN.
SO IT BECOMES A CHESS GAME. THEY PRESENT US WITH ONE STRATEGY. WE EXAMINE IT, THEN OUTTHINK AND OUTMANEUVER THEM ON THE STRATEGY THEY'LL ACTUALLY USE WHEN THEY THINK WE AREN'T LOOKING.
I APPRECIATE THE STRATEGY. BUT WE BOTH KNOW WHAT THIS IS, FLINT.
YOUR TEAM BADLY NEEDS A WIN AFTER THE PAST FEW DEBACLES. AND NOW THAT WILLIAM KESSLER-LATTA HAS FINALLY GIVEN YOU A LEAD, YOU THINK YOU SEE THE SUN SHINING AND YOU NEED TO MAKE HAY.
DUE RESPECT, SIR, BUT I'M DOING EXACTLY WHAT YOU PERSONALLY CHARTERED THIS UNIT TO DO: GATHERING INTELLIGENCE THROUGH IRREGULAR MEANS, AND THEN ACTING ON THAT INTELLIGENCE TO PREVENT SMALLER PROBLEMS FROM BECOMING LARGER ONES.
WHILE YOU'RE HAVING "BLACKHAWK DOWN" IN THE STREETS OF OHIO, THE NIGHT CREEPERS ARE EXACTLY THE KIND OF THREAT WE'RE SUPPOSED TO ENGAGE: INTELLIGENCE-DRIVEN, SMALL-SCALE AND OFF THE BOOKS.

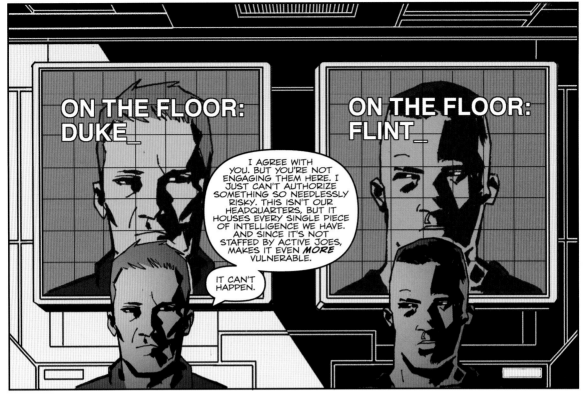

ON THE FLOOR: DUKE_

ON THE FLOOR: FLINT_

I AGREE WITH YOU. BUT YOU'RE NOT ENGAGING THEM HERE. I JUST CAN'T AUTHORIZE SOMETHING SO NEEDLESSLY RISKY. THIS ISN'T OUR HEADQUARTERS, BUT IT HOUSES EVERY SINGLE PIECE OF INTELLIGENCE WE HAVE. AND SINCE IT'S NOT STAFFED BY ACTIVE JOES, MAKES IT EVEN *MORE* VULNERABLE.

IT CAN'T HAPPEN.

THEN I'M VERY SORRY TO SAY THIS, SIR... BUT IT *ALREADY HAS.*

EXCUSE ME?

I HIRED THEM SIX WEEKS AGO. THEY EXECUTED THEIR INITIAL BREAK-IN LAST NIGHT. WE HAVE OUR CONSULTATION MEETING IN THREE HOURS.

SOLDIER, ARE YOU—?

I DID IT AND IT'S DONE. THEY'LL BE COMING, AND WE HAVE TO BE READY.

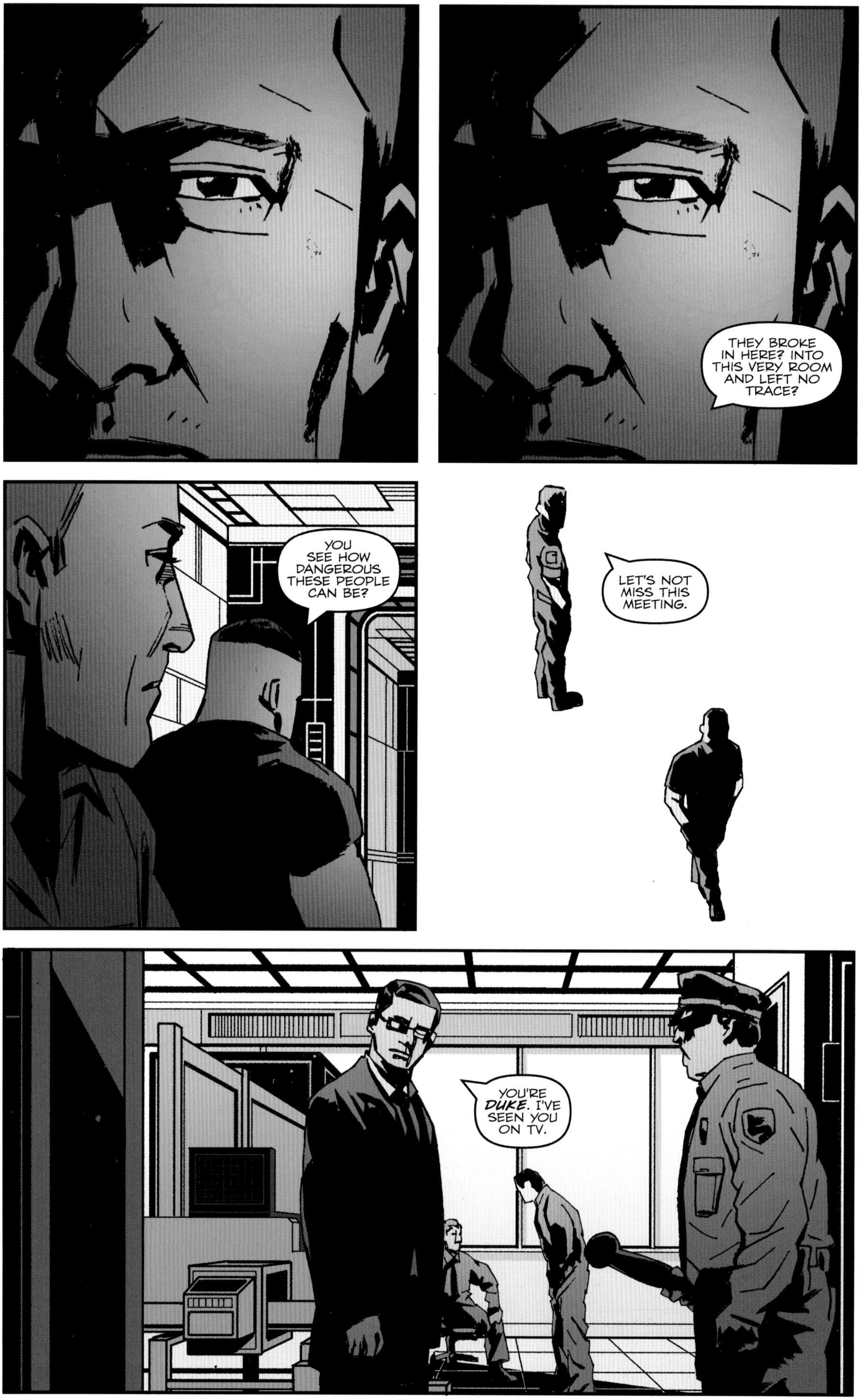
THEY BROKE IN HERE? INTO THIS VERY ROOM AND LEFT NO TRACE?
YOU SEE HOW DANGEROUS THESE PEOPLE CAN BE?
LET'S NOT MISS THIS MEETING.
YOU'RE DUKE. I'VE SEEN YOU ON TV.

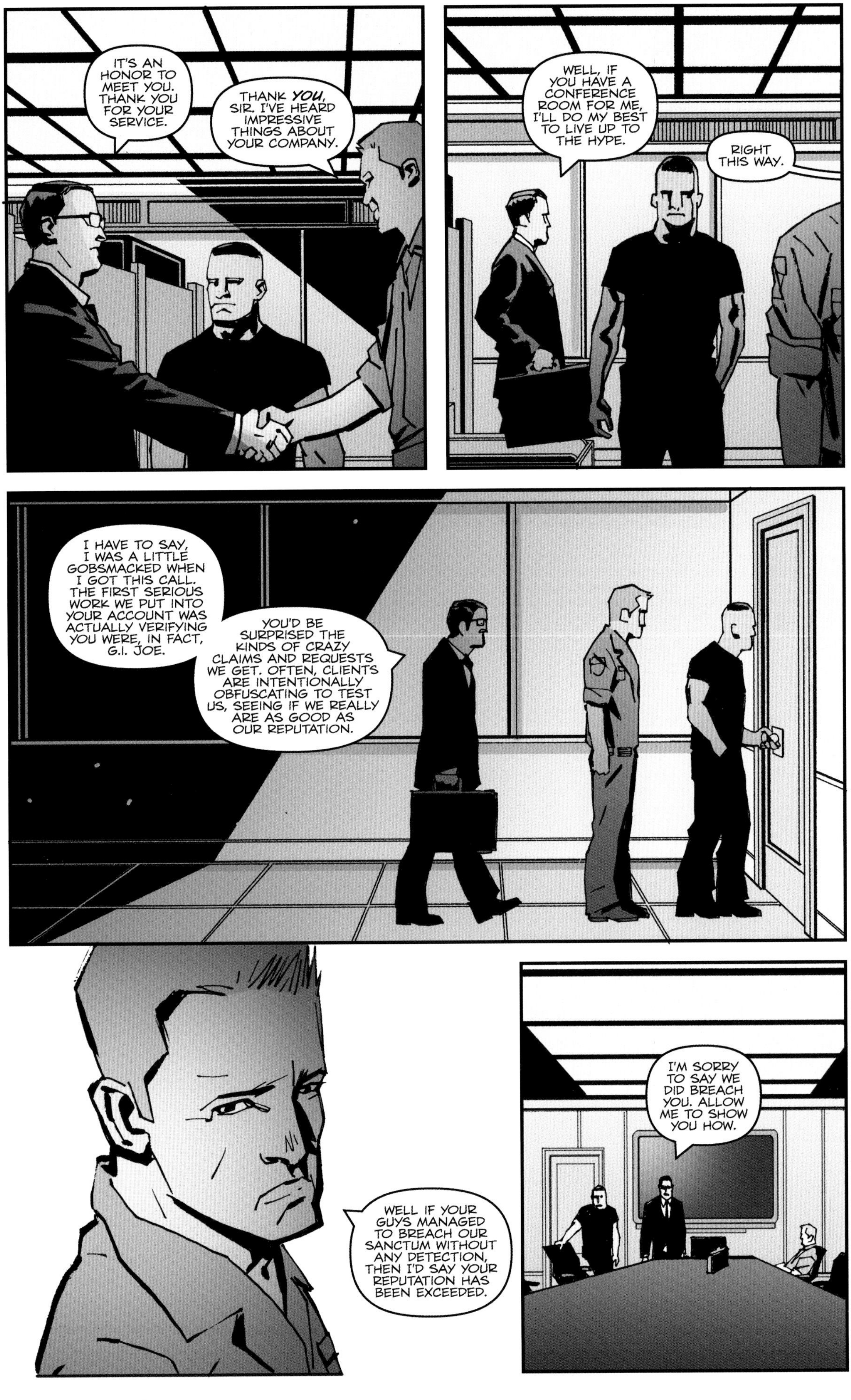
IT'S AN HONOR TO MEET YOU. THANK YOU FOR YOUR SERVICE.
THANK *YOU*, SIR. I'VE HEARD IMPRESSIVE THINGS ABOUT YOUR COMPANY.
WELL, IF YOU HAVE A CONFERENCE ROOM FOR ME, I'LL DO MY BEST TO LIVE UP TO THE HYPE.
RIGHT THIS WAY.
I HAVE TO SAY, I WAS A LITTLE GOBSMACKED WHEN I GOT THIS CALL. THE FIRST SERIOUS WORK WE PUT INTO YOUR ACCOUNT WAS ACTUALLY VERIFYING YOU WERE, IN FACT, G.I. JOE.
YOU'D BE SURPRISED THE KINDS OF CRAZY CLAIMS AND REQUESTS WE GET. OFTEN, CLIENTS ARE INTENTIONALLY OBFUSCATING TO TEST US, SEEING IF WE REALLY ARE AS GOOD AS OUR REPUTATION.
WELL IF YOUR GUYS MANAGED TO BREACH OUR SANCTUM WITHOUT ANY DETECTION, THEN I'D SAY YOUR REPUTATION HAS BEEN EXCEEDED.
I'M SORRY TO SAY WE DID BREACH YOU. ALLOW ME TO SHOW YOU HOW.

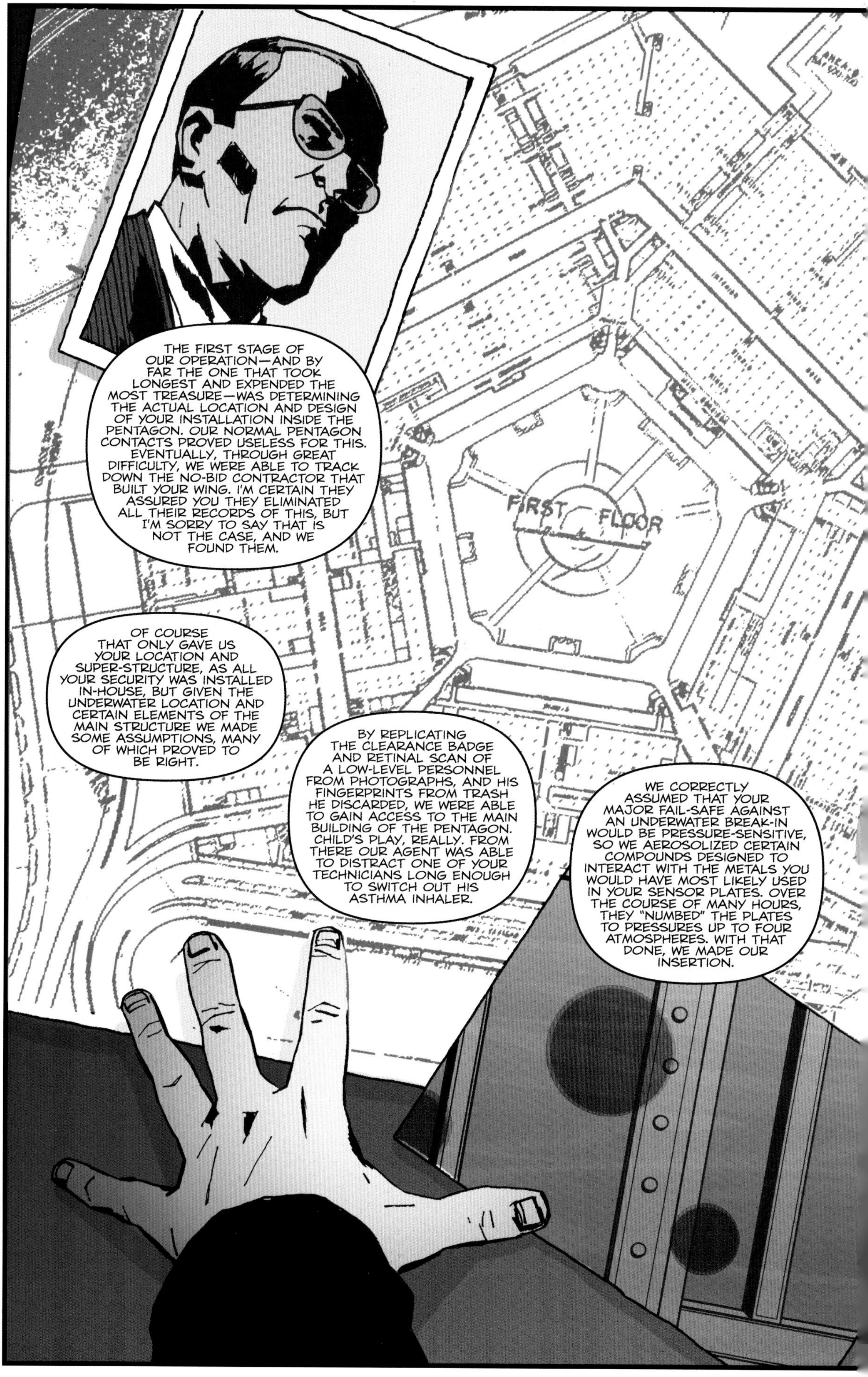
FIRST FLOOR
THE FIRST STAGE OF OUR OPERATION—AND BY FAR THE ONE THAT TOOK LONGEST AND EXPENDED THE MOST TREASURE—WAS DETERMINING THE ACTUAL LOCATION AND DESIGN OF YOUR INSTALLATION INSIDE THE PENTAGON. OUR NORMAL PENTAGON CONTACTS PROVED USELESS FOR THIS. EVENTUALLY, THROUGH GREAT DIFFICULTY, WE WERE ABLE TO TRACK DOWN THE NO-BID CONTRACTOR THAT BUILT YOUR WING. I'M CERTAIN THEY ASSURED YOU THEY ELIMINATED ALL THEIR RECORDS OF THIS, BUT I'M SORRY TO SAY THAT IS NOT THE CASE, AND WE FOUND THEM.
OF COURSE THAT ONLY GAVE US YOUR LOCATION AND SUPER-STRUCTURE, AS ALL YOUR SECURITY WAS INSTALLED IN-HOUSE, BUT GIVEN THE UNDERWATER LOCATION AND CERTAIN ELEMENTS OF THE MAIN STRUCTURE WE MADE SOME ASSUMPTIONS, MANY OF WHICH PROVED TO BE RIGHT.
BY REPLICATING THE CLEARANCE BADGE AND RETINAL SCAN OF A LOW-LEVEL PERSONNEL FROM PHOTOGRAPHS, AND HIS FINGERPRINTS FROM TRASH HE DISCARDED, WE WERE ABLE TO GAIN ACCESS TO THE MAIN BUILDING OF THE PENTAGON. CHILD'S PLAY, REALLY. FROM THERE OUR AGENT WAS ABLE TO DISTRACT ONE OF YOUR TECHNICIANS LONG ENOUGH TO SWITCH OUT HIS ASTHMA INHALER.
WE CORRECTLY ASSUMED THAT YOUR MAJOR FAIL-SAFE AGAINST AN UNDERWATER BREAK-IN WOULD BE PRESSURE-SENSITIVE, SO WE AEROSOLIZED CERTAIN COMPOUNDS DESIGNED TO INTERACT WITH THE METALS YOU WOULD HAVE MOST LIKELY USED IN YOUR SENSOR PLATES. OVER THE COURSE OF MANY HOURS, THEY "NUMBED" THE PLATES TO PRESSURES UP TO FOUR ATMOSPHERES. WITH THAT DONE, WE MADE OUR INSERTION.

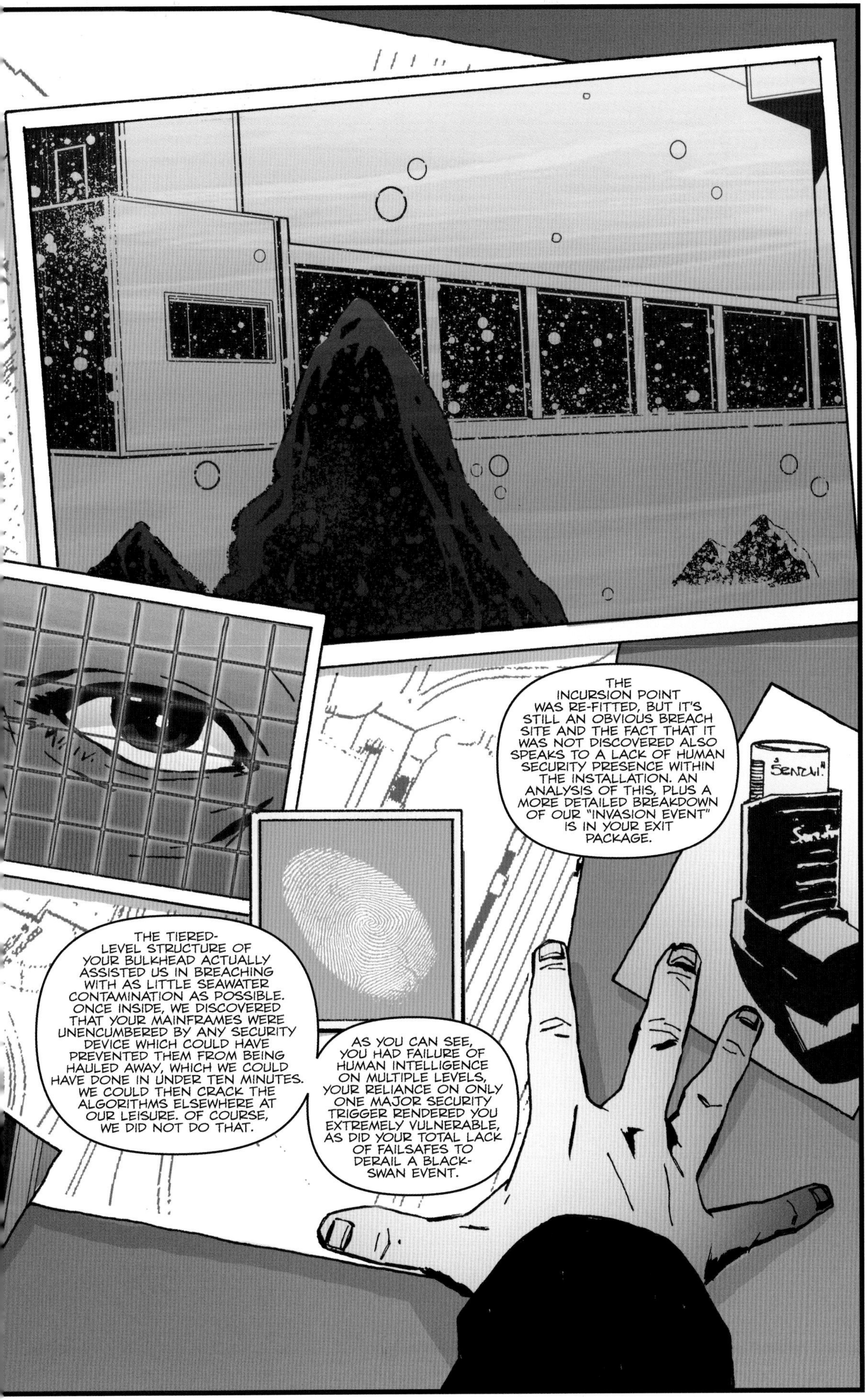
THE INCURSION POINT WAS RE-FITTED, BUT IT'S STILL AN OBVIOUS BREACH SITE AND THE FACT THAT IT WAS NOT DISCOVERED ALSO SPEAKS TO A LACK OF HUMAN SECURITY PRESENCE WITHIN THE INSTALLATION. AN ANALYSIS OF THIS, PLUS A MORE DETAILED BREAKDOWN OF OUR "INVASION EVENT" IS IN YOUR EXIT PACKAGE.
THE TIERED-LEVEL STRUCTURE OF YOUR BULKHEAD ACTUALLY ASSISTED US IN BREACHING WITH AS LITTLE SEAWATER CONTAMINATION AS POSSIBLE. ONCE INSIDE, WE DISCOVERED THAT YOUR MAINFRAMES WERE UNENCUMBERED BY ANY SECURITY DEVICE WHICH COULD HAVE PREVENTED THEM FROM BEING HAULED AWAY, WHICH WE COULD HAVE DONE IN UNDER TEN MINUTES. WE COULD THEN CRACK THE ALGORITHMS ELSEWHERE AT OUR LEISURE. OF COURSE, WE DID NOT DO THAT.
AS YOU CAN SEE, YOU HAD FAILURE OF HUMAN INTELLIGENCE ON MULTIPLE LEVELS, YOUR RELIANCE ON ONLY ONE MAJOR SECURITY TRIGGER RENDERED YOU EXTREMELY VULNERABLE, AS DID YOUR TOTAL LACK OF FAILSAFES TO DERAIL A BLACK-SWAN EVENT.

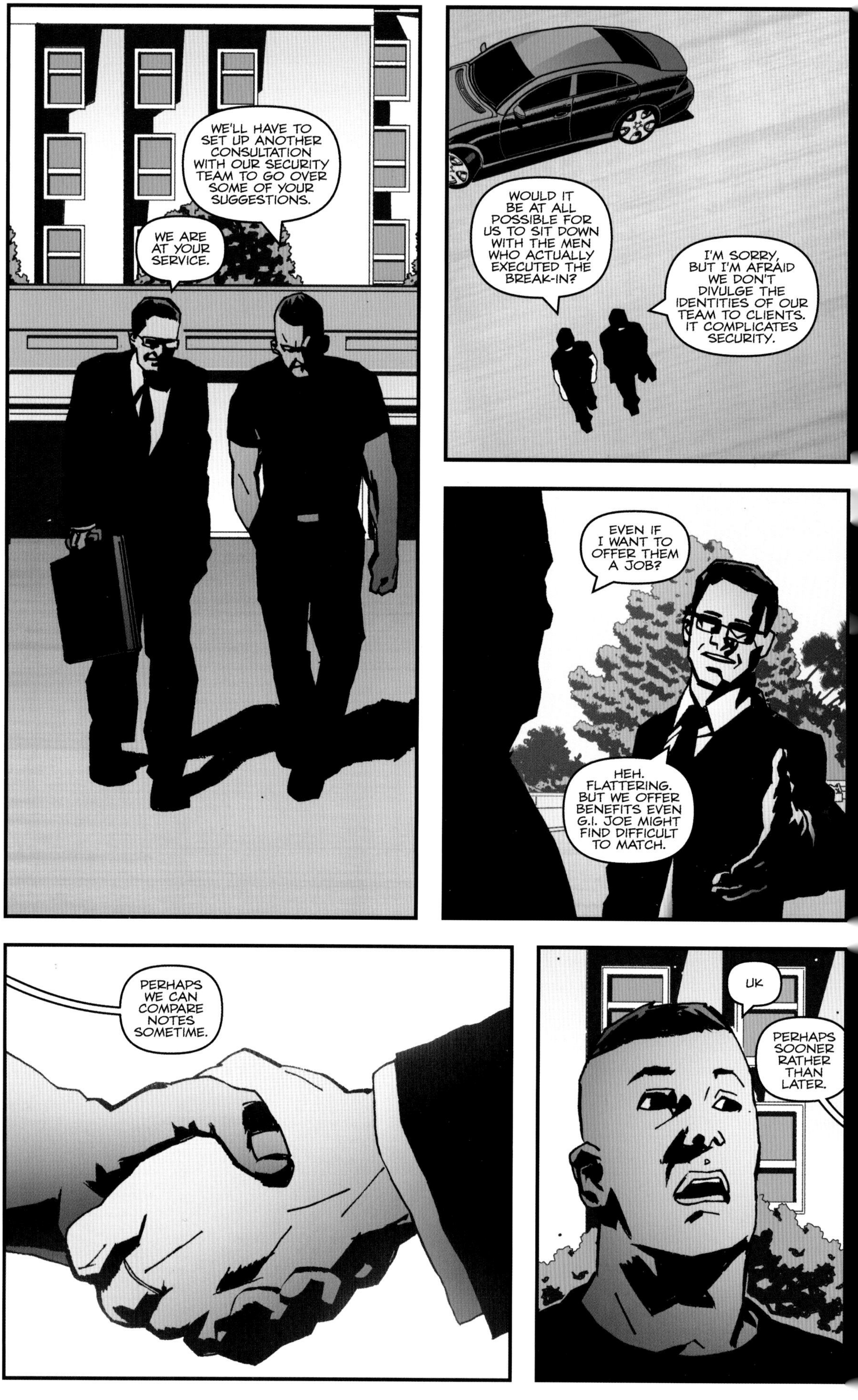
WE'LL HAVE TO SET UP ANOTHER CONSULTATION WITH OUR SECURITY TEAM TO GO OVER SOME OF YOUR SUGGESTIONS.
WE ARE AT YOUR SERVICE.
WOULD IT BE AT ALL POSSIBLE FOR US TO SIT DOWN WITH THE MEN WHO ACTUALLY EXECUTED THE BREAK-IN?
I'M SORRY, BUT I'M AFRAID WE DON'T DIVULGE THE IDENTITIES OF OUR TEAM TO CLIENTS. IT COMPLICATES SECURITY.
EVEN IF I WANT TO OFFER THEM A JOB?
HEH. FLATTERING. BUT WE OFFER BENEFITS EVEN G.I. JOE MIGHT FIND DIFFICULT TO MATCH.
PERHAPS WE CAN COMPARE NOTES SOMETIME.
UK
PERHAPS SOONER RATHER THAN LATER.

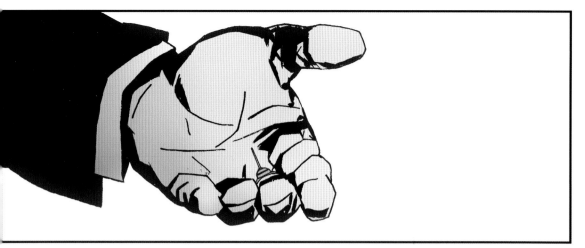

EASY NOW.

YOU LOOK LIKE YOU COULD USE A RIDE.

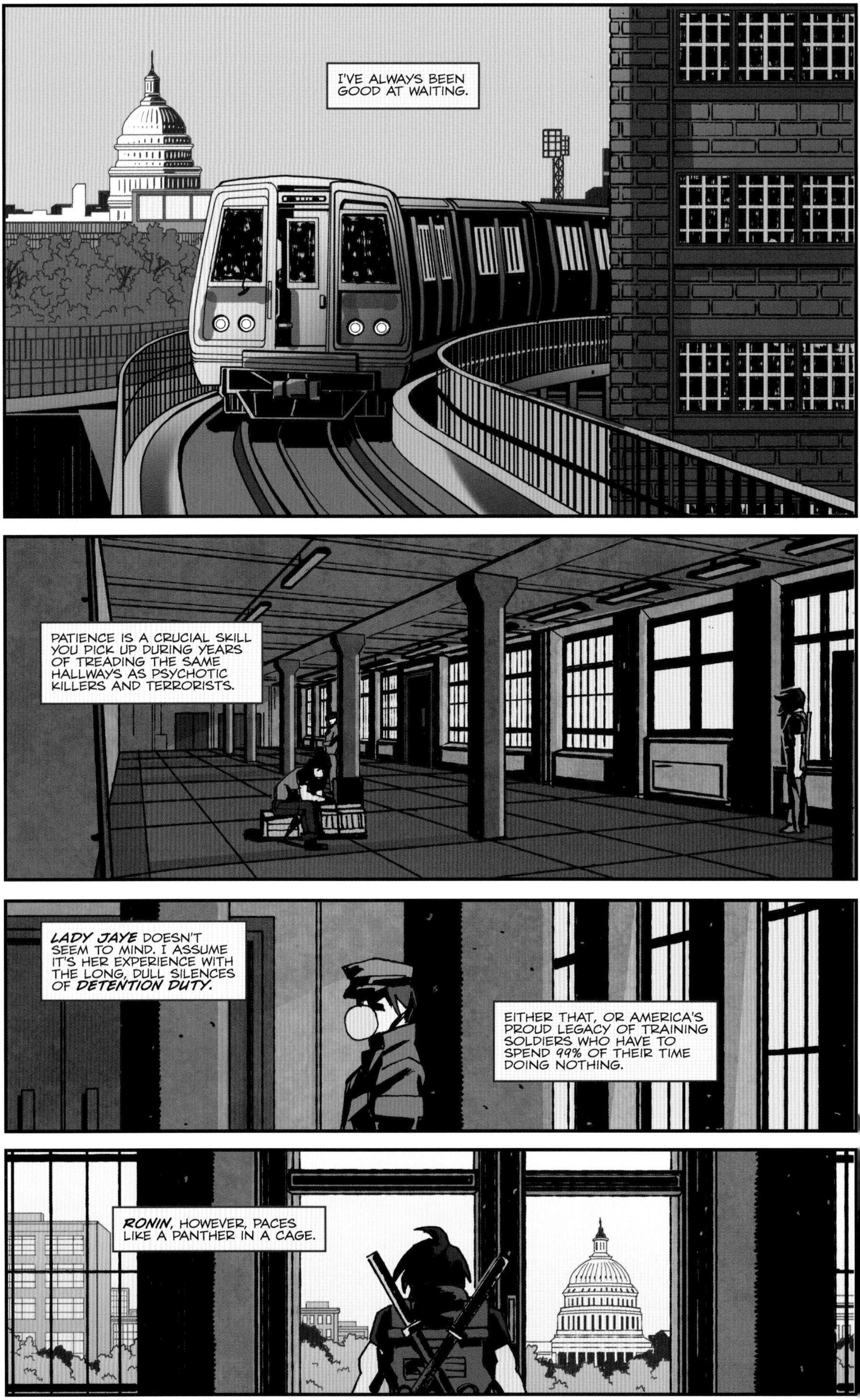
I'VE ALWAYS BEEN GOOD AT WAITING.
PATIENCE IS A CRUCIAL SKILL YOU PICK UP DURING YEARS OF TREADING THE SAME HALLWAYS AS PSYCHOTIC KILLERS AND TERRORISTS.
LADY JAYE DOESN'T SEEM TO MIND. I ASSUME IT'S HER EXPERIENCE WITH THE LONG, DULL SILENCES OF DETENTION DUTY.
EITHER THAT, OR AMERICA'S PROUD LEGACY OF TRAINING SOLDIERS WHO HAVE TO SPEND 99% OF THEIR TIME DOING NOTHING.
RONIN, HOWEVER, PACES LIKE A PANTHER IN A CAGE.

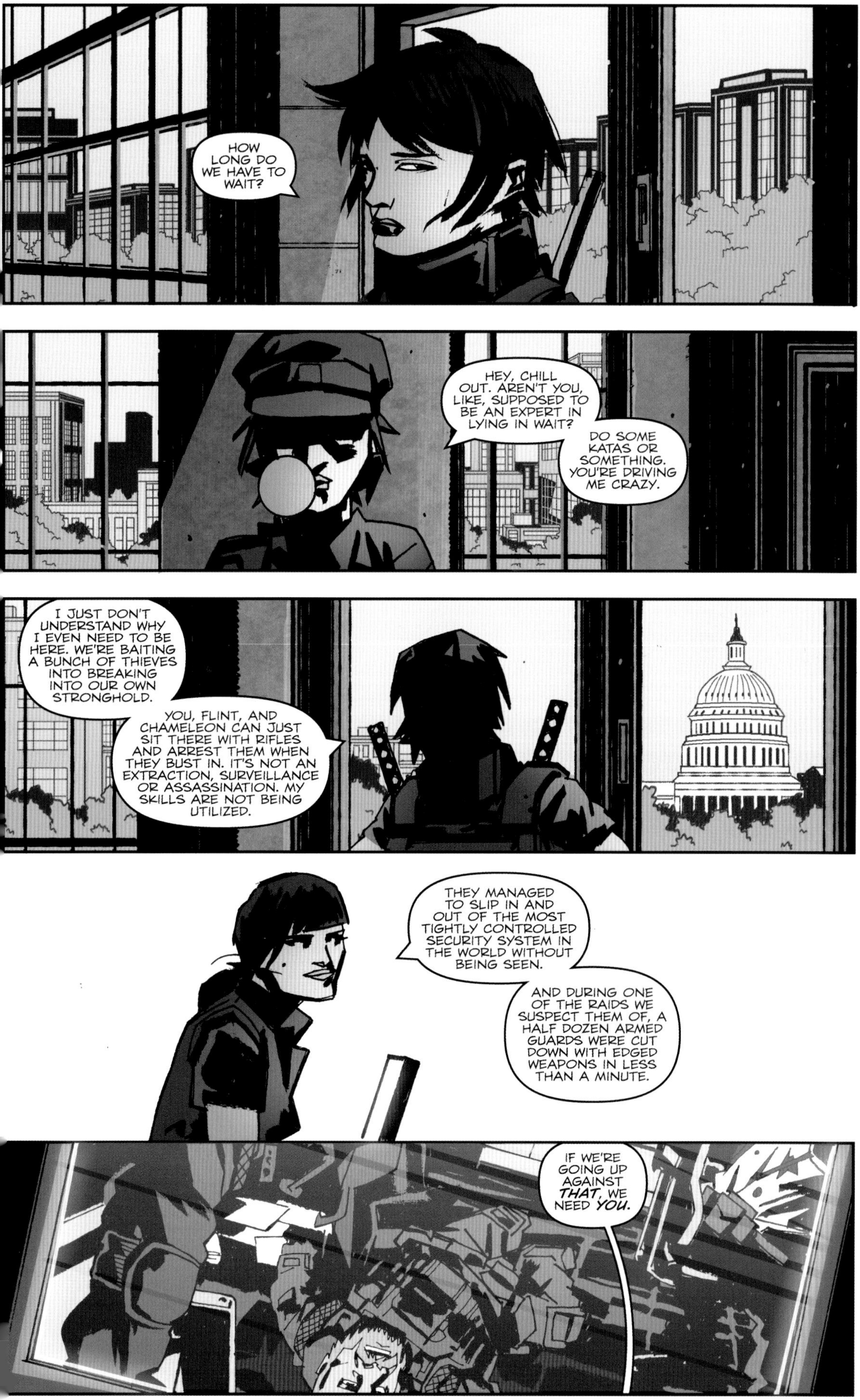
HOW LONG DO WE HAVE TO WAIT?
HEY, CHILL OUT. AREN'T YOU, LIKE, SUPPOSED TO BE AN EXPERT IN LYING IN WAIT?
DO SOME KATAS OR SOMETHING. YOU'RE DRIVING ME CRAZY.
I JUST DON'T UNDERSTAND WHY I EVEN NEED TO BE HERE. WE'RE BAITING A BUNCH OF THIEVES INTO BREAKING INTO OUR OWN STRONGHOLD.
YOU, FLINT, AND CHAMELEON CAN JUST SIT THERE WITH RIFLES AND ARREST THEM WHEN THEY BUST IN. IT'S NOT AN EXTRACTION, SURVEILLANCE OR ASSASSINATION. MY SKILLS ARE NOT BEING UTILIZED.
THEY MANAGED TO SLIP IN AND OUT OF THE MOST TIGHTLY CONTROLLED SECURITY SYSTEM IN THE WORLD WITHOUT BEING SEEN.
AND DURING ONE OF THE RAIDS WE SUSPECT THEM OF, A HALF DOZEN ARMED GUARDS WERE CUT DOWN WITH EDGED WEAPONS IN LESS THAN A MINUTE.
IF WE'RE GOING UP AGAINST *THAT*, WE NEED *YOU*.

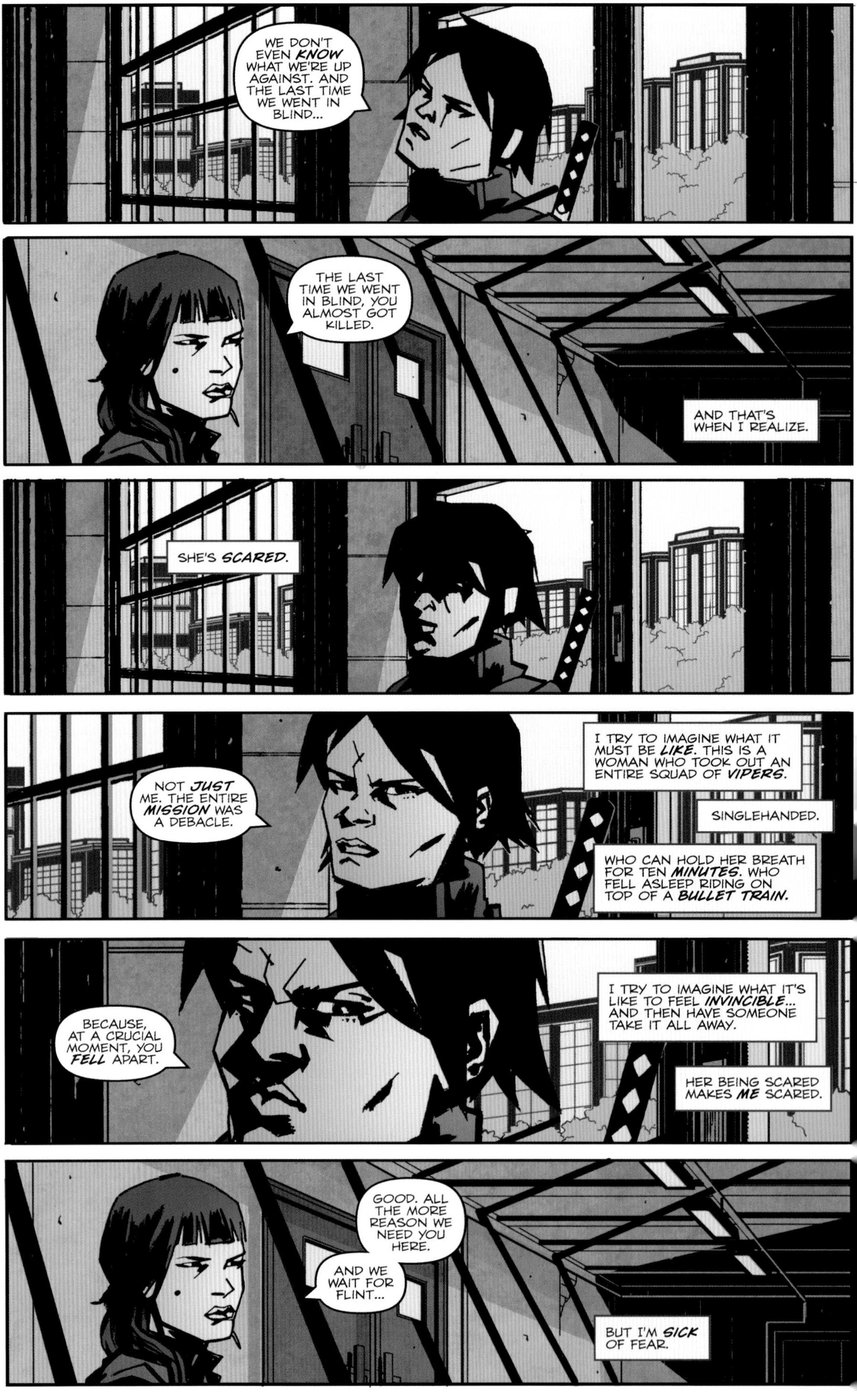

WE DON'T EVEN KNOW WHAT WE'RE UP AGAINST. AND THE LAST TIME WE WENT IN BLIND...
THE LAST TIME WE WENT IN BLIND, YOU ALMOST GOT KILLED.
AND THAT'S WHEN I REALIZE.
SHE'S SCARED.
NOT JUST ME. THE ENTIRE MISSION WAS A DEBACLE.
I TRY TO IMAGINE WHAT IT MUST BE LIKE. THIS IS A WOMAN WHO TOOK OUT AN ENTIRE SQUAD OF VIPERS.
SINGLEHANDED.
WHO CAN HOLD HER BREATH FOR TEN MINUTES. WHO FELL ASLEEP RIDING ON TOP OF A BULLET TRAIN.
BECAUSE, AT A CRUCIAL MOMENT, YOU FELL APART.
I TRY TO IMAGINE WHAT IT'S LIKE TO FEEL INVINCIBLE... AND THEN HAVE SOMEONE TAKE IT ALL AWAY.
HER BEING SCARED MAKES ME SCARED.
GOOD. ALL THE MORE REASON WE NEED YOU HERE.
AND WE WAIT FOR FLINT...
BUT I'M SICK OF FEAR.

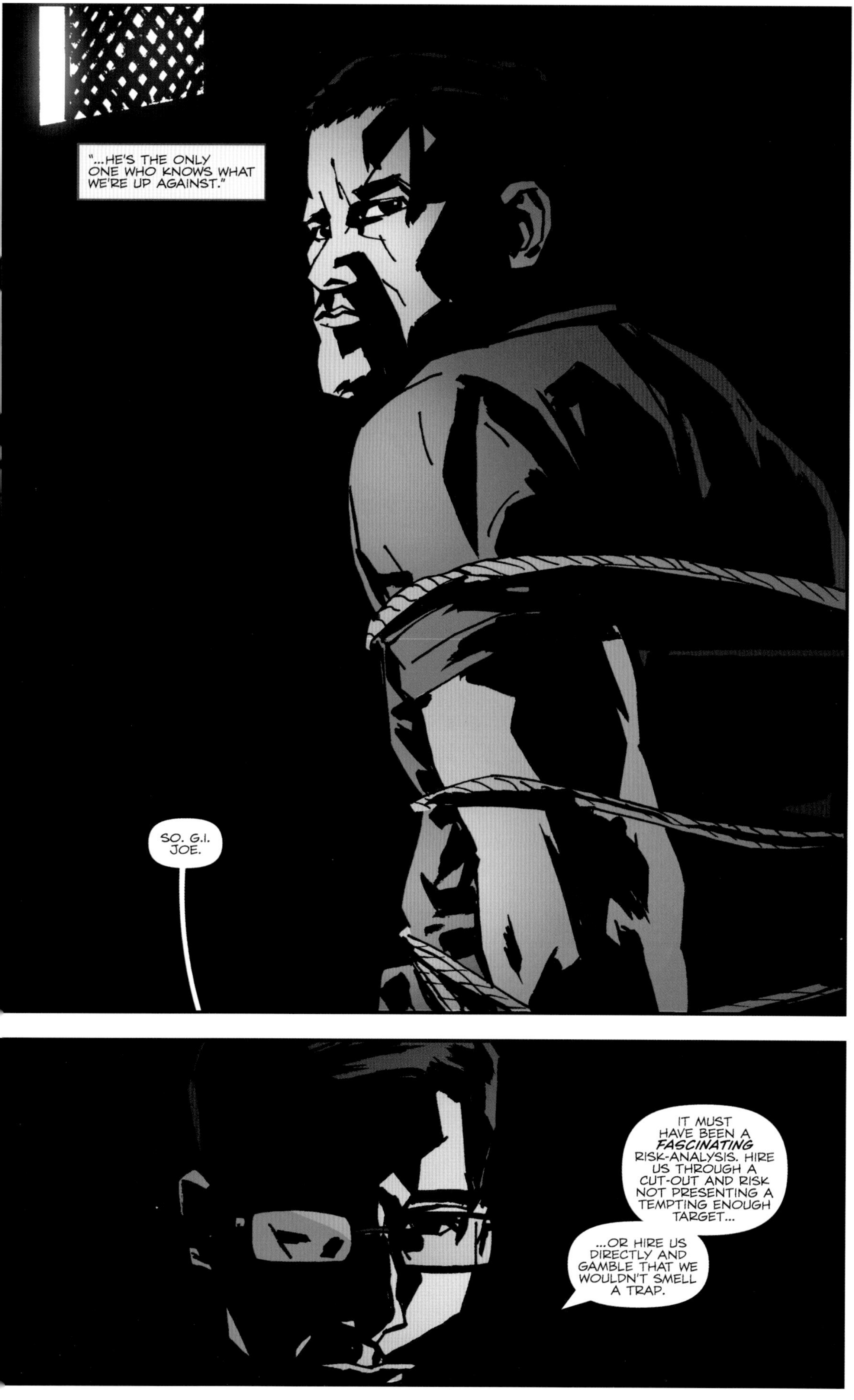
"...HE'S THE ONLY ONE WHO KNOWS WHAT WE'RE UP AGAINST."
SO. G.I. JOE.
IT MUST HAVE BEEN A ***FASCINATING*** RISK-ANALYSIS. HIRE US THROUGH A CUT-OUT AND RISK NOT PRESENTING A TEMPTING ENOUGH TARGET...
...OR HIRE US DIRECTLY AND GAMBLE THAT WE WOULDN'T SMELL A TRAP.

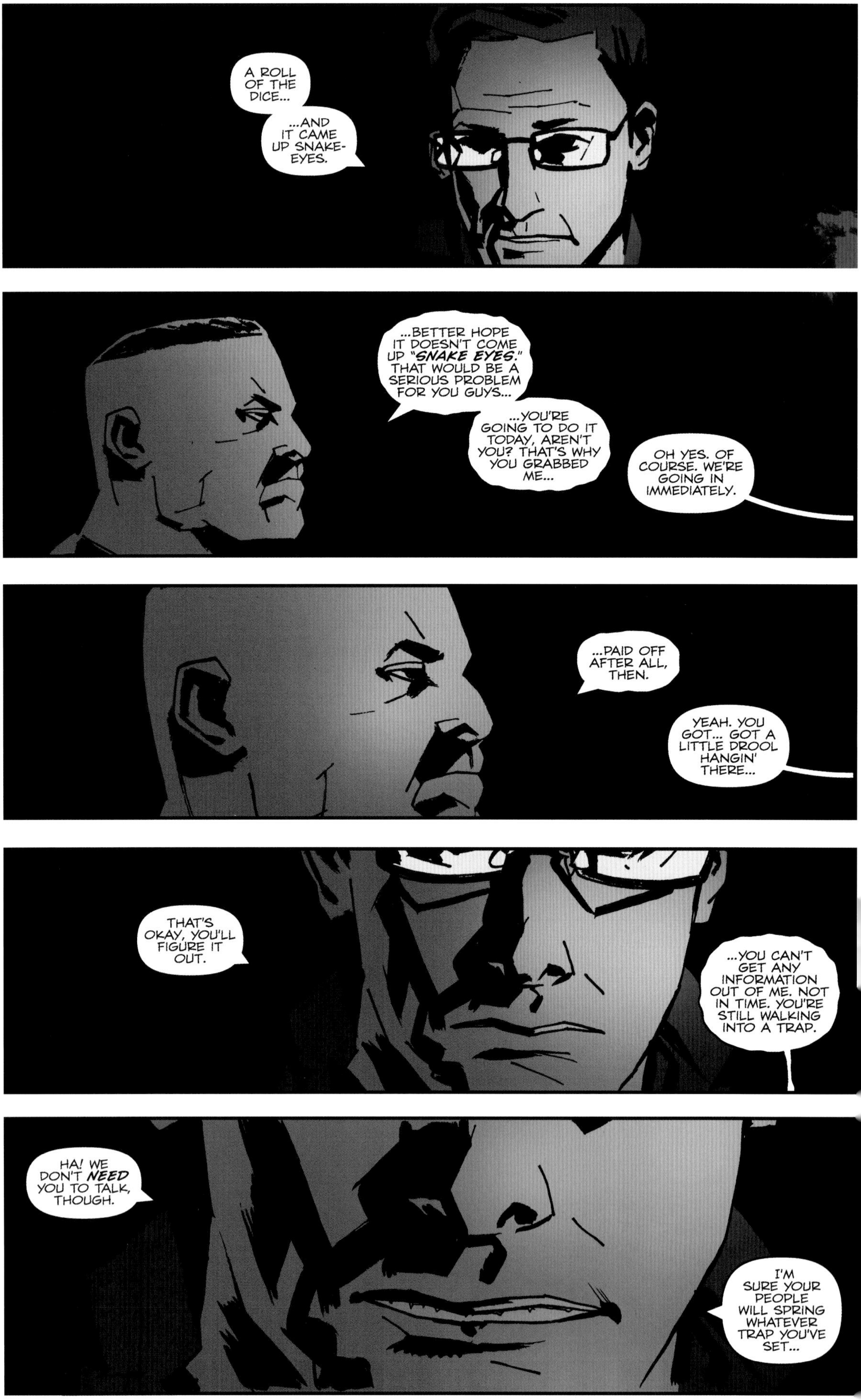
A ROLL OF THE DICE...
...AND IT CAME UP SNAKE-EYES.
...BETTER HOPE IT DOESN'T COME UP "SNAKE EYES." THAT WOULD BE A SERIOUS PROBLEM FOR YOU GUYS...
...YOU'RE GOING TO DO IT TODAY, AREN'T YOU? THAT'S WHY YOU GRABBED ME...
OH YES. OF COURSE. WE'RE GOING IN IMMEDIATELY.
...PAID OFF AFTER ALL, THEN.
YEAH. YOU GOT... GOT A LITTLE DROOL HANGIN' THERE...
THAT'S OKAY, YOU'LL FIGURE IT OUT.
...YOU CAN'T GET ANY INFORMATION OUT OF ME. NOT IN TIME. YOU'RE STILL WALKING INTO A TRAP.
HA! WE DON'T NEED YOU TO TALK, THOUGH.
I'M SURE YOUR PEOPLE WILL SPRING WHATEVER TRAP YOU'VE SET...

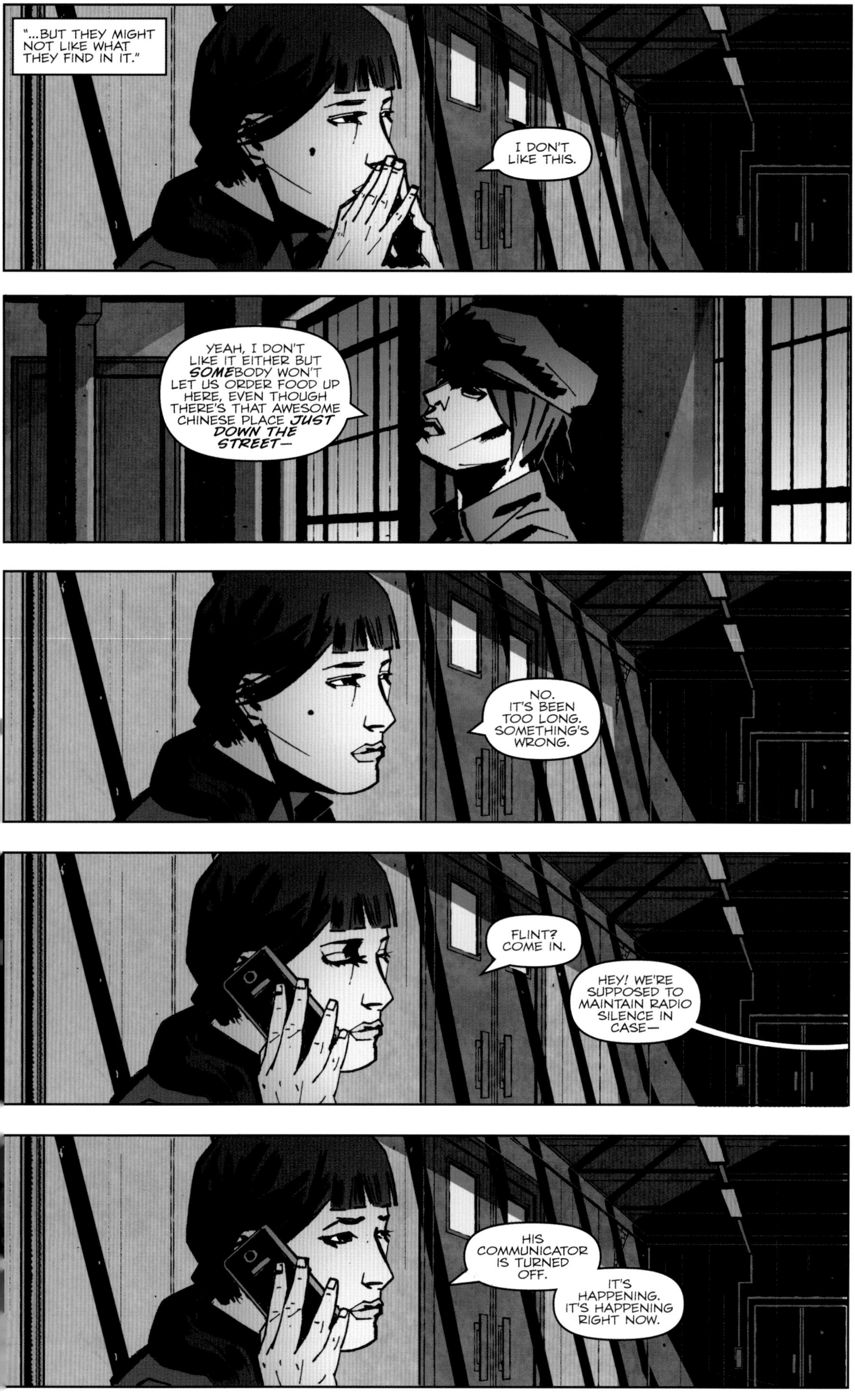
"...BUT THEY MIGHT NOT LIKE WHAT THEY FIND IN IT."
I DON'T LIKE THIS.
YEAH, I DON'T LIKE IT EITHER BUT **SOME**BODY WON'T LET US ORDER FOOD UP HERE, EVEN THOUGH THERE'S THAT AWESOME CHINESE PLACE ***JUST DOWN THE STREET***—
NO. IT'S BEEN TOO LONG. SOMETHING'S WRONG.
FLINT? COME IN.
HEY! WE'RE SUPPOSED TO MAINTAIN RADIO SILENCE IN CASE—
HIS COMMUNICATOR IS TURNED OFF.
IT'S HAPPENING. IT'S HAPPENING RIGHT NOW.

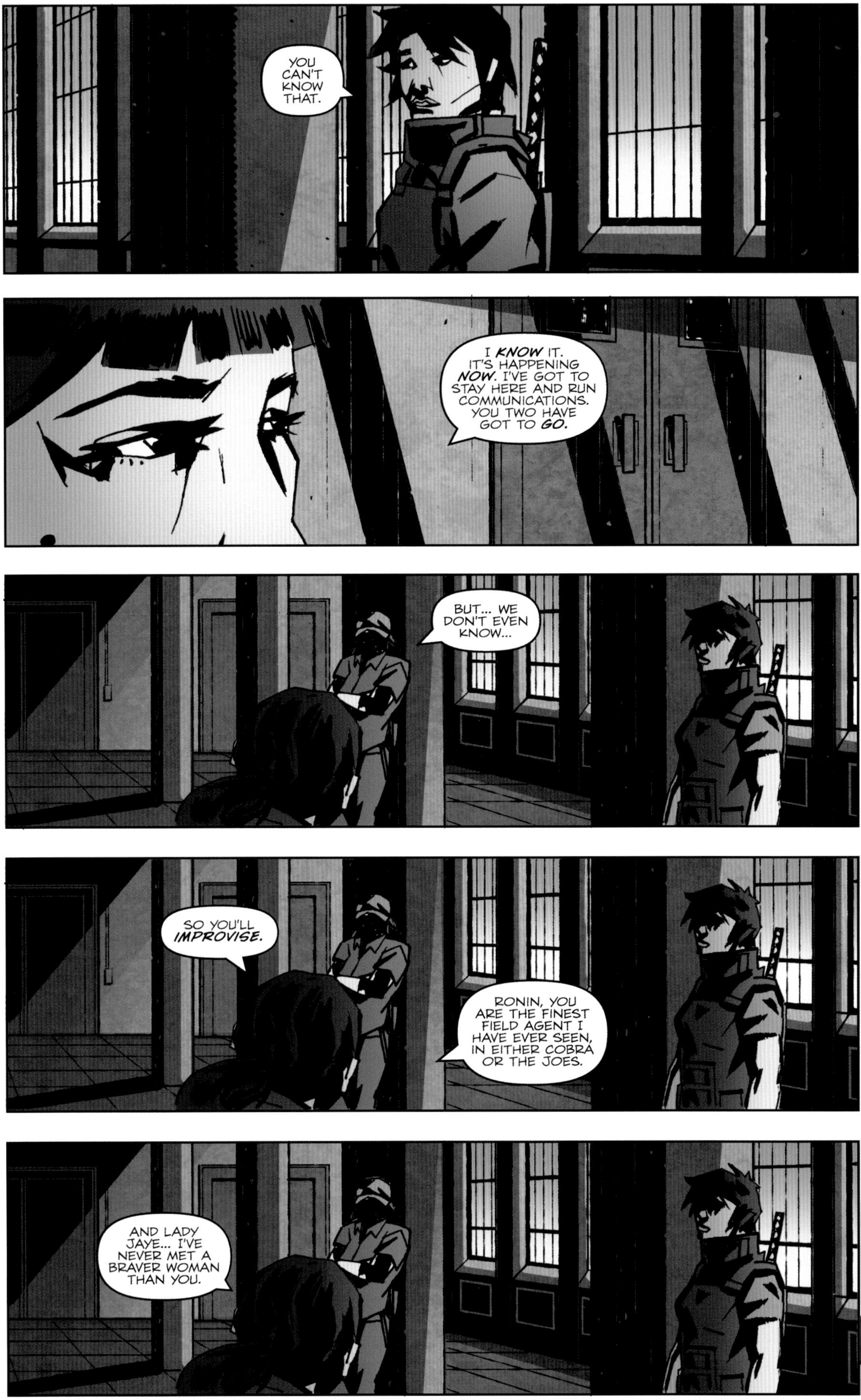
YOU CAN'T KNOW THAT.
I *KNOW* IT. IT'S HAPPENING *NOW*. I'VE GOT TO STAY HERE AND RUN COMMUNICATIONS. YOU TWO HAVE GOT TO *GO*.
BUT... WE DON'T EVEN KNOW...
SO YOU'LL *IMPROVISE*.
RONIN, YOU ARE THE FINEST FIELD AGENT I HAVE EVER SEEN, IN EITHER COBRA OR THE JOES.
AND LADY JAYE... I'VE NEVER MET A BRAVER WOMAN THAN YOU.

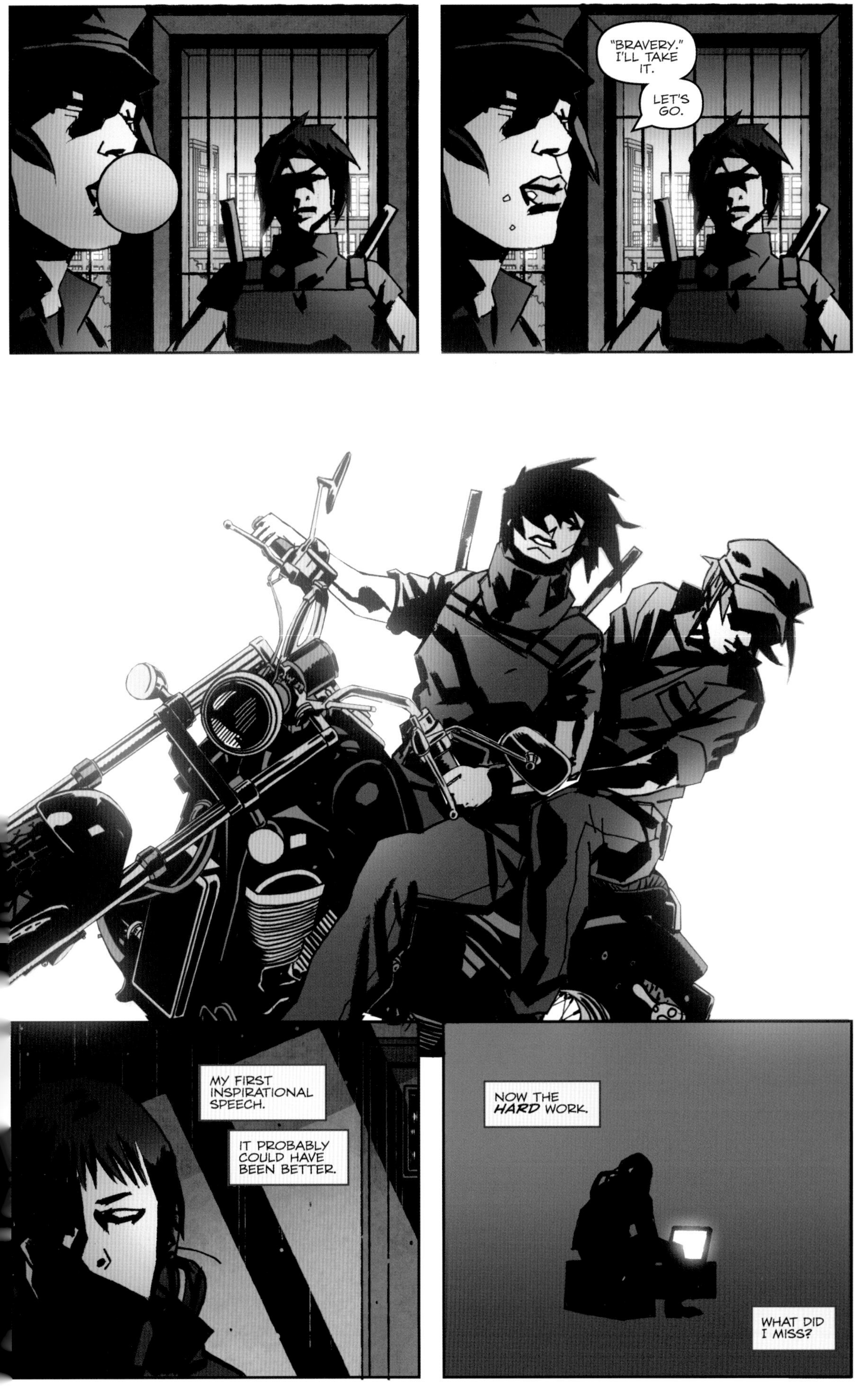
"BRAVERY." I'LL TAKE IT.
LET'S GO.
MY FIRST INSPIRATIONAL SPEECH.
IT PROBABLY COULD HAVE BEEN BETTER.
NOW THE **HARD** WORK.
WHAT DID I MISS?

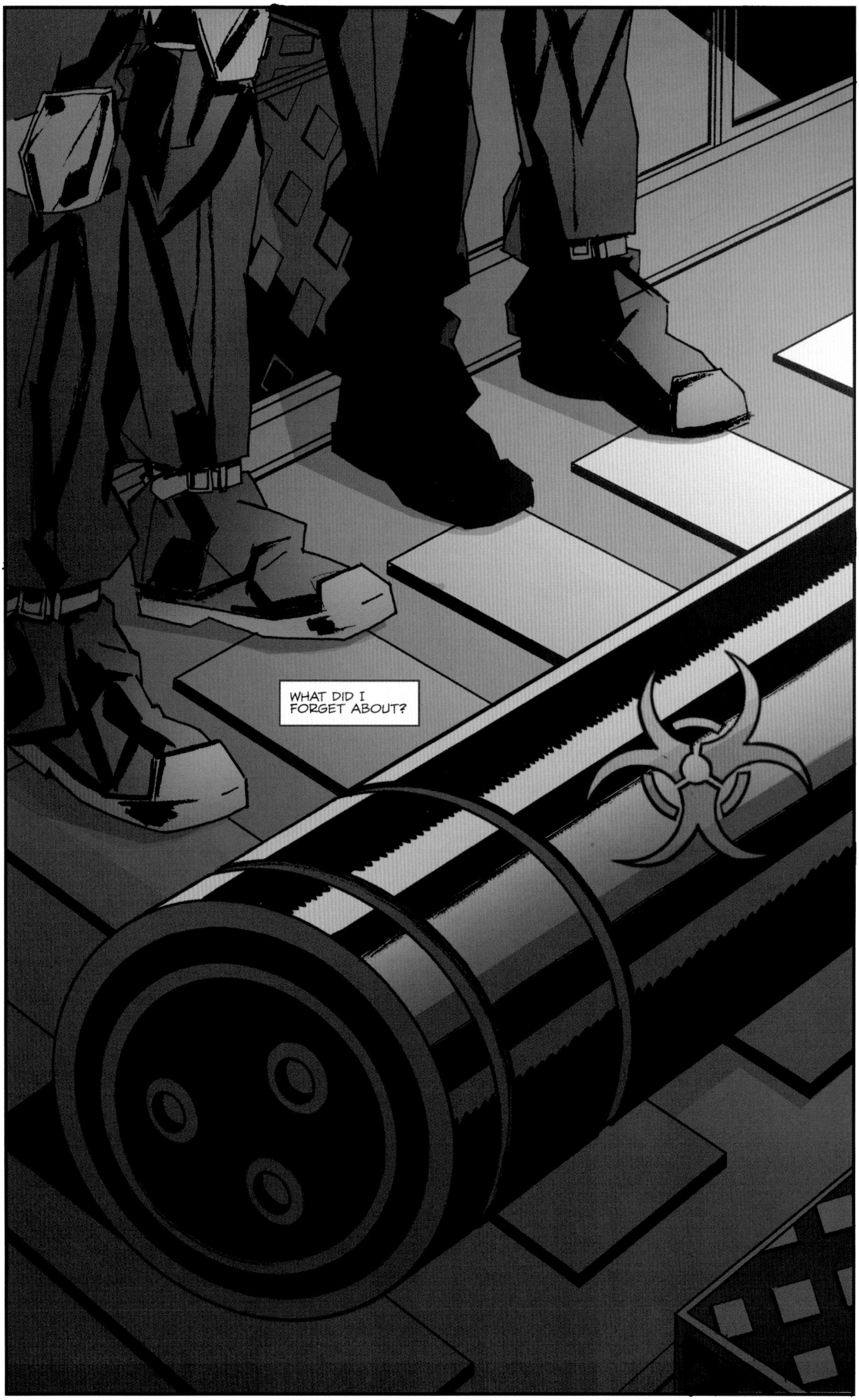
WHAT DID I
FORGET ABOUT?

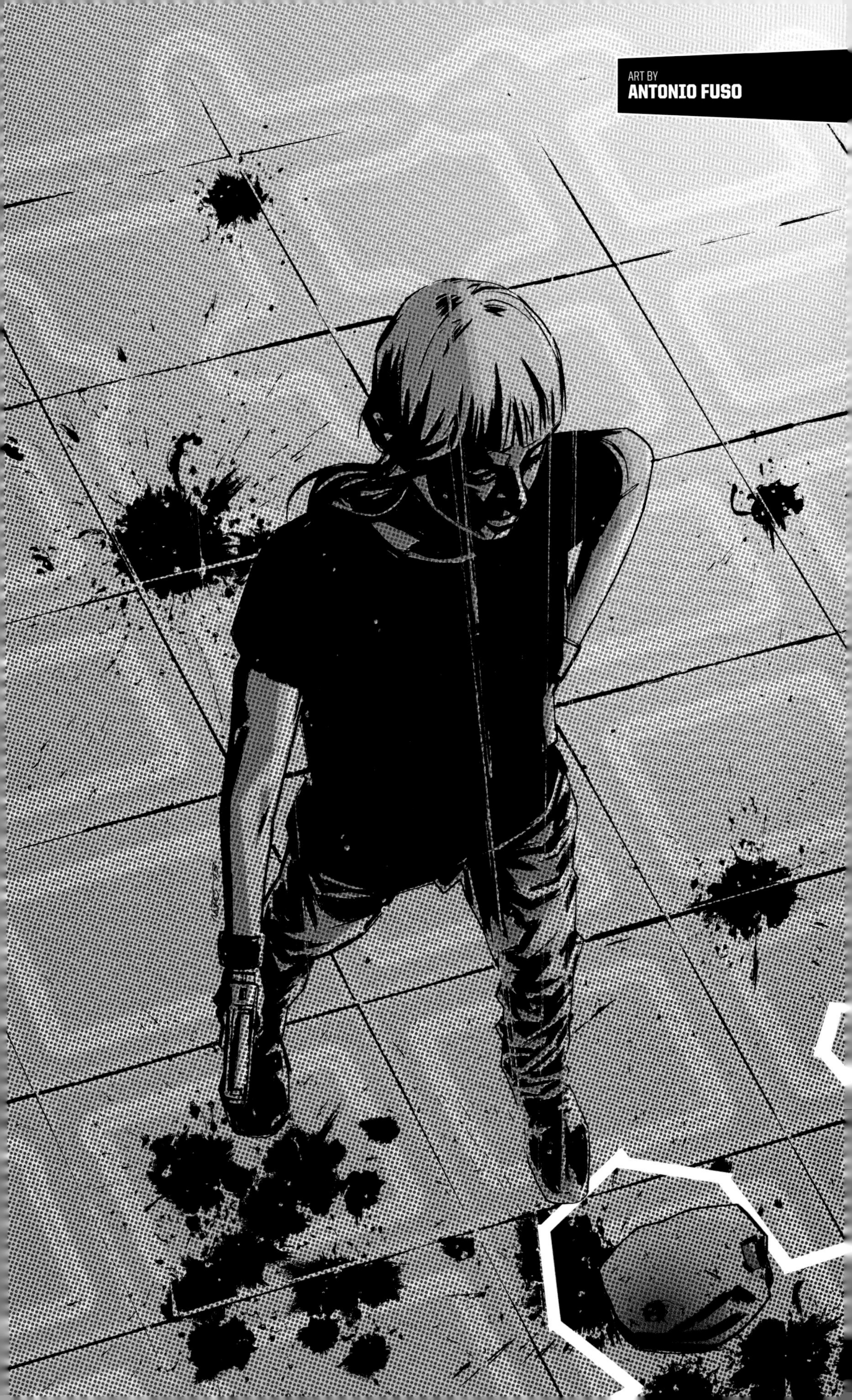
ART BY
ANTONIO FUSO

ART BY
**MICHAEL LARK**

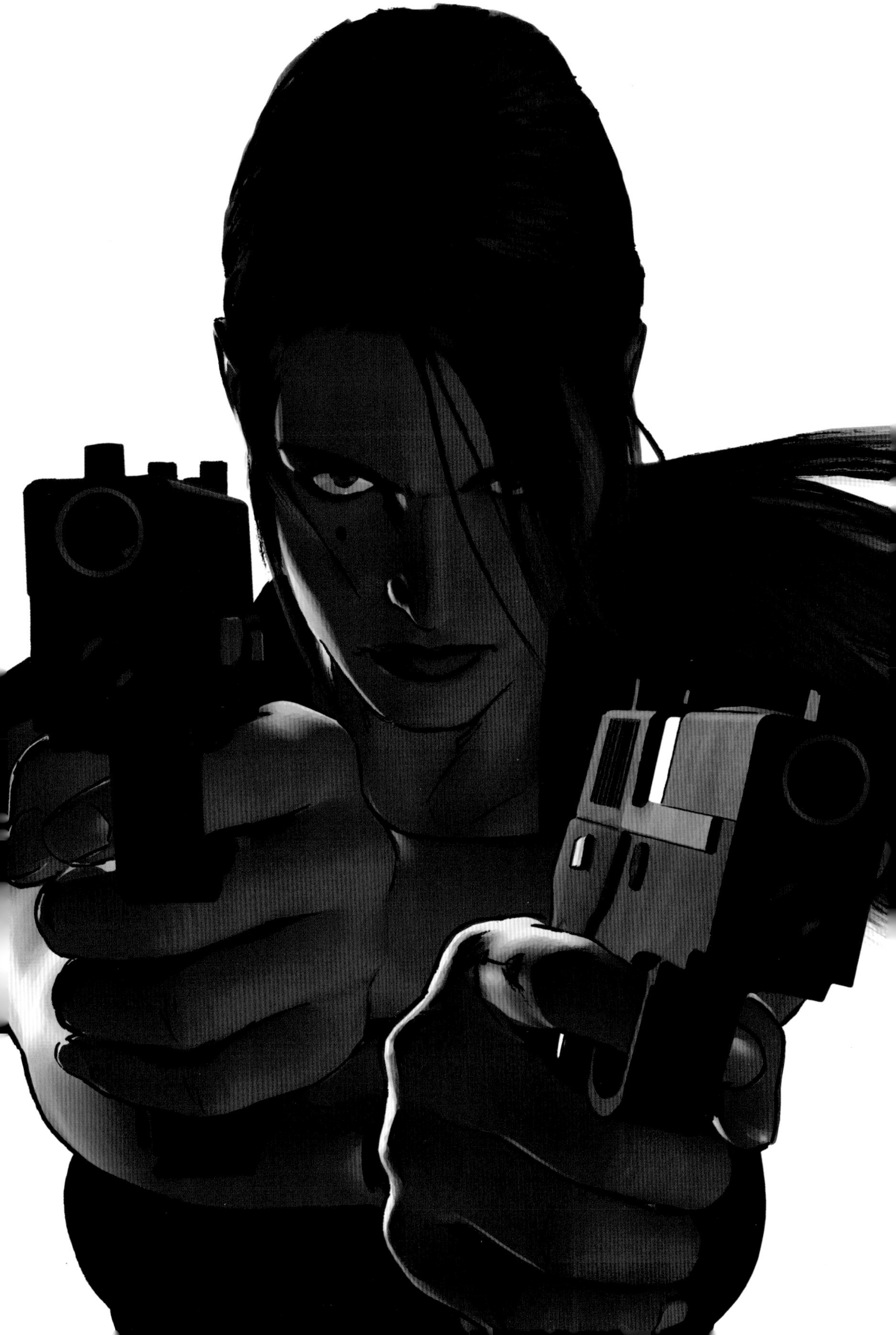

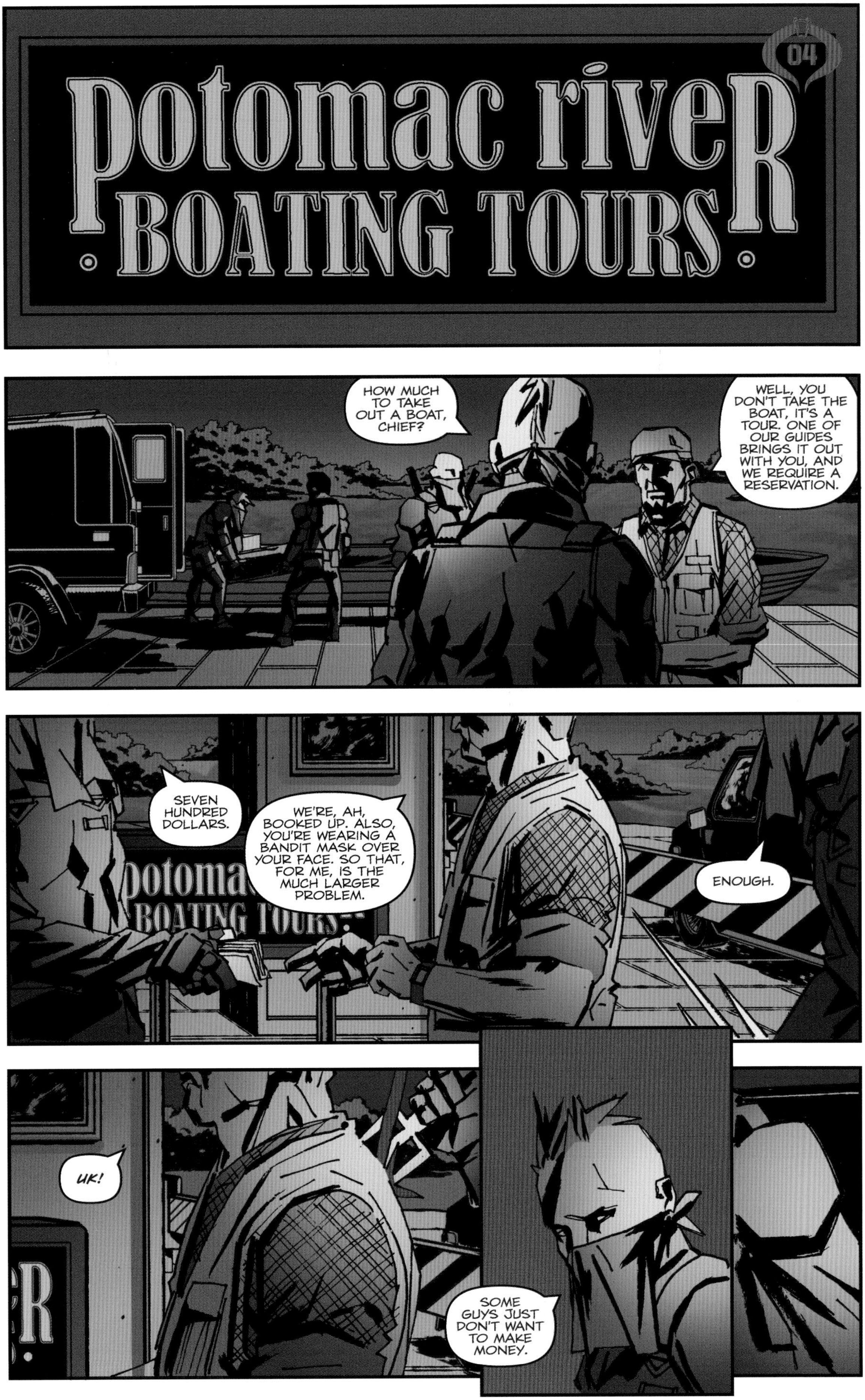
04
potomac river
BOATING TOURS
HOW MUCH TO TAKE OUT A BOAT, CHIEF?
WELL, YOU DON'T TAKE THE BOAT, IT'S A TOUR. ONE OF OUR GUIDES BRINGS IT OUT WITH YOU, AND WE REQUIRE A RESERVATION.
SEVEN HUNDRED DOLLARS.
WE'RE, AH, BOOKED UP. ALSO, YOU'RE WEARING A BANDIT MASK OVER YOUR FACE. SO THAT, FOR ME, IS THE MUCH LARGER PROBLEM.
potomac
BOATING TOURS
ENOUGH.
UK!
SOME GUYS JUST DON'T WANT TO MAKE MONEY.

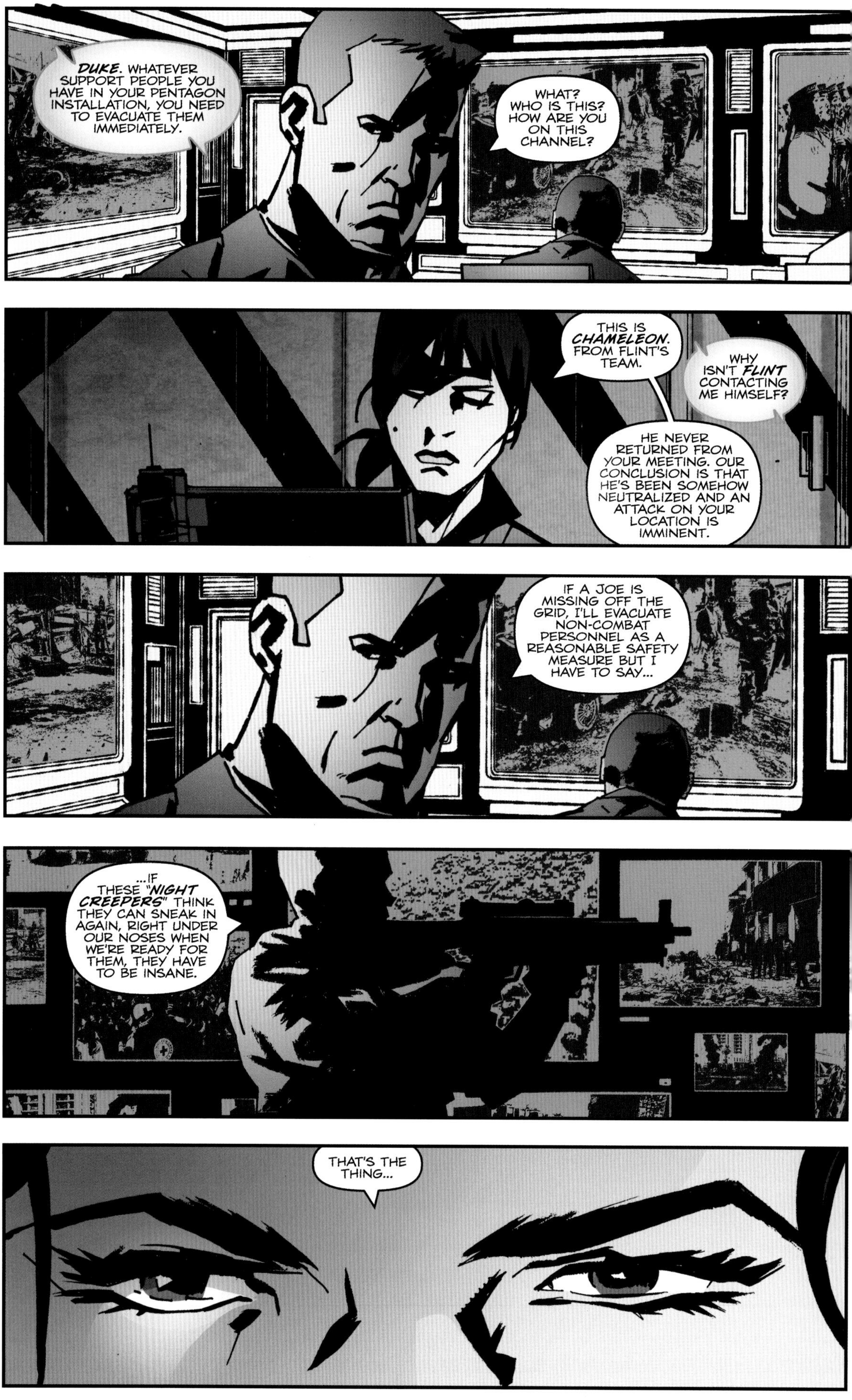
DUKE. WHATEVER SUPPORT PEOPLE YOU HAVE IN YOUR PENTAGON INSTALLATION, YOU NEED TO EVACUATE THEM IMMEDIATELY.
WHAT? WHO IS THIS? HOW ARE YOU ON THIS CHANNEL?
THIS IS CHAMELEON. FROM FLINT'S TEAM.
WHY ISN'T FLINT CONTACTING ME HIMSELF?
HE NEVER RETURNED FROM YOUR MEETING. OUR CONCLUSION IS THAT HE'S BEEN SOMEHOW NEUTRALIZED AND AN ATTACK ON YOUR LOCATION IS IMMINENT.
IF A JOE IS MISSING OFF THE GRID, I'LL EVACUATE NON-COMBAT PERSONNEL AS A REASONABLE SAFETY MEASURE BUT I HAVE TO SAY...
...IF THESE "NIGHT CREEPERS" THINK THEY CAN SNEAK IN AGAIN, RIGHT UNDER OUR NOSES WHEN WE'RE READY FOR THEM, THEY HAVE TO BE INSANE.
THAT'S THE THING...

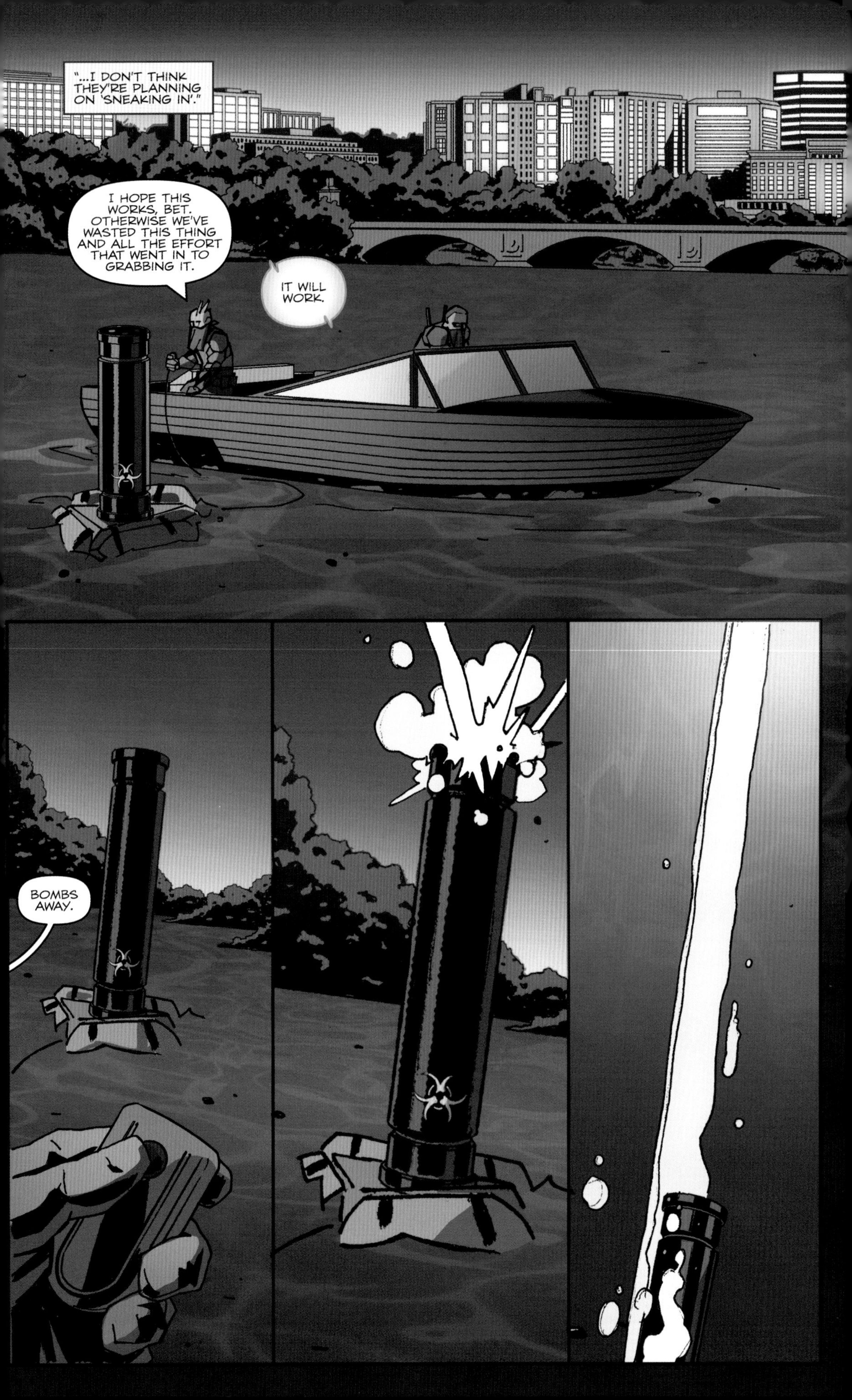
"...I DON'T THINK THEY'RE PLANNING ON 'SNEAKING IN'."
I HOPE THIS WORKS, BET. OTHERWISE WE'VE WASTED THIS THING AND ALL THE EFFORT THAT WENT IN TO GRABBING IT.
IT WILL WORK.
BOMBS AWAY.

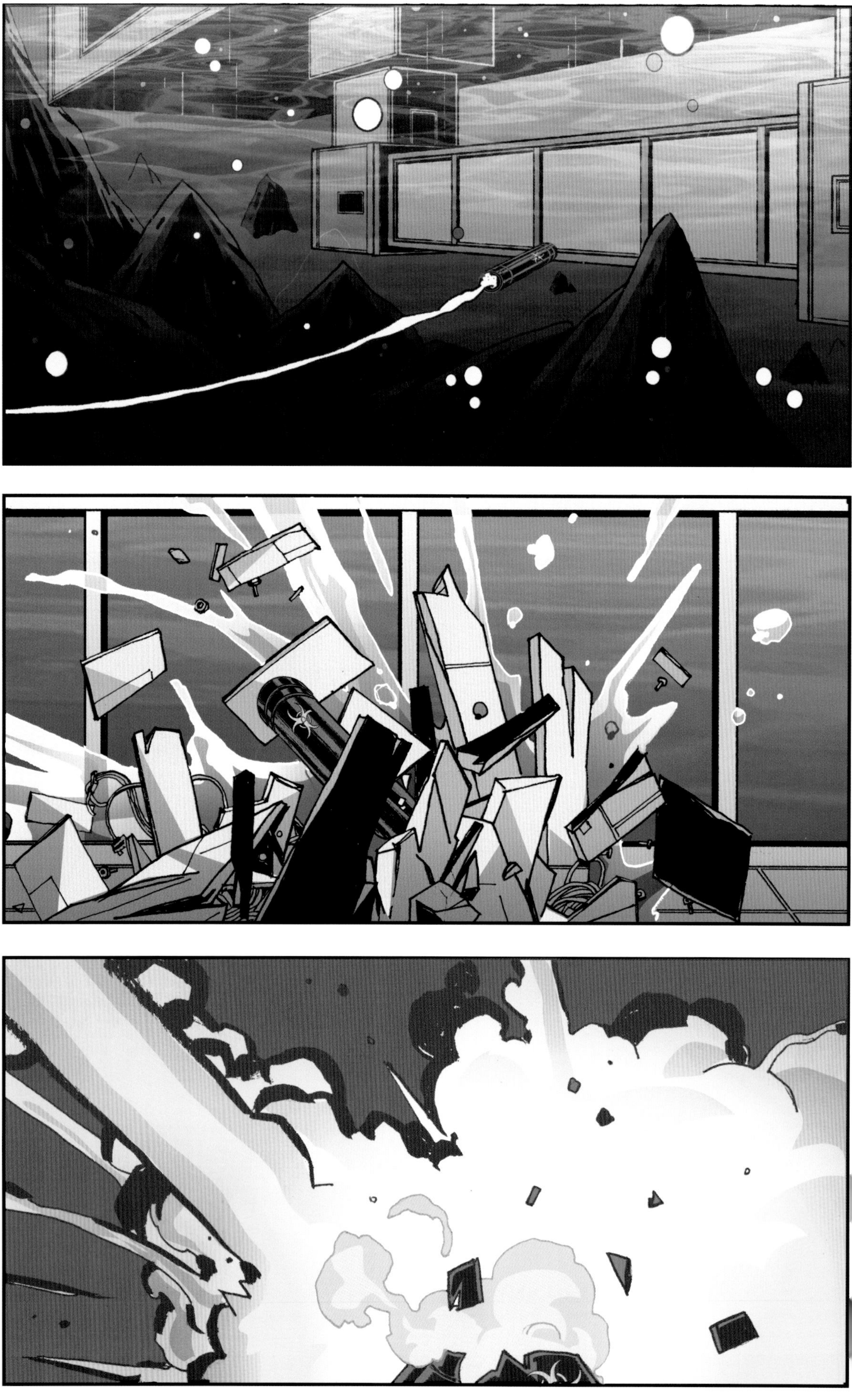

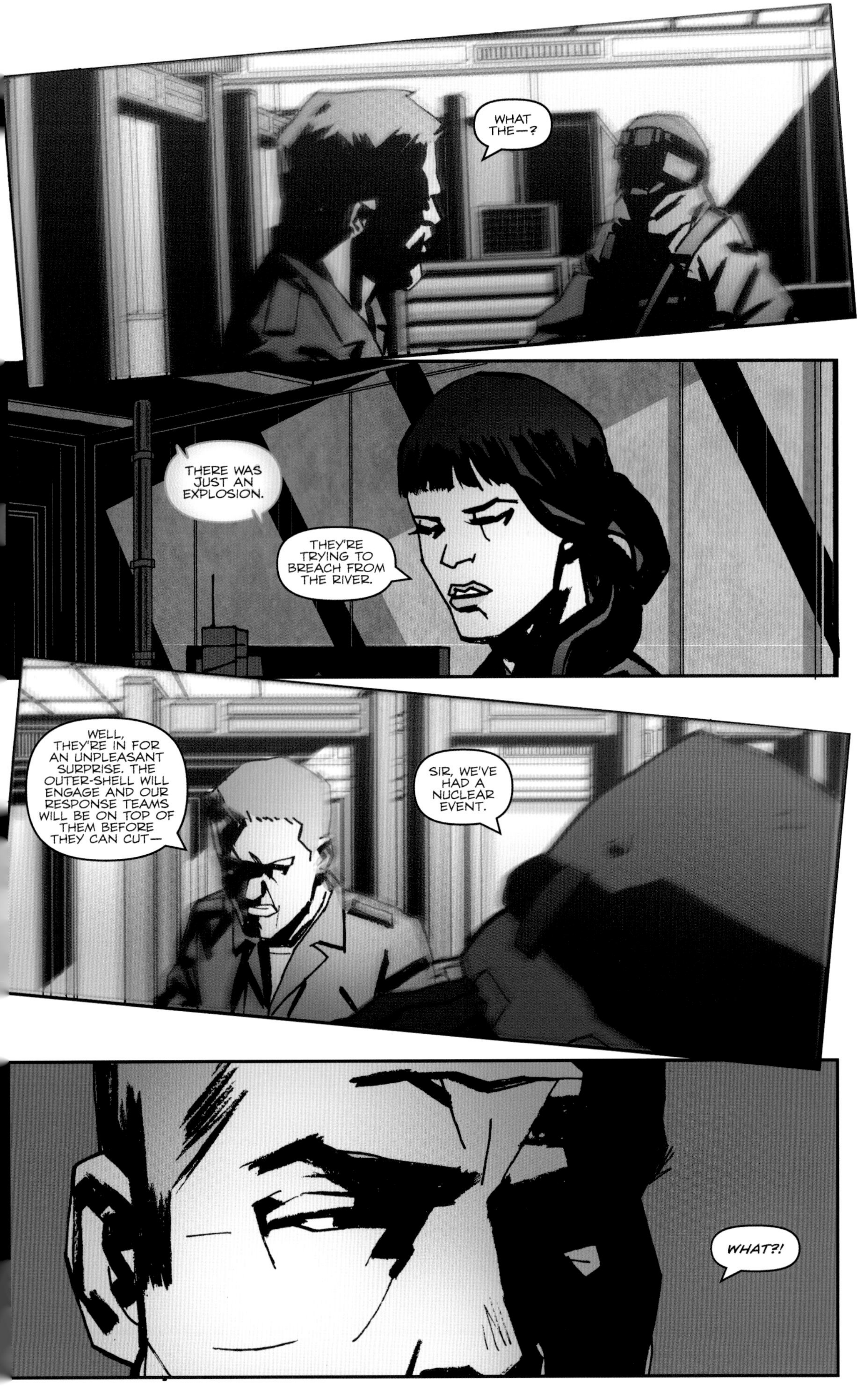
WHAT THE—?
THERE WAS JUST AN EXPLOSION.
THEY'RE TRYING TO BREACH FROM THE RIVER.
WELL, THEY'RE IN FOR AN UNPLEASANT SURPRISE. THE OUTER-SHELL WILL ENGAGE AND OUR RESPONSE TEAMS WILL BE ON TOP OF THEM BEFORE THEY CAN CUT—
SIR, WE'VE HAD A NUCLEAR EVENT.
WHAT?!

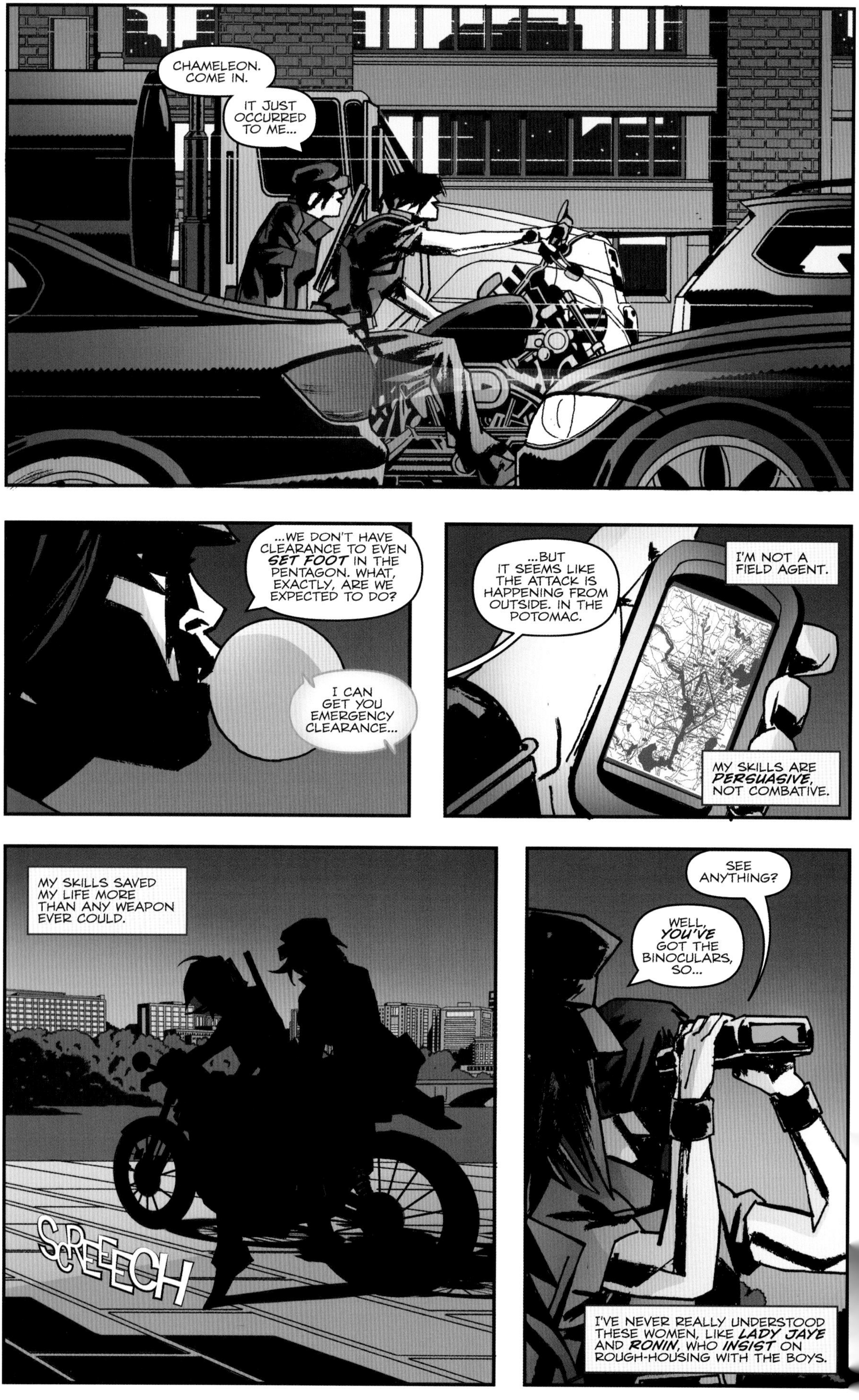
CHAMELEON. COME IN.
IT JUST OCCURRED TO ME...
...WE DON'T HAVE CLEARANCE TO EVEN SET FOOT IN THE PENTAGON. WHAT, EXACTLY, ARE WE EXPECTED TO DO?
I CAN GET YOU EMERGENCY CLEARANCE...
...BUT IT SEEMS LIKE THE ATTACK IS HAPPENING FROM OUTSIDE. IN THE POTOMAC.
I'M NOT A FIELD AGENT.
MY SKILLS ARE PERSUASIVE, NOT COMBATIVE.
MY SKILLS SAVED MY LIFE MORE THAN ANY WEAPON EVER COULD.
SCREEECH
SEE ANYTHING?
WELL, YOU'VE GOT THE BINOCULARS, SO...
I'VE NEVER REALLY UNDERSTOOD THESE WOMEN, LIKE LADY JAYE AND RONIN, WHO INSIST ON ROUGH-HOUSING WITH THE BOYS.

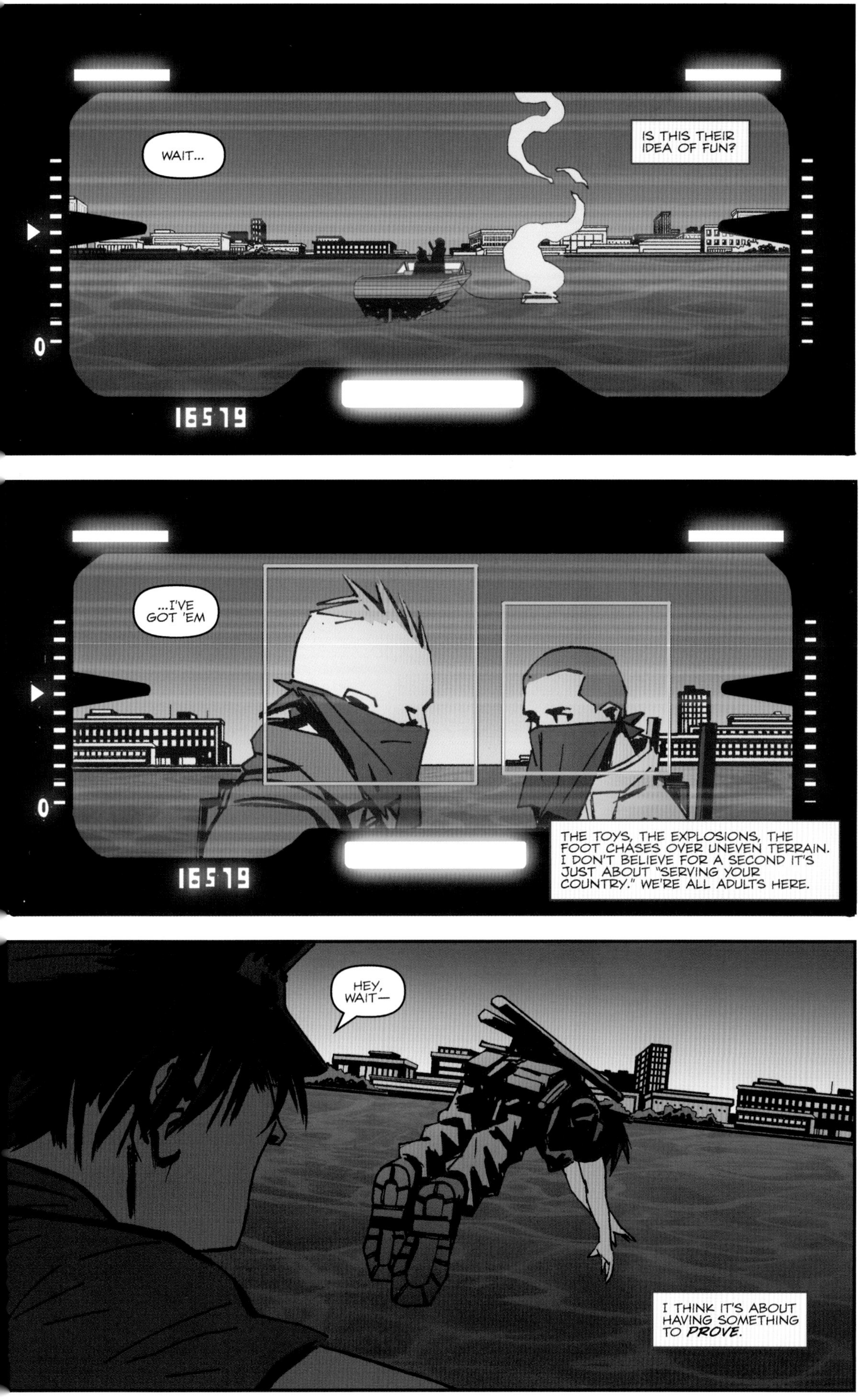
IS THIS THEIR IDEA OF FUN?
WAIT...
16579
...I'VE GOT 'EM
THE TOYS, THE EXPLOSIONS, THE FOOT CHASES OVER UNEVEN TERRAIN. I DON'T BELIEVE FOR A SECOND IT'S JUST ABOUT "SERVING YOUR COUNTRY." WE'RE ALL ADULTS HERE.
16579
HEY, WAIT—
I THINK IT'S ABOUT HAVING SOMETHING TO ***PROVE***.

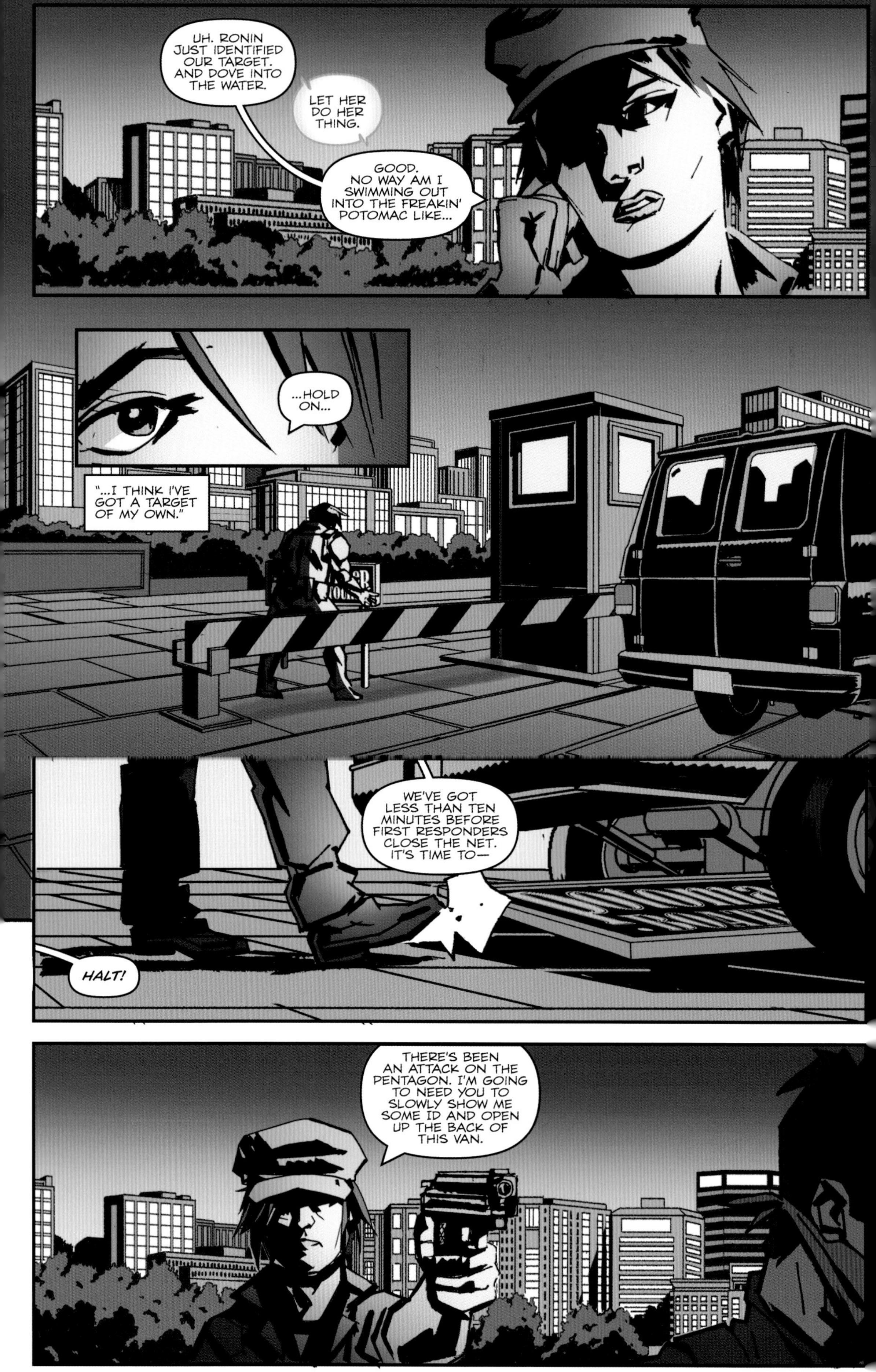
UH. RONIN JUST IDENTIFIED OUR TARGET. AND DOVE INTO THE WATER.
LET HER DO HER THING.
GOOD. NO WAY AM I SWIMMING OUT INTO THE FREAKIN' POTOMAC LIKE...
...HOLD ON...
"...I THINK I'VE GOT A TARGET OF MY OWN."
WE'VE GOT LESS THAN TEN MINUTES BEFORE FIRST RESPONDERS CLOSE THE NET. IT'S TIME TO—
HALT!
THERE'S BEEN AN ATTACK ON THE PENTAGON. I'M GOING TO NEED YOU TO SLOWLY SHOW ME SOME ID AND OPEN UP THE BACK OF THIS VAN.

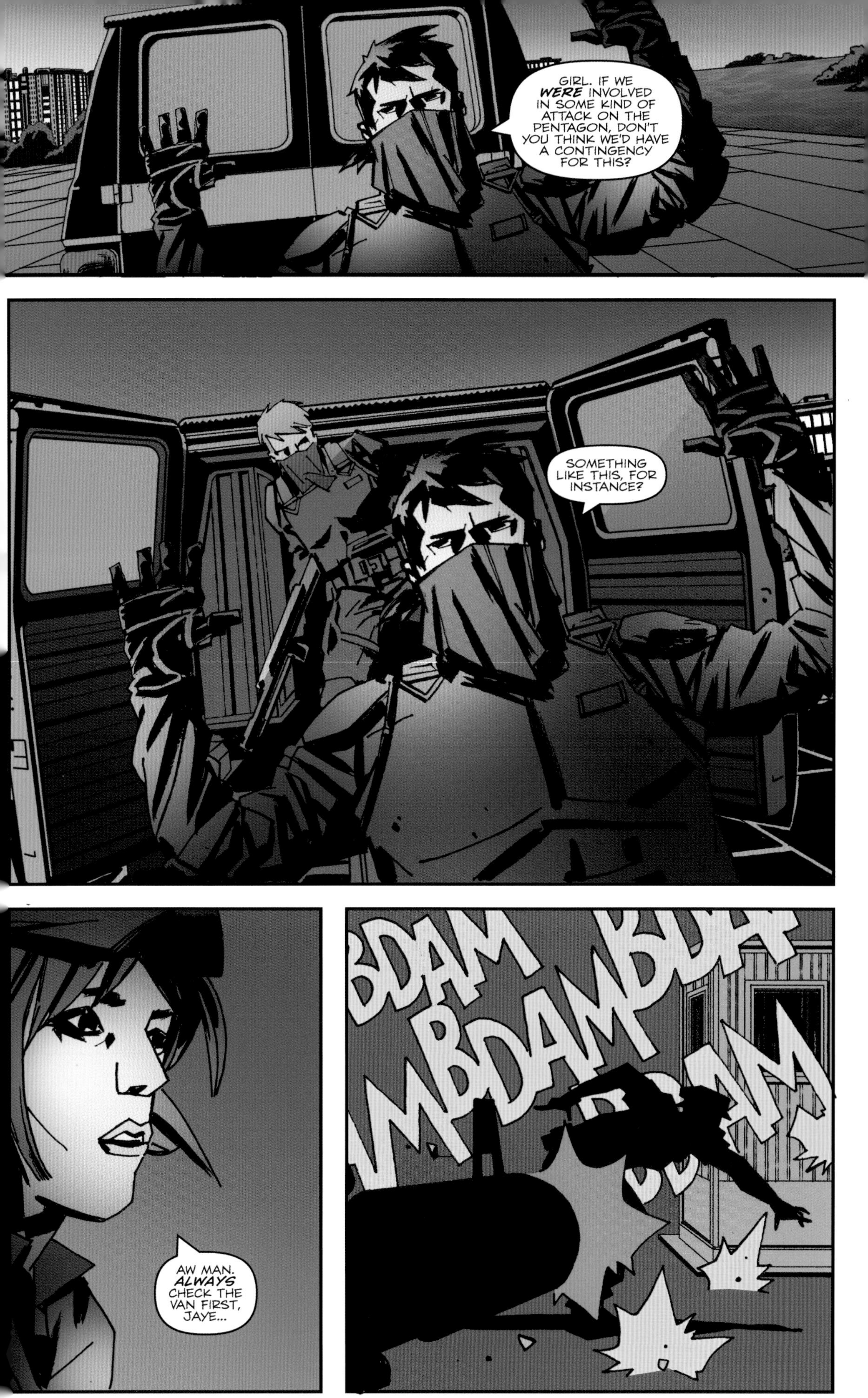
GIRL. IF WE *WERE* INVOLVED IN SOME KIND OF ATTACK ON THE PENTAGON, DON'T YOU THINK WE'D HAVE A CONTINGENCY FOR THIS?
SOMETHING LIKE THIS, FOR INSTANCE?
AW MAN. *ALWAYS* CHECK THE VAN FIRST, JAYE...
BDAM
BDAM

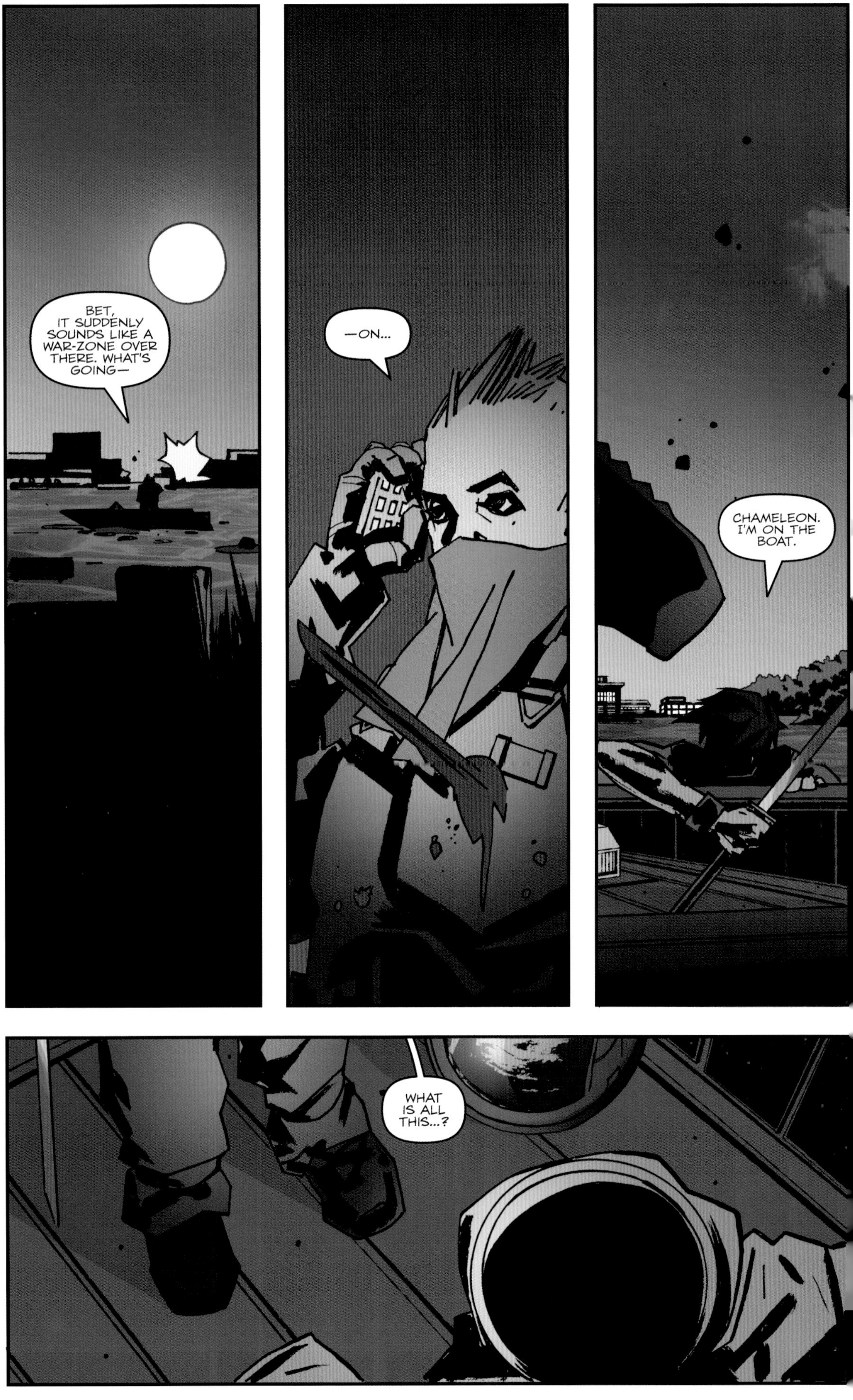
BET, IT SUDDENLY SOUNDS LIKE A WAR-ZONE OVER THERE. WHAT'S GOING—
—ON...
CHAMELEON. I'M ON THE BOAT.
WHAT IS ALL THIS...?

BEST I CAN TELL, IT LOOKS LIKE THE NIGHT CREEPERS ARE ATTEMPTING A BREACH AT THEIR PREVIOUS ENTRY POINT. THEY'RE NOT BEING SUBTLE ABOUT IT, BUT THEY DON'T HAVE TO BE.

THEY'RE CONFUSING AND DELAYING OUR RESPONSE BY CONTAMINATING THE ENTIRE AREA WITH SOME KIND OF RADIOACTIVE *DIRTY BOMB.*

YEAH. I GOT THAT IMPRESSION. THE GUY ON THE BOAT HAD A RADIATION SUIT, BUT HE WON'T BE NEEDING IT NOW.

INTERNAL RESPIRATOR ON THE SUIT?

NO. IT'S ONLY TYVEK. THIS GUY I JUST KILLED WASN'T PLANNING ON DIVING ALL THE WAY DOWN THERE.

BUT IF *I* DON'T, THE *ENTIRE G.I. JOE PROGRAM* COULD GO UNDER.

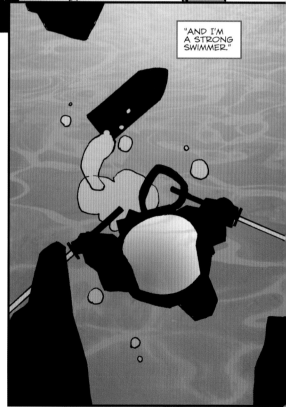

"AND I'M A STRONG SWIMMER."

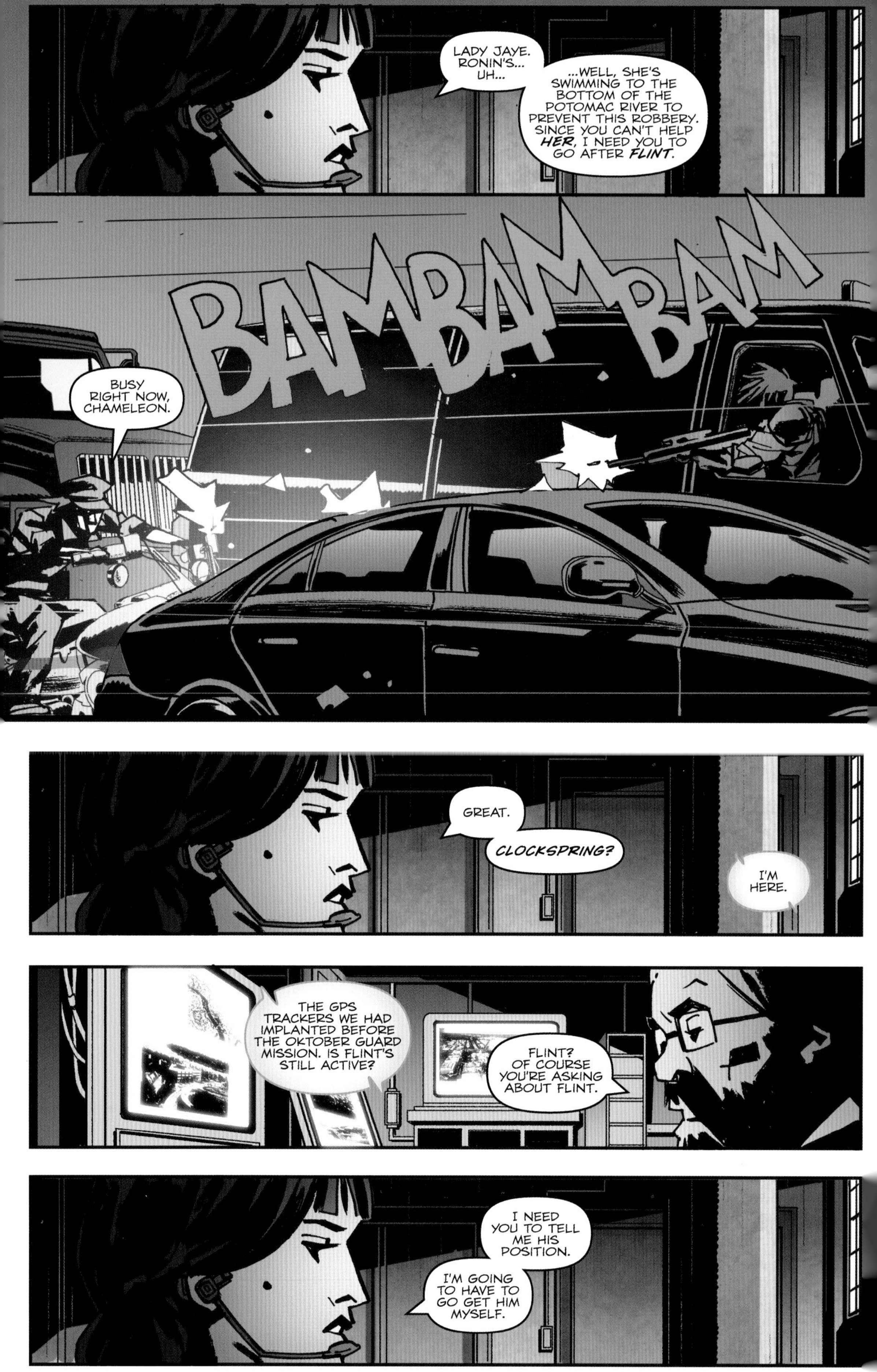

LADY JAYE. RONIN'S... UH...
...WELL, SHE'S SWIMMING TO THE BOTTOM OF THE POTOMAC RIVER TO PREVENT THIS ROBBERY. SINCE YOU CAN'T HELP *HER*, I NEED YOU TO GO AFTER *FLINT*.
BAMBAMBAM
BUSY RIGHT NOW, CHAMELEON.
GREAT.
*CLOCKSPRING?*
I'M HERE.
THE GPS TRACKERS WE HAD IMPLANTED BEFORE THE OKTOBER GUARD MISSION. IS FLINT'S STILL ACTIVE?
FLINT? OF COURSE YOU'RE ASKING ABOUT FLINT.
I NEED YOU TO TELL ME HIS POSITION.
I'M GOING TO HAVE TO GO GET HIM MYSELF.

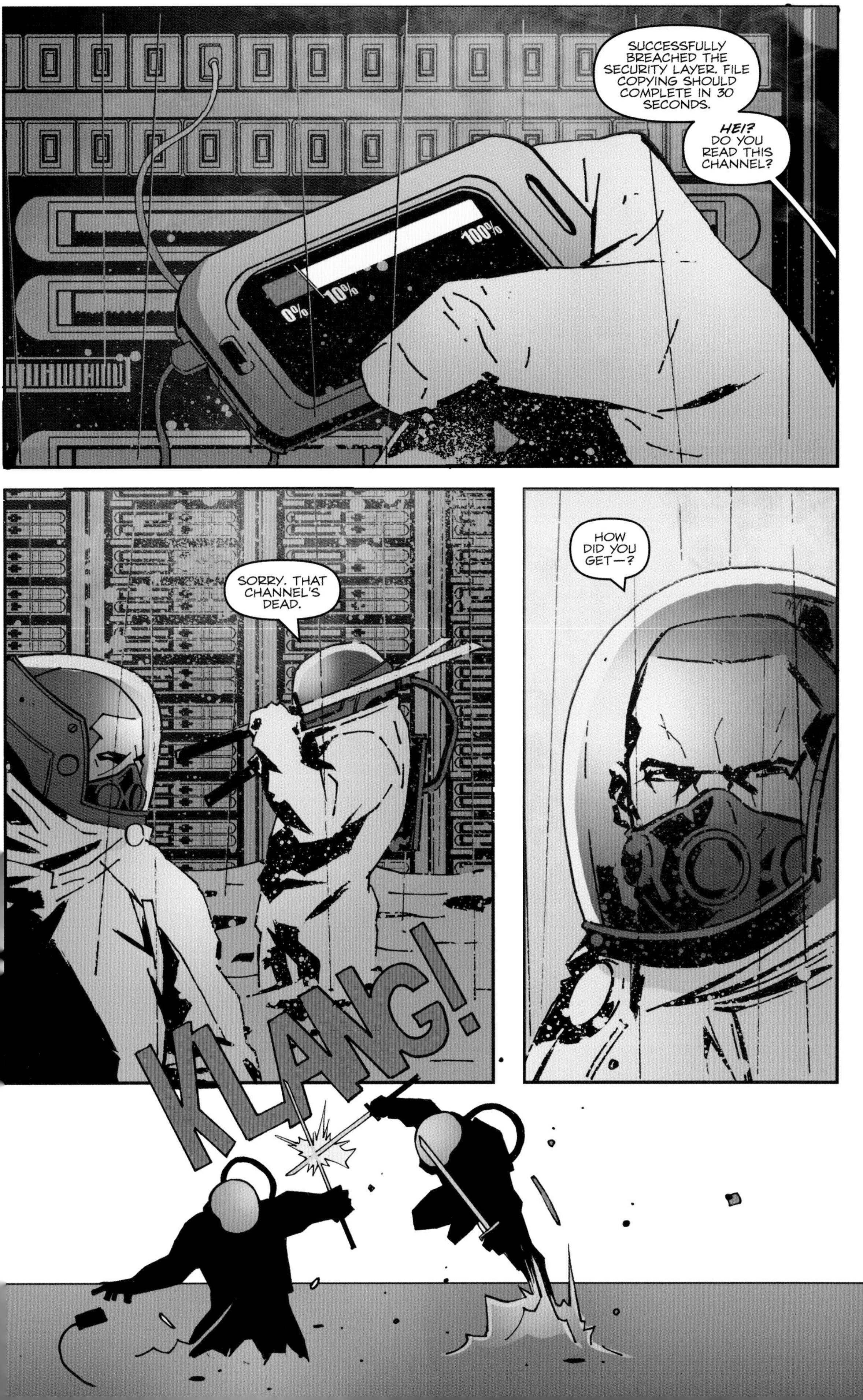

SUCCESSFULLY BREACHED THE SECURITY LAYER. FILE COPYING SHOULD COMPLETE IN 30 SECONDS.
HEI? DO YOU READ THIS CHANNEL?
0%
10%
100%
SORRY. THAT CHANNEL'S DEAD.
HOW DID YOU GET—?
KLANG!
HEI?

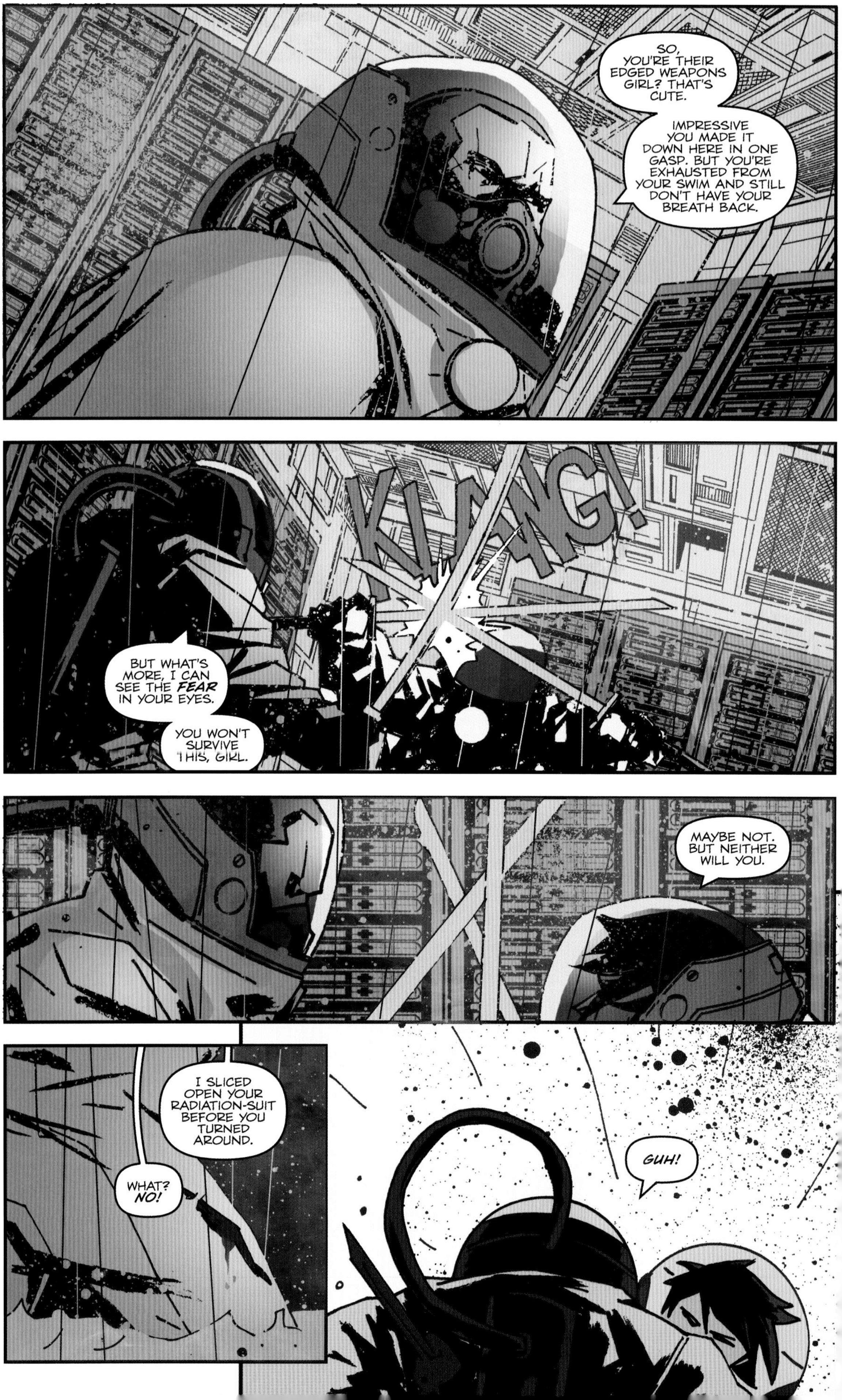
SO, YOU'RE THEIR EDGED WEAPONS GIRL? THAT'S CUTE.
IMPRESSIVE YOU MADE IT DOWN HERE IN ONE GASP. BUT YOU'RE EXHAUSTED FROM YOUR SWIM AND STILL DON'T HAVE YOUR BREATH BACK.
KLANG!
BUT WHAT'S MORE, I CAN SEE THE ***FEAR*** IN YOUR EYES.
YOU WON'T SURVIVE THIS, GIRL.
MAYBE NOT. BUT NEITHER WILL YOU.
I SLICED OPEN YOUR RADIATION-SUIT BEFORE YOU TURNED AROUND.
WHAT? ***NO!***
***GUH!***

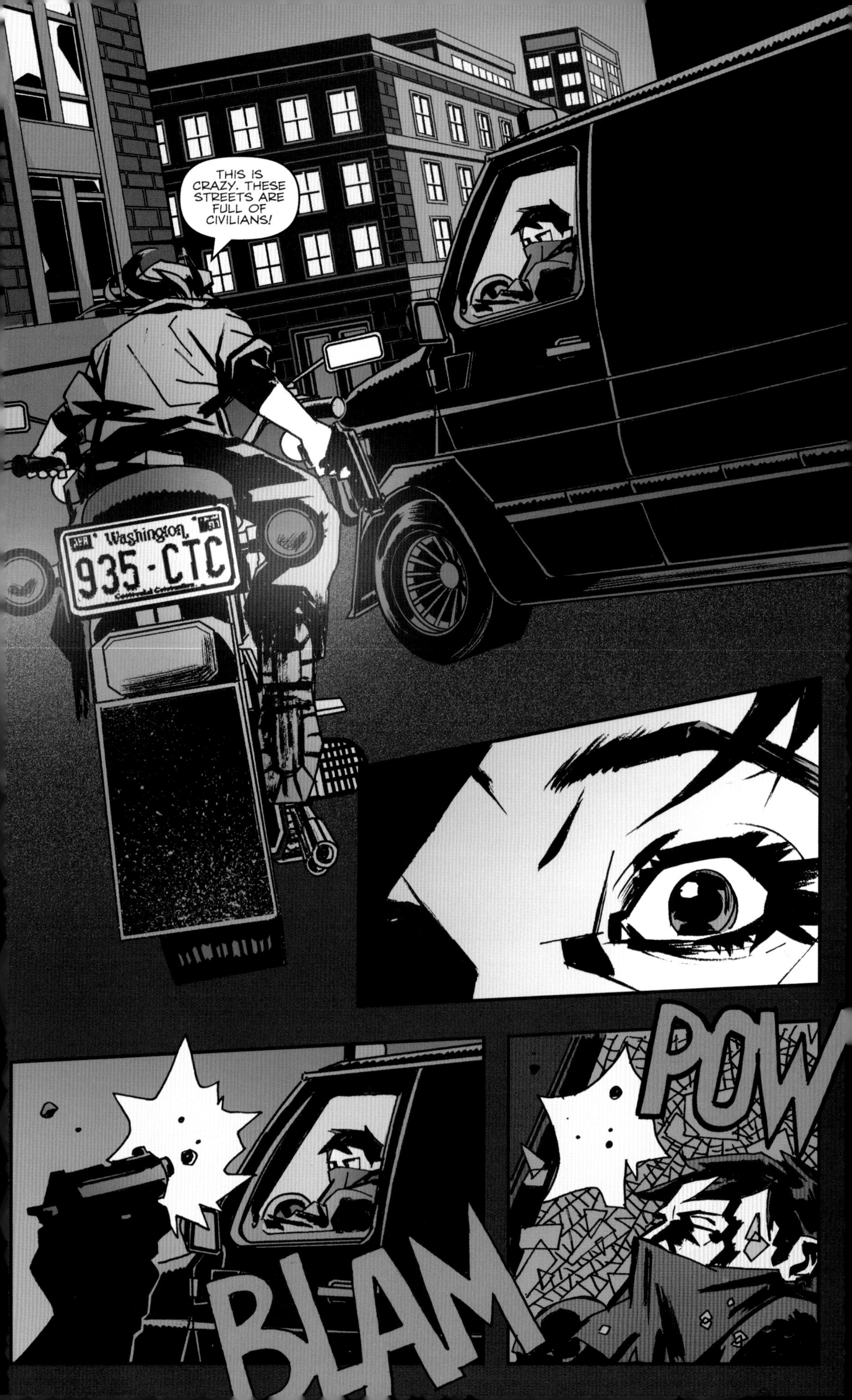
THIS IS CRAZY. THESE STREETS ARE FULL OF CIVILIANS!
Washington
935-CTC
BLAM
POW

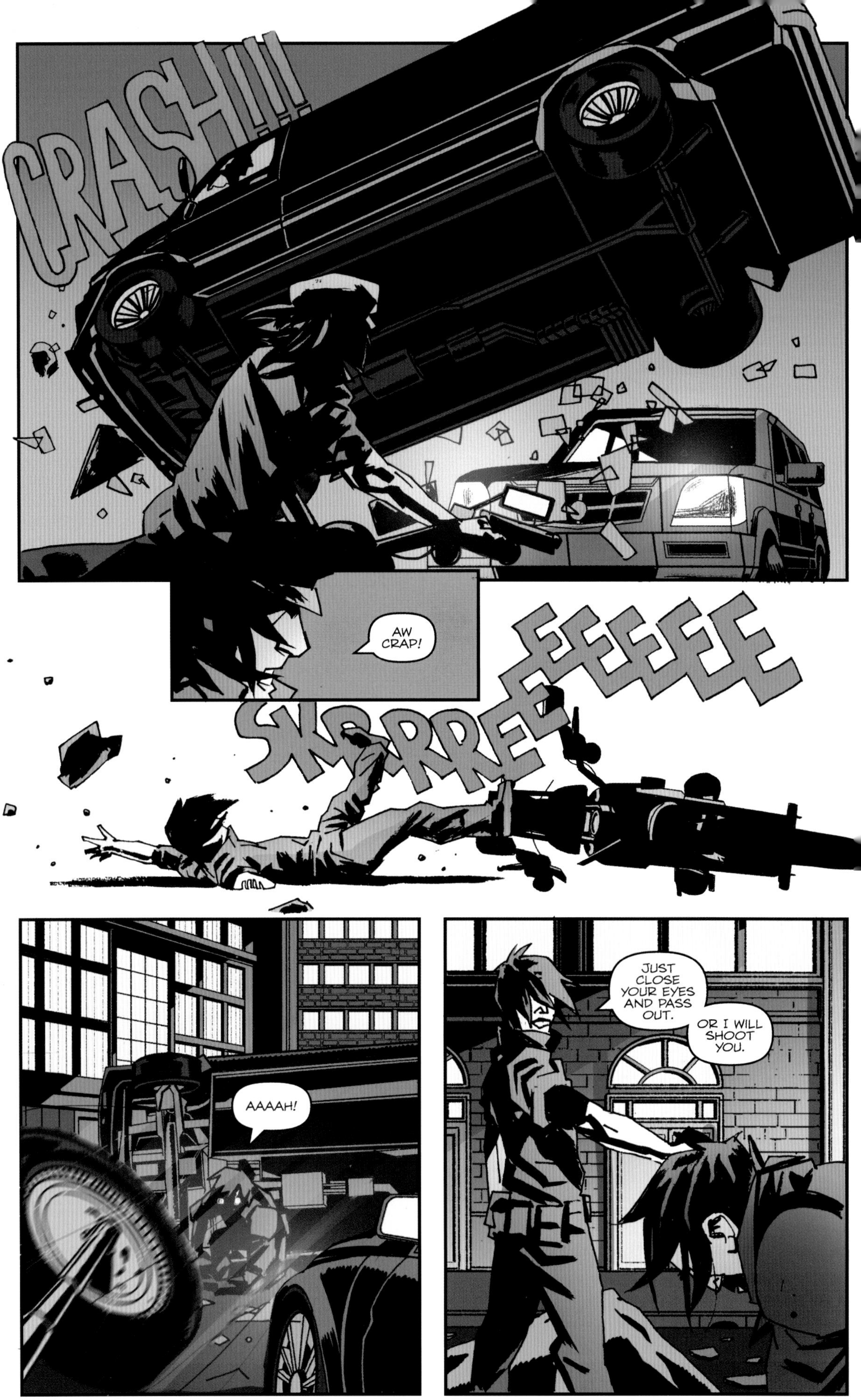
CRASH!!!
AW CRAP!
SKRRREEEEEEEE
AAAAH!
JUST CLOSE YOUR EYES AND PASS OUT.
OR I WILL SHOOT YOU.

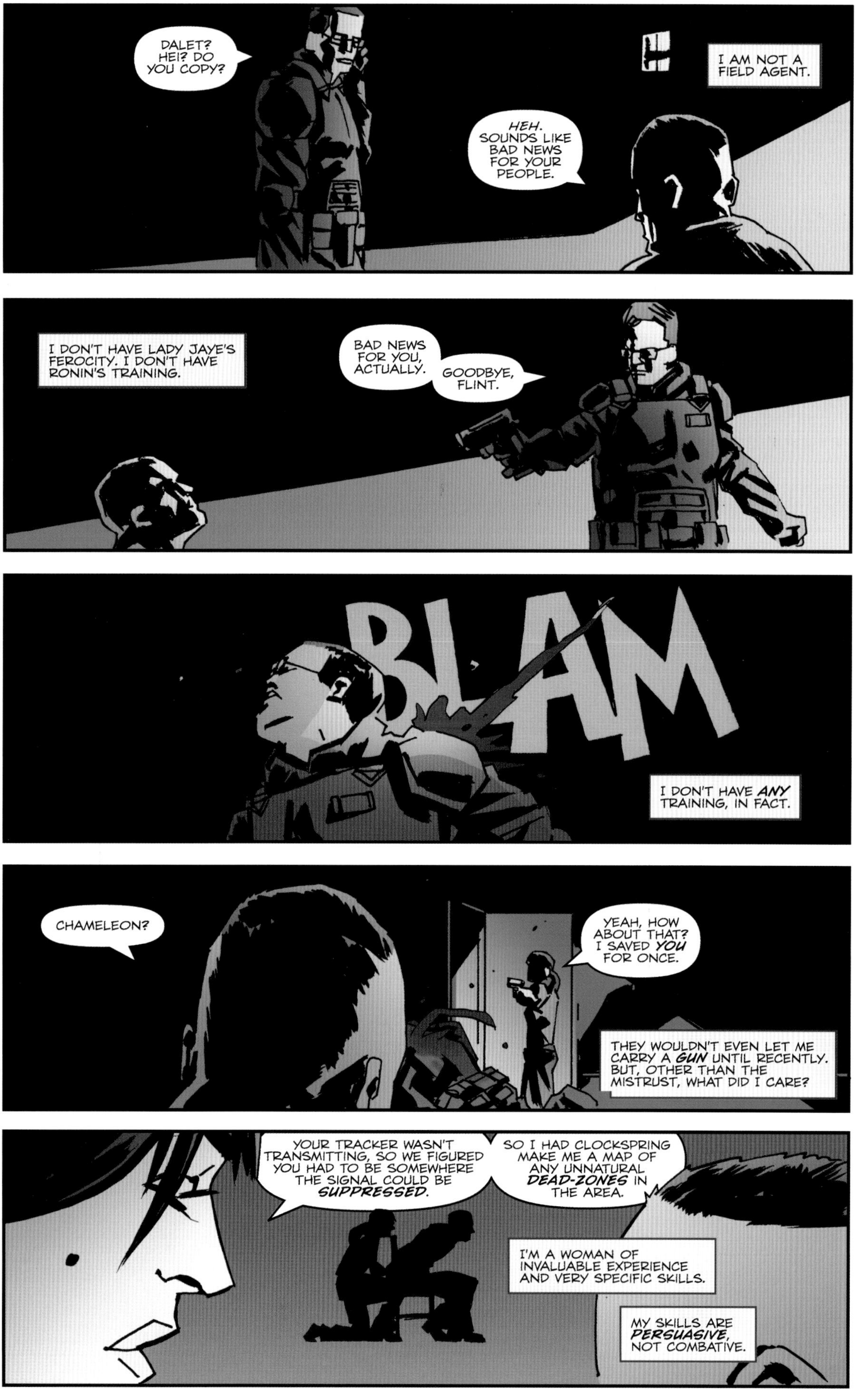
DALET? HEI? DO YOU COPY?
I AM NOT A FIELD AGENT.
*HEH.* SOUNDS LIKE BAD NEWS FOR YOUR PEOPLE.
I DON'T HAVE LADY JAYE'S FEROCITY. I DON'T HAVE RONIN'S TRAINING.
BAD NEWS FOR YOU, ACTUALLY.
GOODBYE, FLINT.
BLAM
I DON'T HAVE ***ANY*** TRAINING, IN FACT.
CHAMELEON?
YEAH, HOW ABOUT THAT? I SAVED ***YOU*** FOR ONCE.
THEY WOULDN'T EVEN LET ME CARRY A ***GUN*** UNTIL RECENTLY. BUT, OTHER THAN THE MISTRUST, WHAT DID I CARE?
YOUR TRACKER WASN'T TRANSMITTING, SO WE FIGURED YOU HAD TO BE SOMEWHERE THE SIGNAL COULD BE ***SUPPRESSED.***
SO I HAD CLOCKSPRING MAKE ME A MAP OF ANY UNNATURAL ***DEAD-ZONES*** IN THE AREA.
I'M A WOMAN OF INVALUABLE EXPERIENCE AND VERY SPECIFIC SKILLS.
MY SKILLS ARE ***PERSUASIVE,*** NOT COMBATIVE.

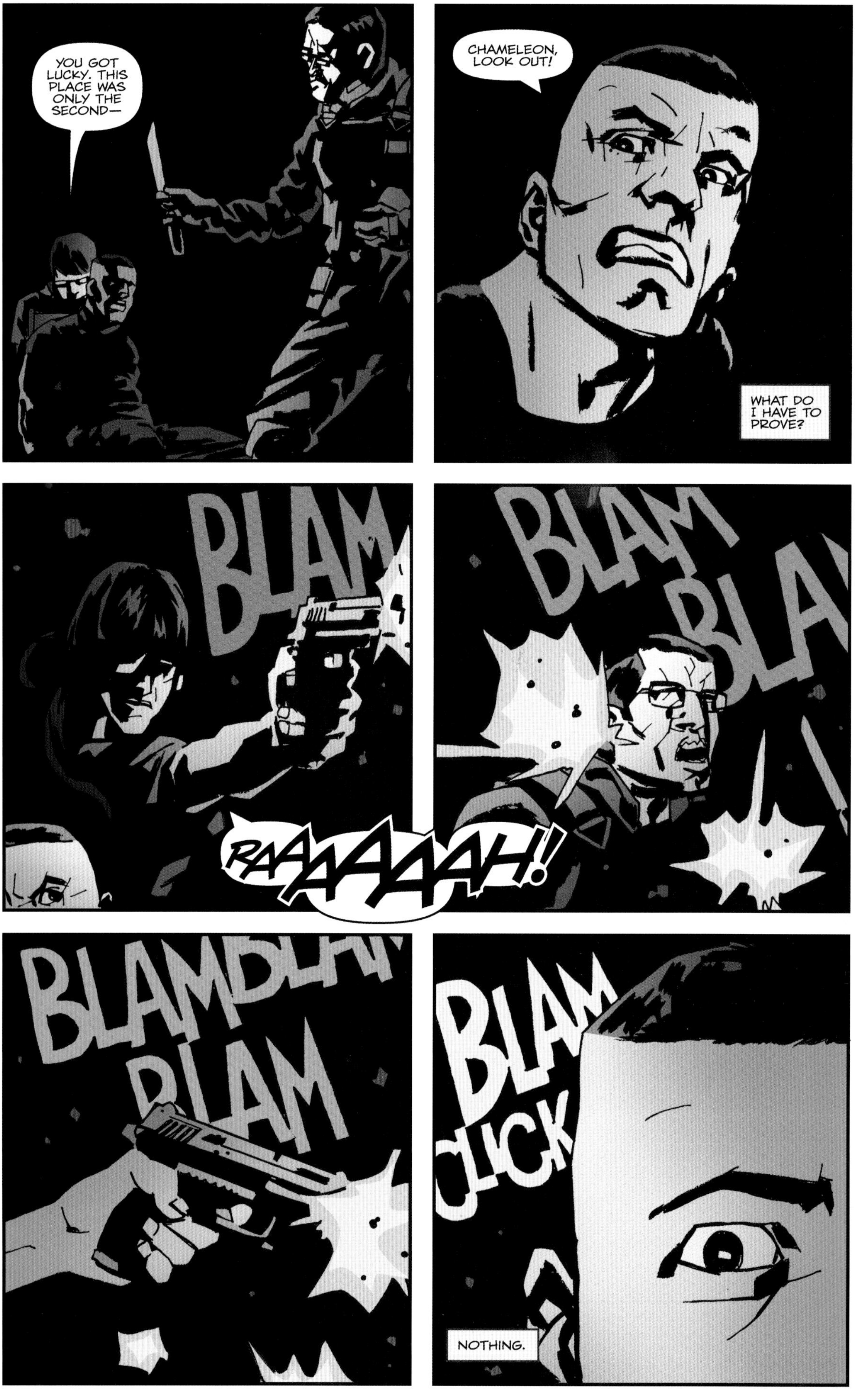
YOU GOT LUCKY. THIS PLACE WAS ONLY THE SECOND—
CHAMELEON, LOOK OUT!
WHAT DO I HAVE TO PROVE?
BLAM
BLAM
BLA
RAAAAAAH!
BLAMBLAM
BLAM
BLAM
CLICK
NOTHING.

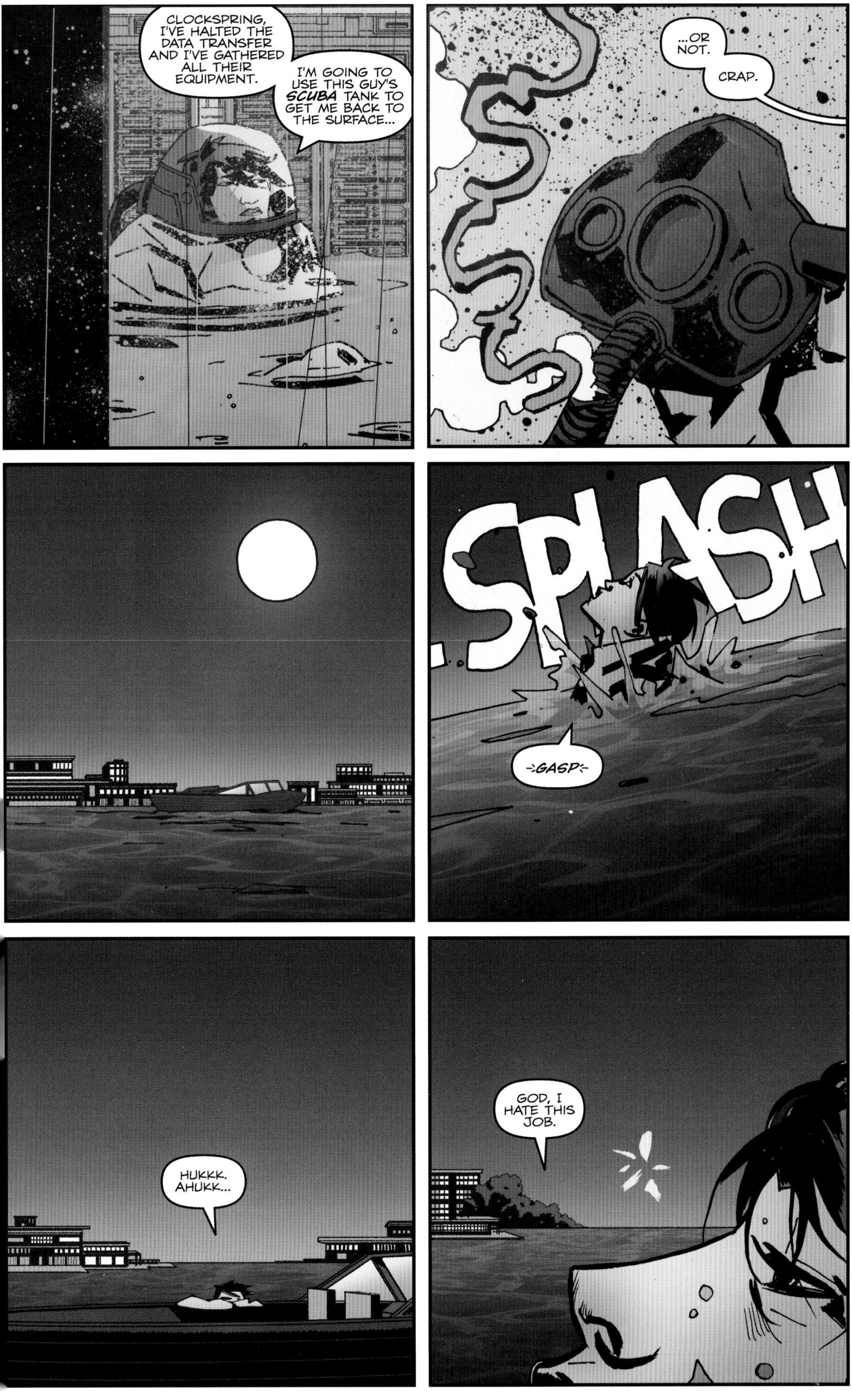
CLOCKSPRING, I'VE HALTED THE DATA TRANSFER AND I'VE GATHERED ALL THEIR EQUIPMENT.
I'M GOING TO USE THIS GUY'S SCUBA TANK TO GET ME BACK TO THE SURFACE...
...OR NOT.
CRAP.
SPLASH
GASP
HUKKK. AHUKK...
GOD, I HATE THIS JOB.

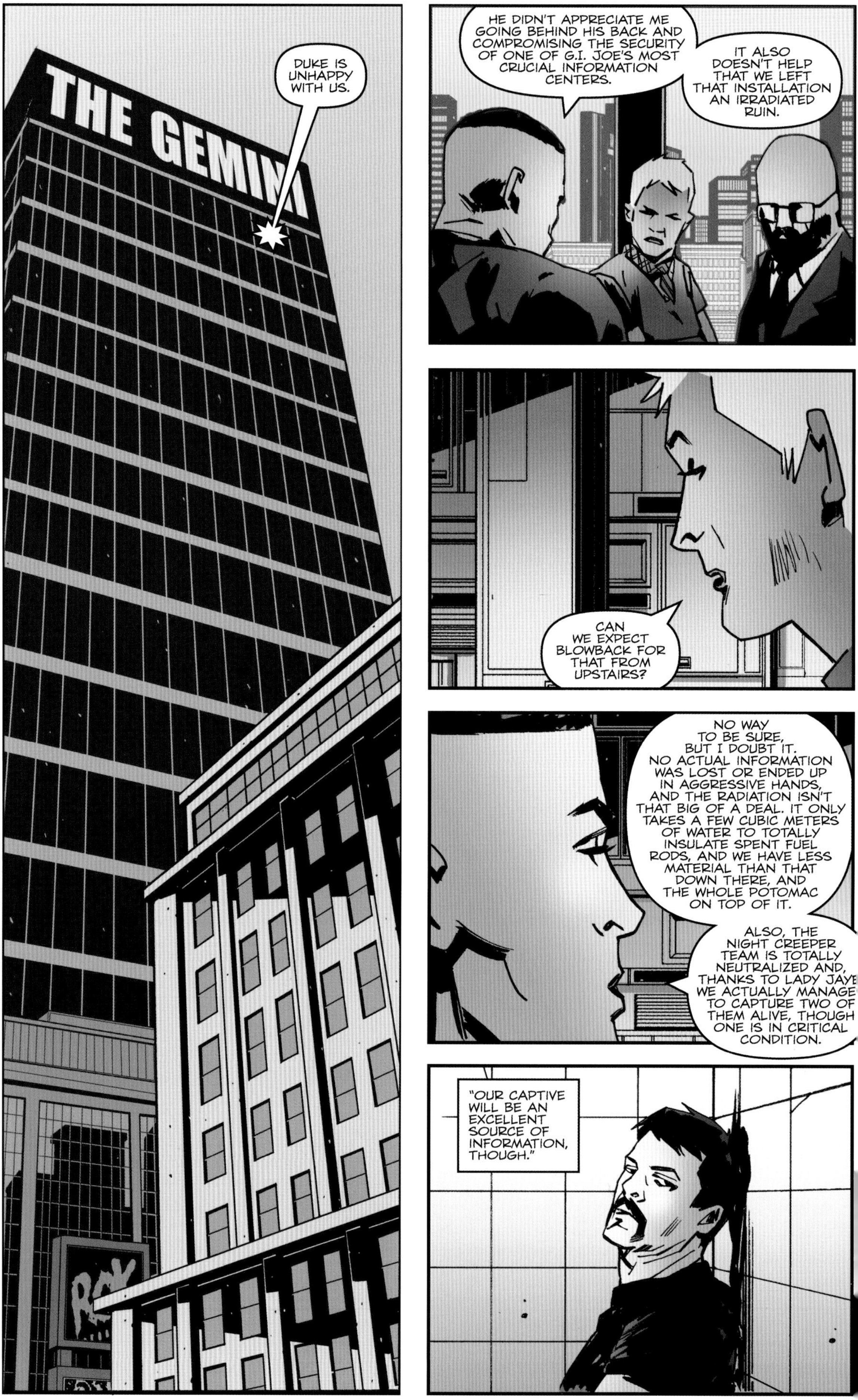
THE GEMINI
DUKE IS UNHAPPY WITH US.
HE DIDN'T APPRECIATE ME GOING BEHIND HIS BACK AND COMPROMISING THE SECURITY OF ONE OF G.I. JOE'S MOST CRUCIAL INFORMATION CENTERS.
IT ALSO DOESN'T HELP THAT WE LEFT THAT INSTALLATION AN IRRADIATED RUIN.
CAN WE EXPECT BLOWBACK FOR THAT FROM UPSTAIRS?
NO WAY TO BE SURE, BUT I DOUBT IT. NO ACTUAL INFORMATION WAS LOST OR ENDED UP IN AGGRESSIVE HANDS, AND THE RADIATION ISN'T THAT BIG OF A DEAL. IT ONLY TAKES A FEW CUBIC METERS OF WATER TO TOTALLY INSULATE SPENT FUEL RODS, AND WE HAVE LESS MATERIAL THAN THAT DOWN THERE, AND THE WHOLE POTOMAC ON TOP OF IT.
ALSO, THE NIGHT CREEPER TEAM IS TOTALLY NEUTRALIZED AND, THANKS TO LADY JAYE WE ACTUALLY MANAGE TO CAPTURE TWO OF THEM ALIVE, THOUGH ONE IS IN CRITICAL CONDITION.
"OUR CAPTIVE WILL BE AN EXCELLENT SOURCE OF INFORMATION, THOUGH."

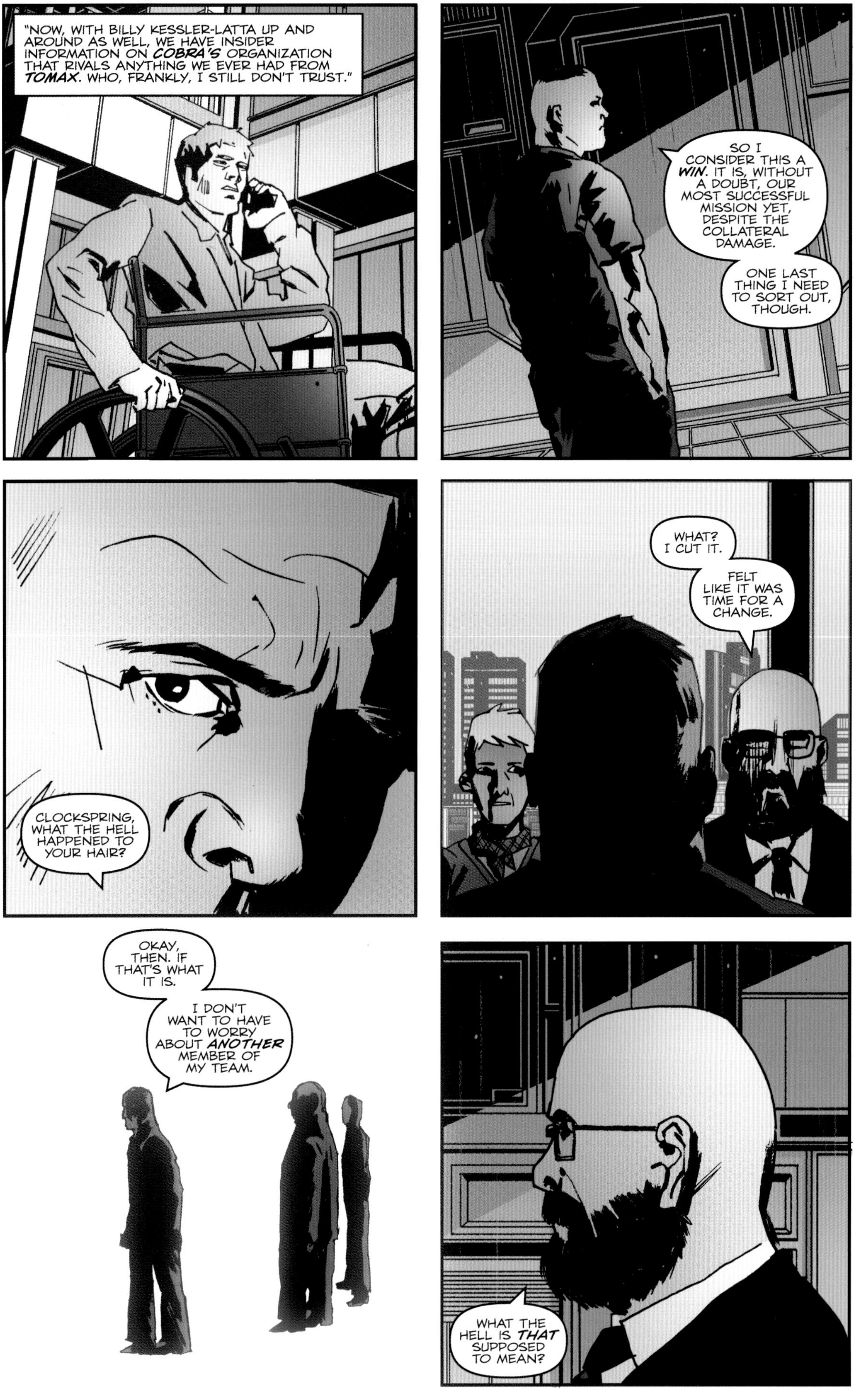
"NOW, WITH BILLY KESSLER-LATTA UP AND AROUND AS WELL, WE HAVE INSIDER INFORMATION ON COBRA'S ORGANIZATION THAT RIVALS ANYTHING WE EVER HAD FROM TOMAX. WHO, FRANKLY, I STILL DON'T TRUST."
SO I CONSIDER THIS A WIN. IT IS, WITHOUT A DOUBT, OUR MOST SUCCESSFUL MISSION YET, DESPITE THE COLLATERAL DAMAGE.
ONE LAST THING I NEED TO SORT OUT, THOUGH.
CLOCKSPRING, WHAT THE HELL HAPPENED TO YOUR HAIR?
WHAT? I CUT IT.
FELT LIKE IT WAS TIME FOR A CHANGE.
OKAY, THEN. IF THAT'S WHAT IT IS.
I DON'T WANT TO HAVE TO WORRY ABOUT ANOTHER MEMBER OF MY TEAM.
WHAT THE HELL IS THAT SUPPOSED TO MEAN?

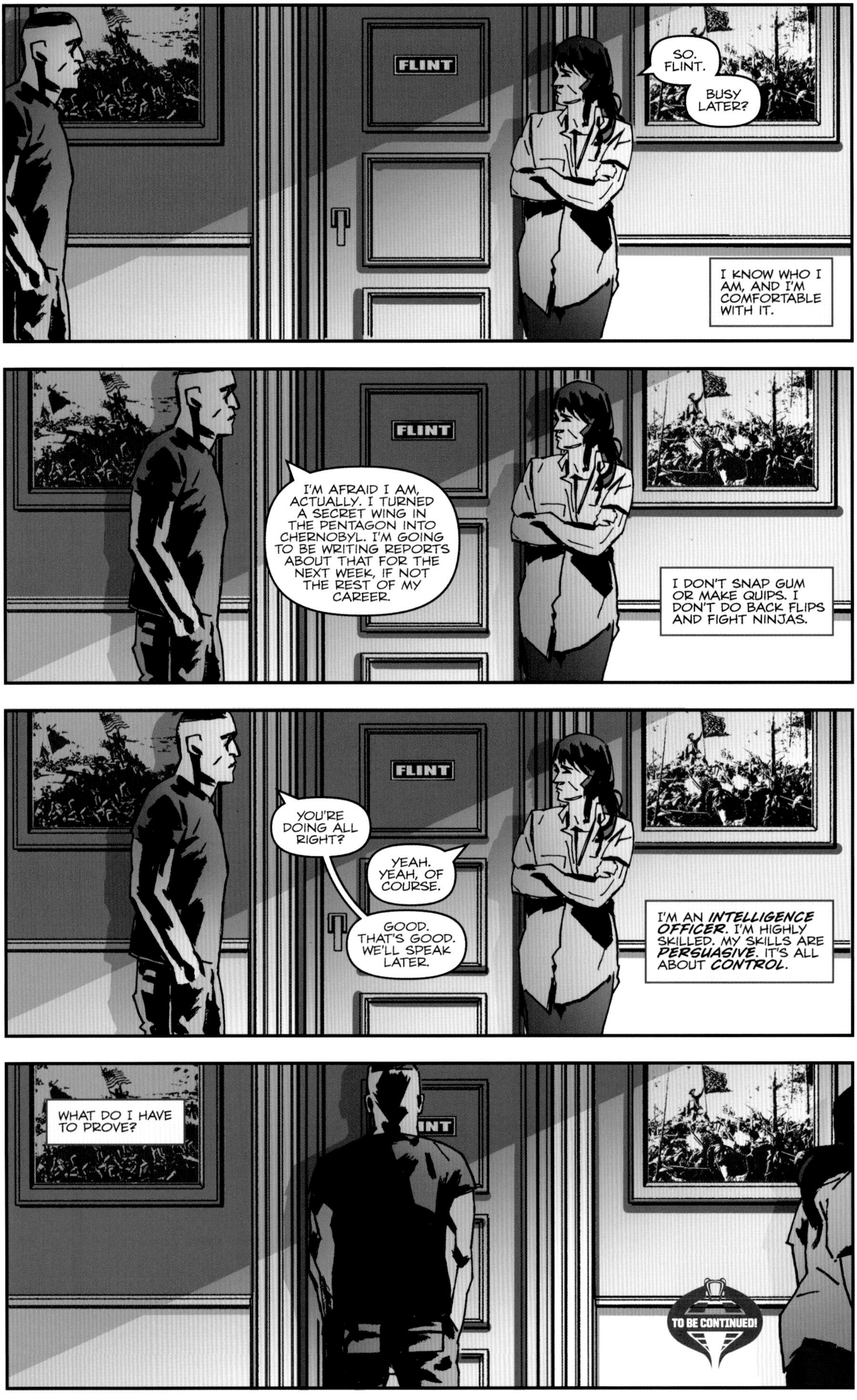
FLINT
SO. FLINT.
BUSY LATER?
I KNOW WHO I AM, AND I'M COMFORTABLE WITH IT.
FLINT
I'M AFRAID I AM, ACTUALLY. I TURNED A SECRET WING IN THE PENTAGON INTO CHERNOBYL. I'M GOING TO BE WRITING REPORTS ABOUT THAT FOR THE NEXT WEEK, IF NOT THE REST OF MY CAREER.
I DON'T SNAP GUM OR MAKE QUIPS. I DON'T DO BACK FLIPS AND FIGHT NINJAS.
FLINT
YOU'RE DOING ALL RIGHT?
YEAH. YEAH, OF COURSE.
GOOD. THAT'S GOOD. WE'LL SPEAK LATER.
I'M AN INTELLIGENCE OFFICER. I'M HIGHLY SKILLED. MY SKILLS ARE PERSUASIVE. IT'S ALL ABOUT CONTROL.
WHAT DO I HAVE TO PROVE?
TO BE CONTINUED!

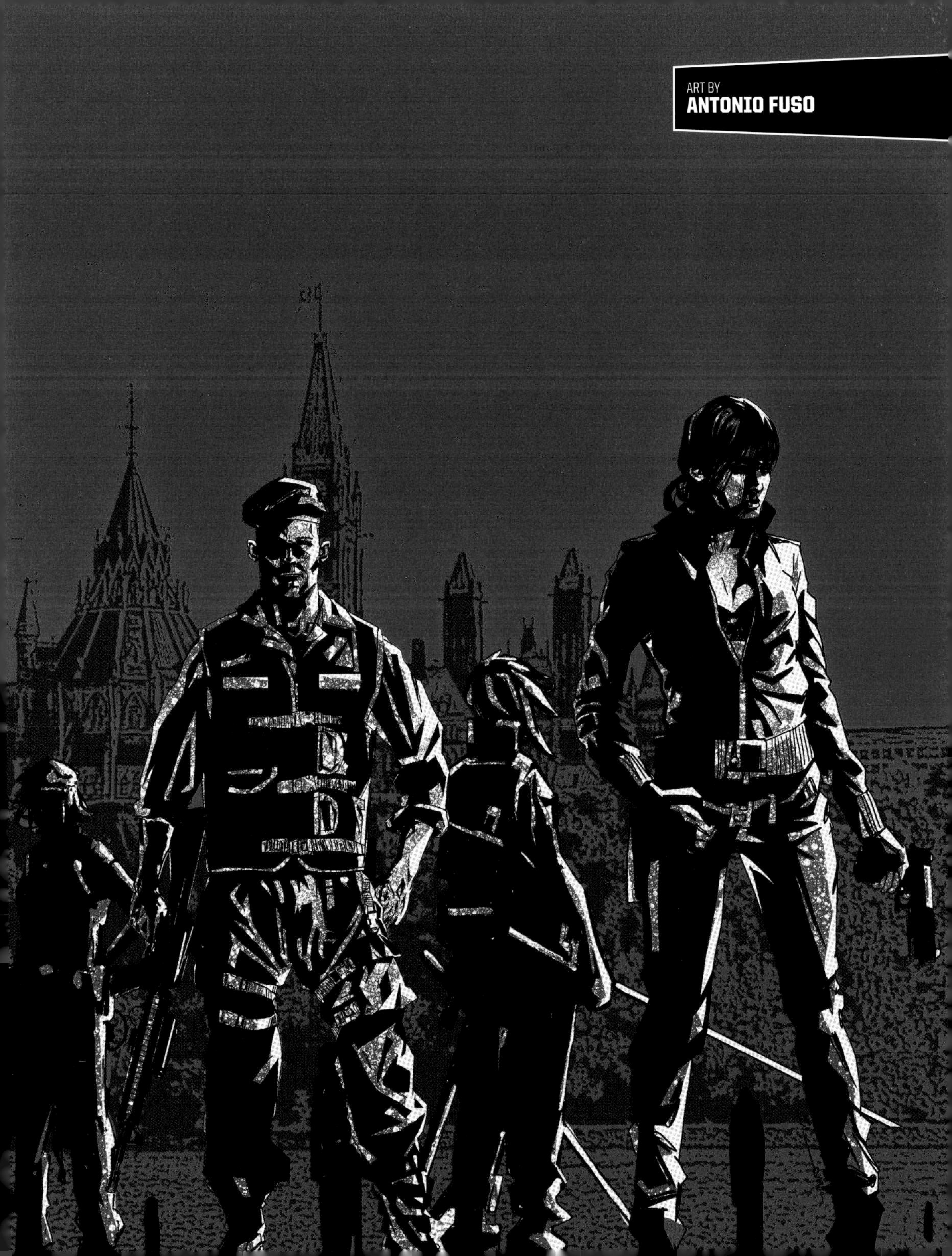

ART BY
**ANTONIO FUSO**

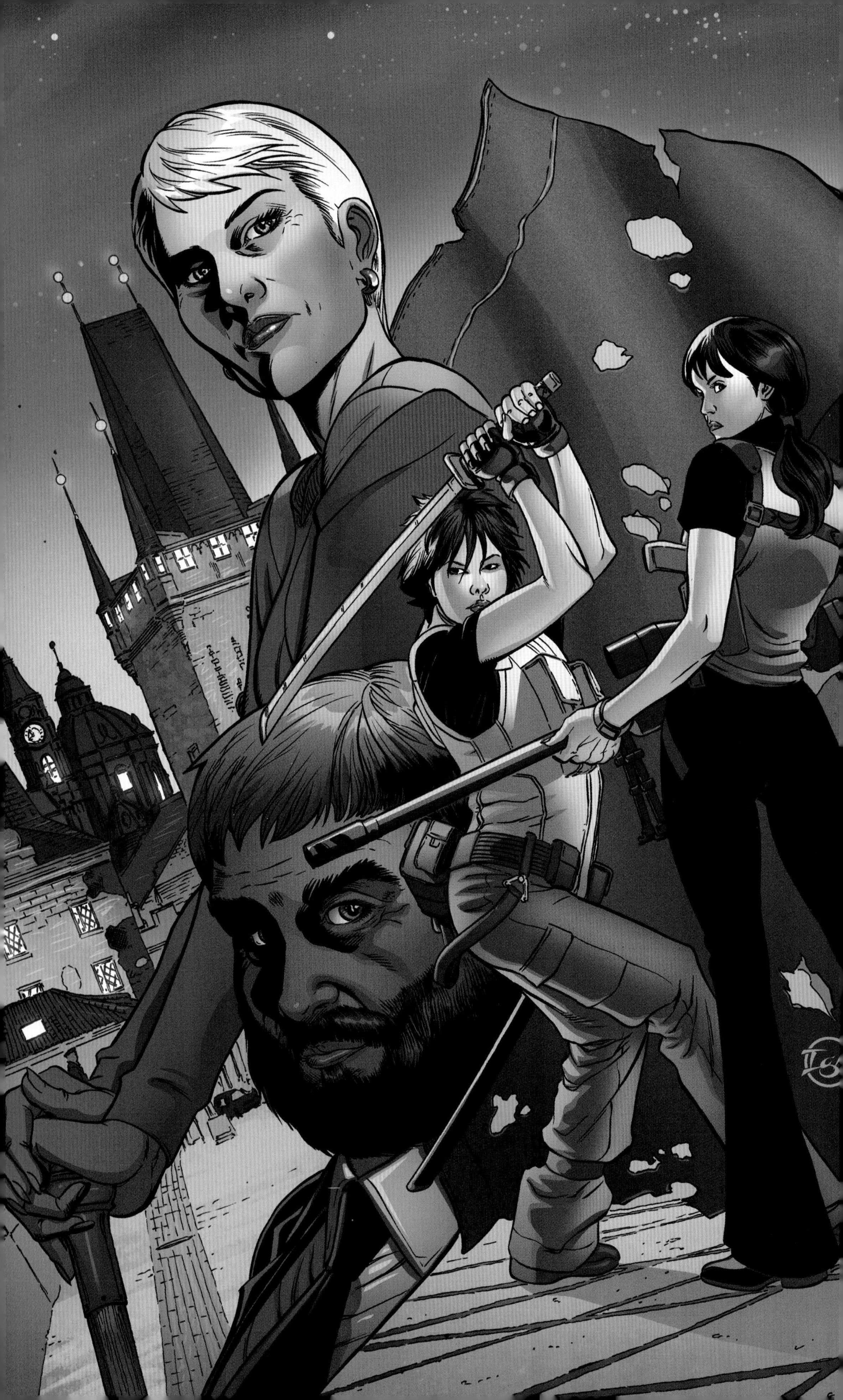

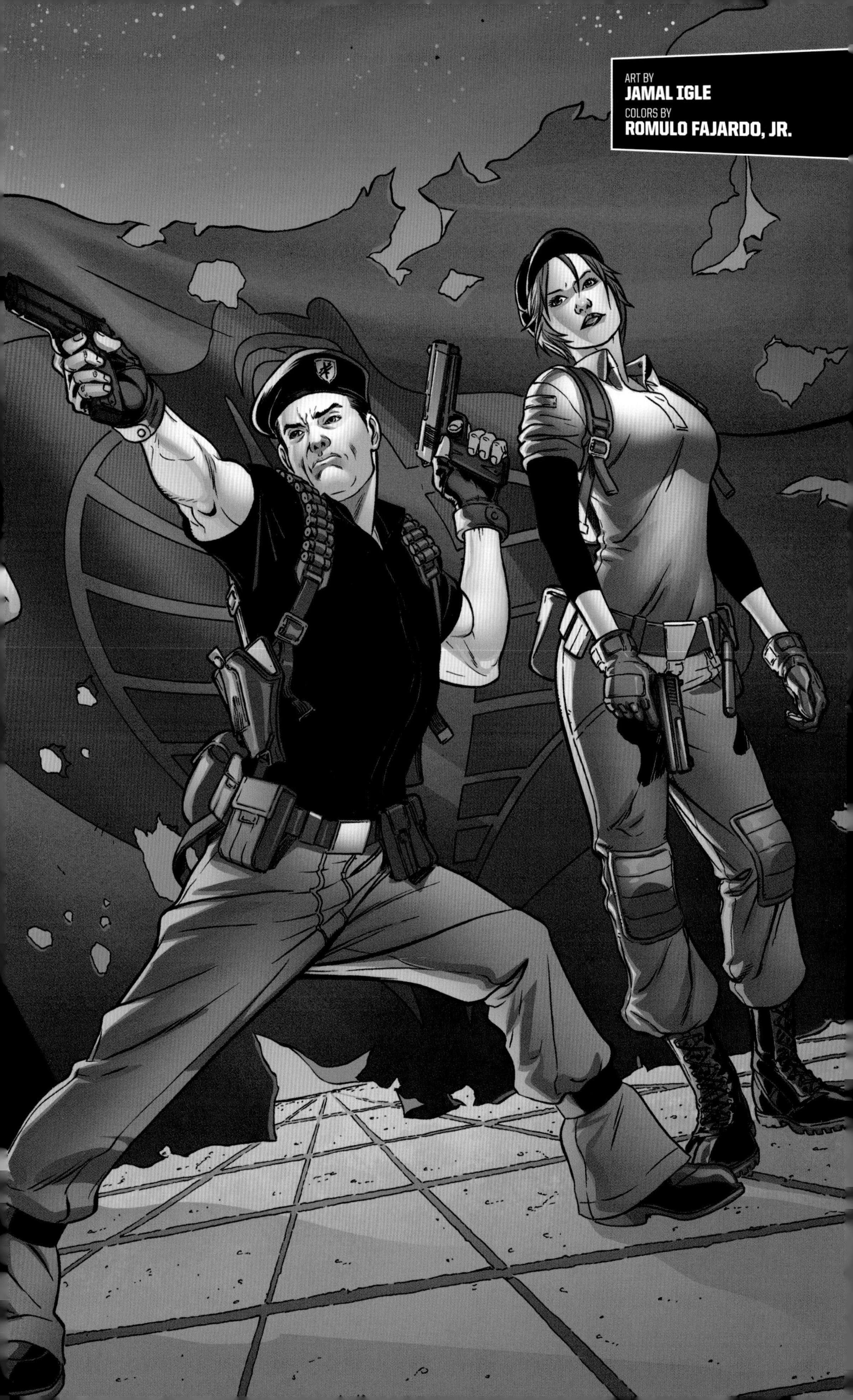
ART BY
JAMAL IGLE
COLORS BY
ROMULO FAJARDO, JR.

ART BY
**ANTONIO FUSO**

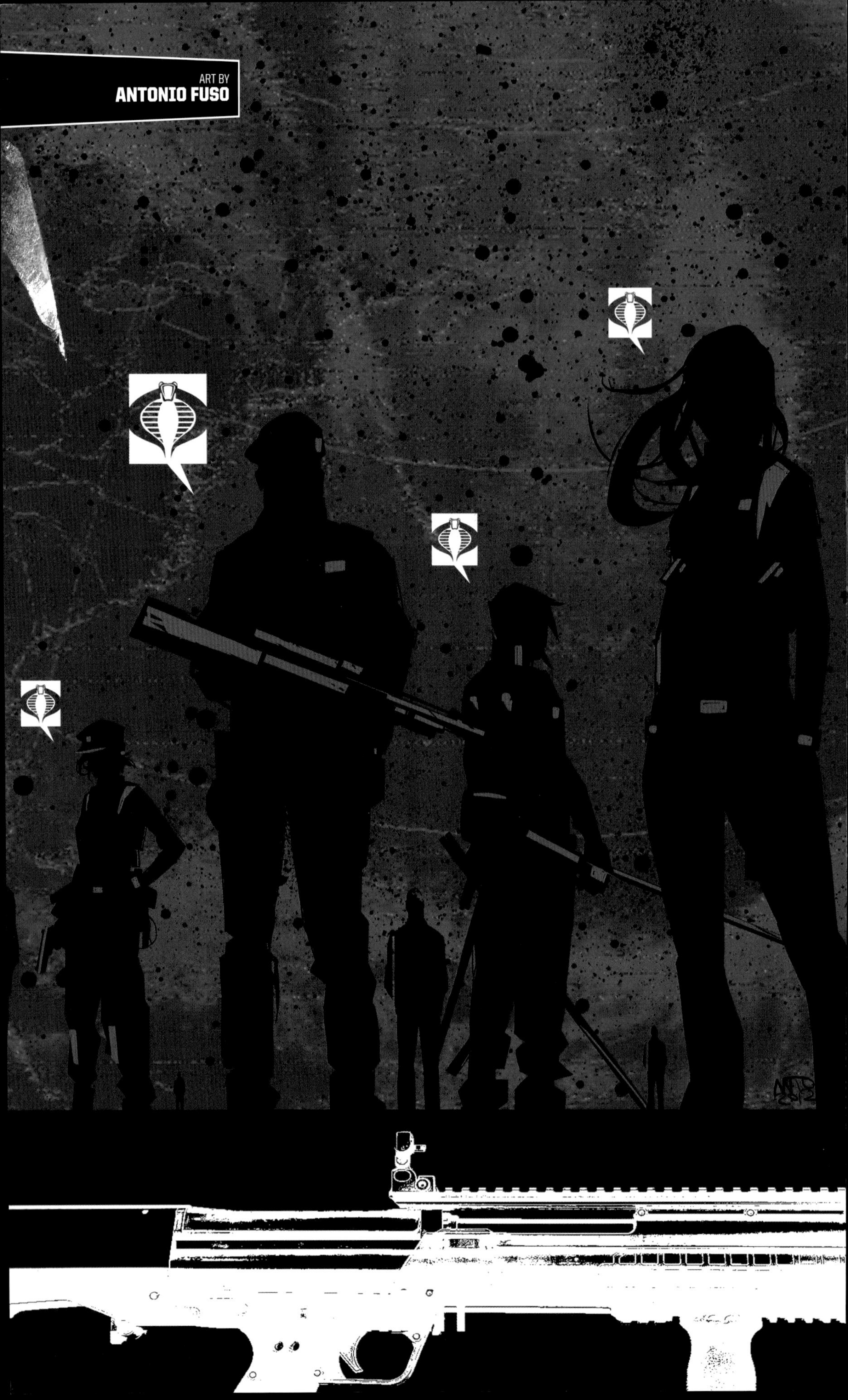

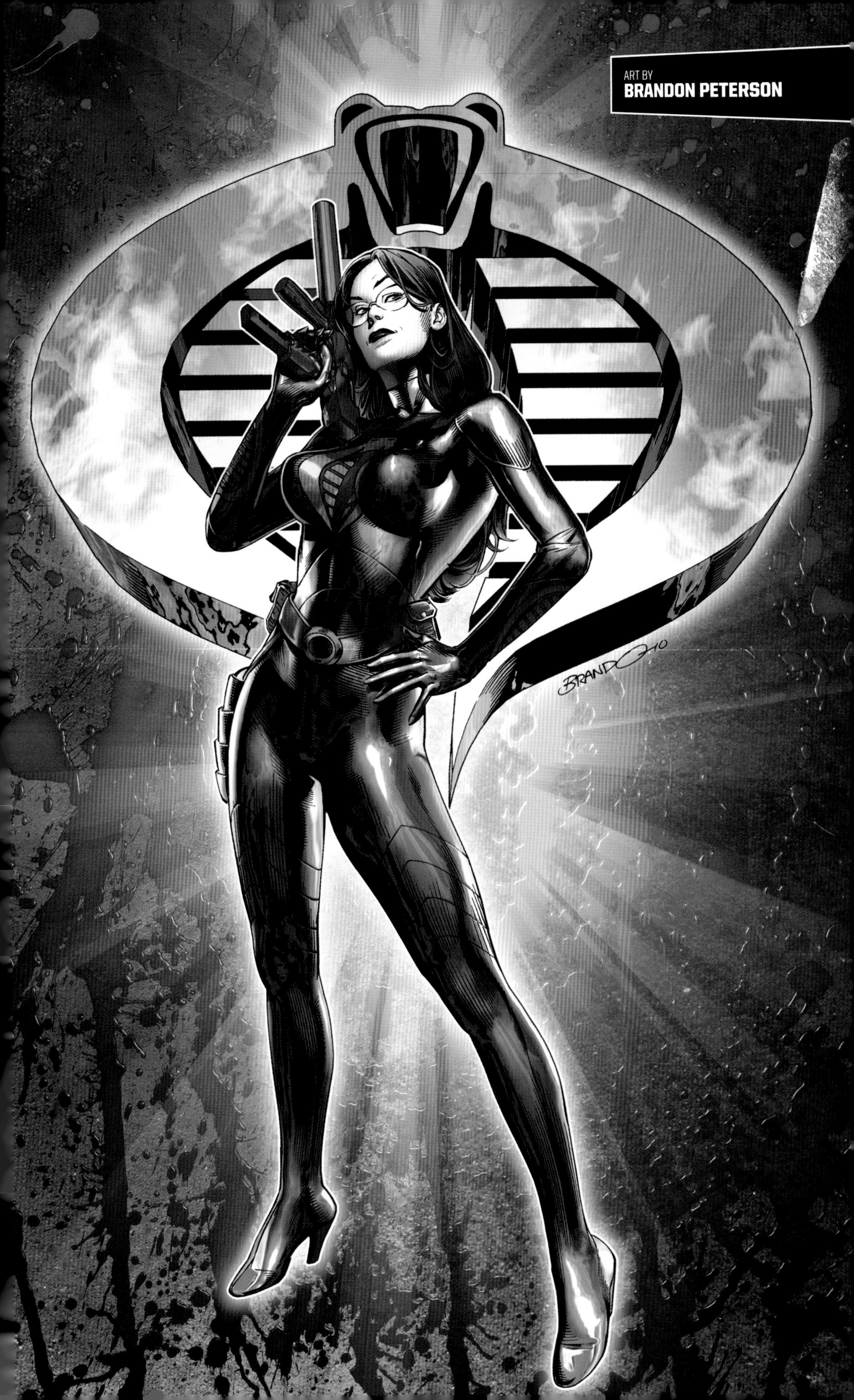

ART BY
**BRANDON PETERSON**

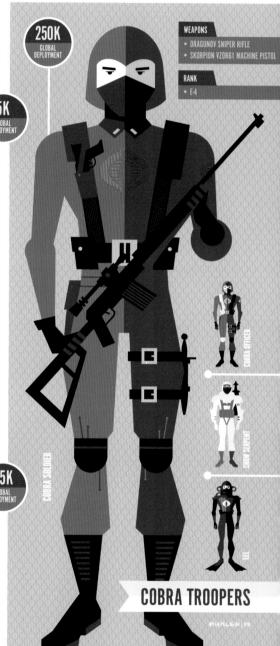

**3K**
GLOBAL
DEPLOYMENT

**5K**
GLOBAL
DEPLOYMENT

TECHNO-VIPER

**250K**
GLOBAL
DEPLOYMENT

**WEAPONS**
• DRAGUNOV SNIPER RIFLE
• SKORPION VZOR61 MACHINE PISTOL

**RANK**
• E-4

NIGHT-VIPER  ASTRO-VIPER  KITCHEN VIPER

**VIPERS**

**WEAPON**
AK-47

**RANK**
E-4

**CRIMSON GUARD**

COBRA OFFICER

SNOW SERPENT

EEL

**7.5K**
GLOBAL
DEPLOYMENT

COBRA SOLDIER

HISS TANK DRIVER

STRATO-VIPER

TELE-VIPER

**VEHICLE DRIVERS**

**COBRA TROOPERS**

WHALEN|13

# KNOW YOUR VIPER

ART BY
**DAN MATUTINA**

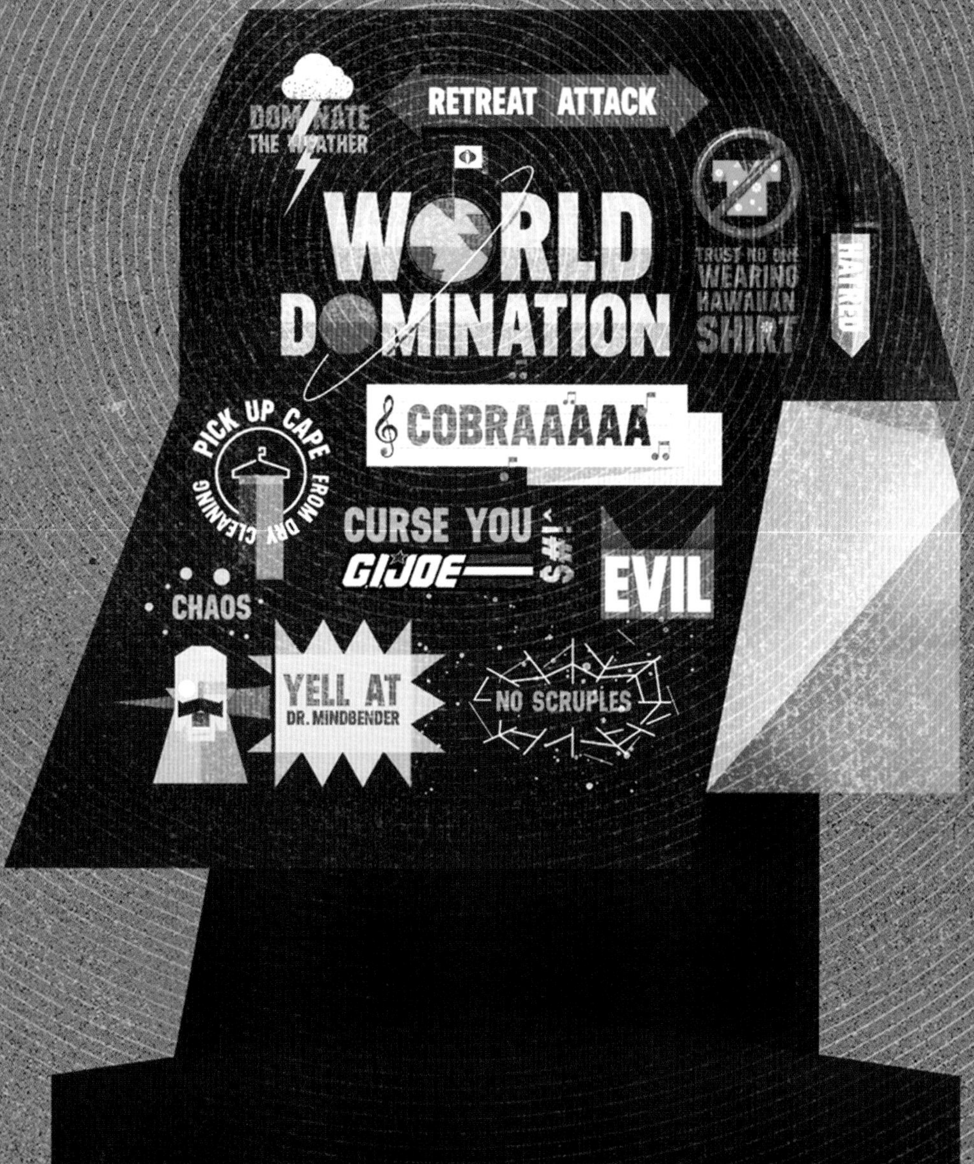
DOMINATE THE WEATHER
RETREAT ATTACK
WORLD DOMINATION
TRUST NO ONE WEARING HAWAIIAN SHIRT
HATRED
COBRAAAAAA
PICK UP CAPE FROM DRY CLEANING
CURSE YOU G.I. JOE
EVIL
CHAOS
YELL AT DR. MINDBENDER
NO SCRUPLES

# WHAT IS ON COBRA COMMANDER'S MIND?

ART BY
**TOM WHALEN**

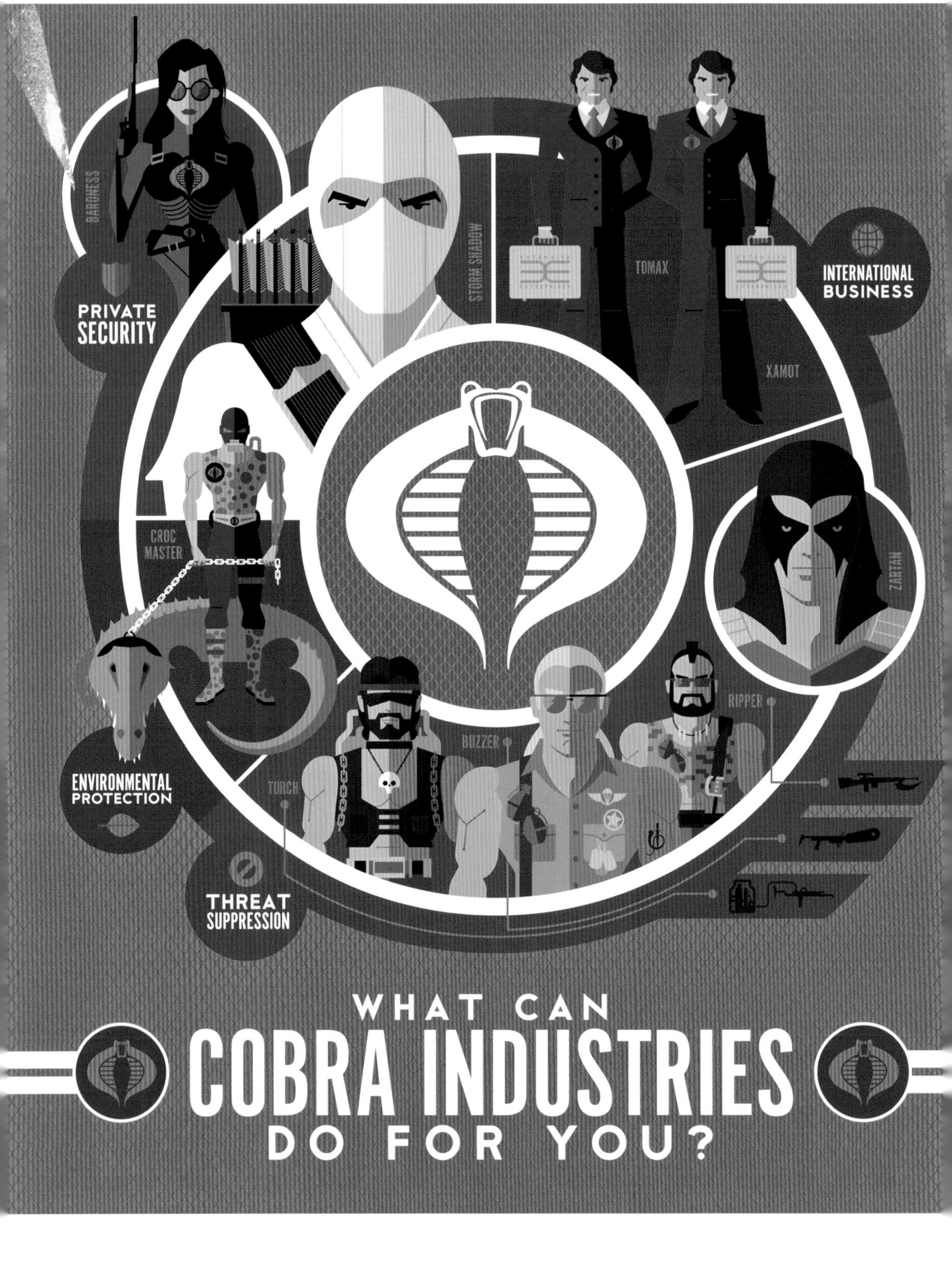

BARONESS
PRIVATE SECURITY
STORM SHADOW
TOMAX
XAMOT
INTERNATIONAL BUSINESS
CROC MASTER
ZARTAN
ENVIRONMENTAL PROTECTION
TORCH
BUZZER
RIPPER
THREAT SUPPRESSION
WHAT CAN
COBRA INDUSTRIES
DO FOR YOU?

ART BY
**JAMES BIGGIE**

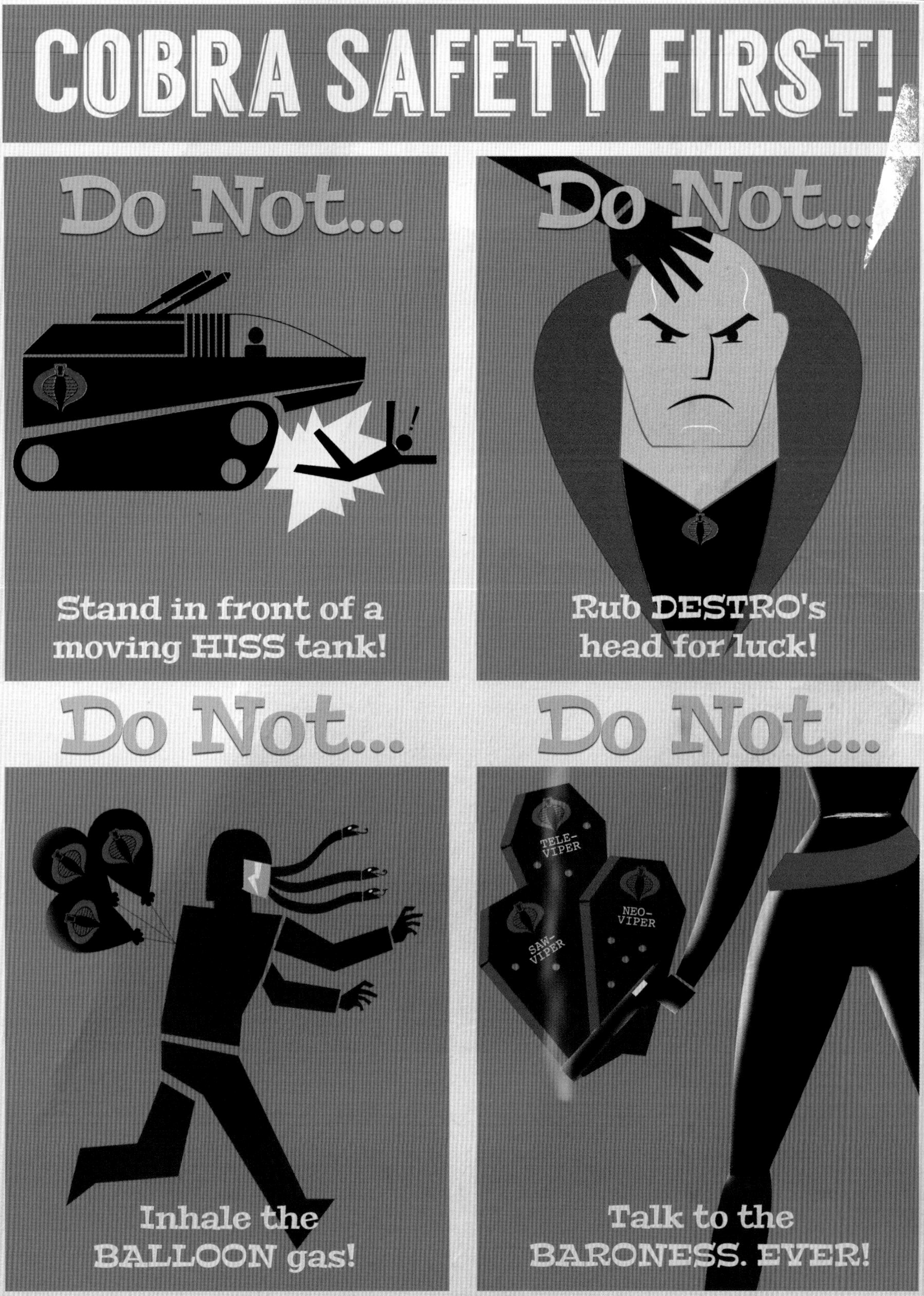
COBRA SAFETY FIRST!
Do Not...
Stand in front of a moving HISS tank!
Do Not...
Rub DESTRO's head for luck!
Do Not...
Inhale the BALLOON gas!
Do Not...
TELE-VIPER
NEO-VIPER
SAW-VIPER
Talk to the BARONESS. EVER!

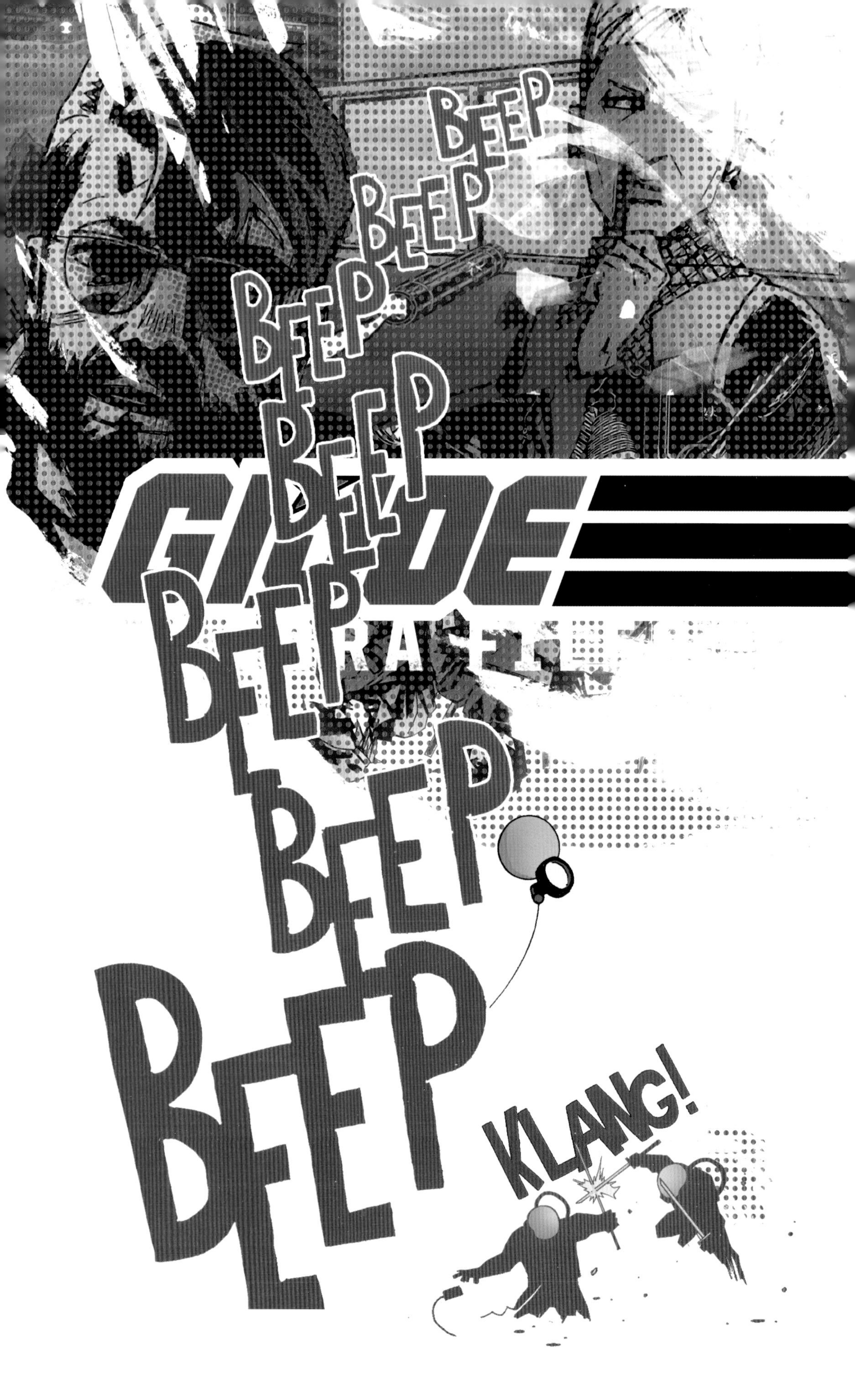

BEEP
BEEP
BEEP
BEEP
G.I. JOE
BEEP
BEEP
BEEP
KLANG!